THE MIDI

LANGUEDOC
and
ROUSSILLON

THE MIDI

LANGUEDOC
and
ROUSSILLON

JOY LAW

JOHN MURRAY

Dedicated to
DILYS, ROGER AND MANDY

© Joy Law 1991

First published in 1991
by John Murray (Publishers) Ltd
50 Albemarle Street, London W1X 4BD

The moral right of the author has been asserted

British Library Cataloguing in Publication Data
Law, Joy *1927*–
   The Midi.
   1. Southern France. Description & travel
   I. Title
914.4804839

ISBN 0-7195-4807-1

Photoset by Rowland Phototypesetting Ltd
Bury St Edmunds, Suffolk
Printed and bound in Great Britain
by Biddles Ltd, Guildford and King's Lynn

Contents

Illustrations

Acknowledgements

I ACKNOWLEDGE with gratitude the help of Monsieur Soulier, Director of the Comité Régional du Tourisme at Montpellier, many museum directors, the staff of Syndicats d'Initiatives, Mairies and municipal libraries throughout the region; Noilly Prat; Parfums Berdoues, Toulouse; Perrier; Le Réverbère, Narbonne; Compagnie des Salins du Midi et des Salins de l'Est; the Chamber of Commerce, Sète; the National Gallery, London; the Royal Danish Embassy, London; the Institut Français and French Government Tourist Office (FGTO), London; and the staff of the London Library.

I should also like to thank Madame d'Andoque, Domaine de Sériège; Françoise Clavairolle, Le Chemin de la Soie, Lassalle; John Danzer; Monsieur Bernard Dudot, Caunes-Minervois; Monsieur Alain Girard, Monsieur Patrick Schumacher, Monique and Martine, Bagnols-sur-Cèze; Sue Harris-Browne; Madame Martine Durif; Mademoiselle Lamache, Fanjeaux; Nicholas Law; Mademoiselle Monique Monifacier, Mallenches; Francesca Phillips and Nick Ould; Monsieur Louis Le Pottier of the Confrérie de la Jubilation, Toulouse; Cyril Ray; Jane Reilly; Lucia S. Stanton of Monticello, Virginia; General Victor Tanguy; Mademoiselle Tapié de Céleyran; Loretta Warnock; John Whiskard; and Diana and Dick Wrathall.

A special word must go to Mandy McMahon, who travelled with me in some discomfort on country buses and whose architectural expertise was of inestimable help; to Roger Toulmin, who undertook the translations of the greater part of the quotations with fine stylistic variations; to Dilys MacCrindle, who spent untold hours chasing references in obscure Parisian libraries and coming up with some splendid anecdotes; Ariane Goodman, for her encouragement, patience and editorial skills and, as always, to Richard, for driving me round the region and for putting up so uncomplainingly with skimpy meals and competition from the word processor.

The author and the publisher would like to thank the following for permission to reproduce copyright material in this book: Cambridge University Press (Steven Runciman, *The Medieval Manichee*, 1960); David Higham Associates (Elizabeth David, *An Omelette and a Glass of Wine*, 1984); The Estate of C. Day Lewis, Jonathan Cape and The Hogarth Press (C. Day Lewis, 'The Graveyard by the Sea', *Collected Poems*, 1954); Faber and Faber Ltd (Erik de Mauny, *A Time to Keep* (André Chamson), 1954); Frederick Muller (Seán Jennett, *Felix Platter, Beloved Son Felix*, 1961, and *Thomas Platter, Journal of a Younger Brother*, 1963); Editions Payot (Adrienne Durand-Tullou, *Le pays des asphodèles*, 1989); Peters, Fraser and Dunlop (Nancy Mitford, *The Sun King*, 1960); Sheldon Press (SPCK) (Thomas Merton, *The Seven-Storey Mountain*, 1975).

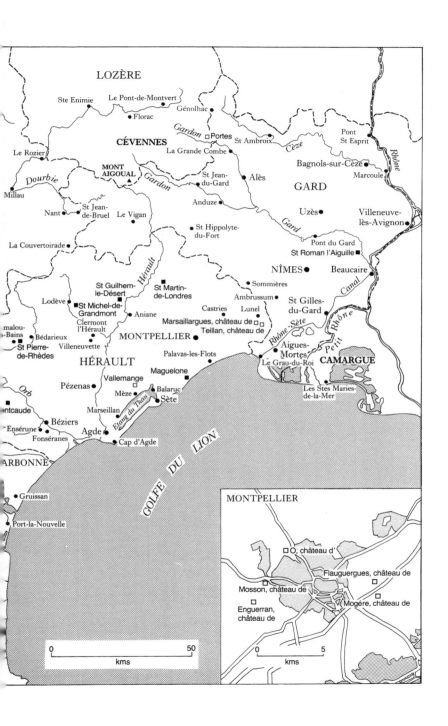

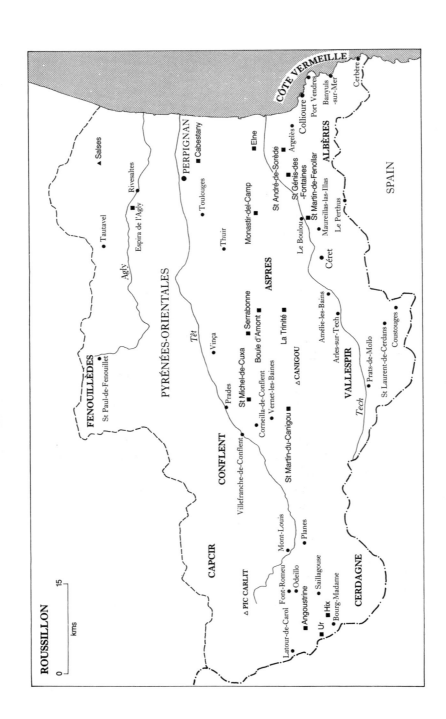

ROUSSILLON

CÔTE VERMEILLE

PYRÉNÉES-ORIENTALES

SPAIN

FENOUILLÈDES

CONFLENT

CAPCIR

CERDAGNE

ASPRES

VALLESPIR

ALBÈRES

▲ Salses
• Tautavel
Rivesaltes
Espira de l'Agly
Agly

• PERPIGNAN
■ Cabestany
■ Eline
• Toulouges
• Thuir

• St André-de-Sorède
Argelès •
Collioure •
Port Vendres •
Banyuls-sur-Mer •
Cerbère •

St Génis-des-Fontaines ■
St Martin-de-Fenollar ■
• Maureillas-las-Illas
Le Perthus

Le Boulou •
• Céret

St Paul-de-Fenouillet •

■ Serrabonne
St Michel-de-Cuxa ■
Boule d'Amont ■
• Vinça
La Trinité ■

Corneilla-de-Conflent •
• Vernet-les-Bains
△ CANIGOU

Amélie-les-Bains •
Arles-sur-Tech •

Prades •
Têt

Villefranche-de-Conflent •

St Martin-du-Canigou •

• Coustouges
St Laurent-de-Cerdans •
• Prats-de-Mollo
Tech

Mont-Louis •
• Planès
△ PIC CARLIT
Font-Romeu
Odeillo •
• Saillagouse
Latour-de-Carol •
Angoustrine •
Ur ■
Hix ■
Bourg-Madame •

0   15
kms

Introduction

'MIDI' in French is noon, and the South of France – where the sun shines more often than not – is simply referred to as 'le Midi'. For too many Britons the South of France constitutes either Provence or the Côte d'Azur, but west of the Rhône stretching right across to the Pyrenees lies Languedoc-Roussillon, a region that the French claim to have been keeping quietly to themselves. It is a countryside of infinite variety where the landscape changes from the savagely dramatic to the quietly domestic and wears a coat of many colours.

The roseate granitic uplands of the Cévennes make a stark contrast to the bleached brilliance of the littoral fringing the ultramarine sea; the golden cornfields of the Lauragais blend into the sun-baked vineyards of the Corbières and the lush green orchards of the Vallespir. The Petite Camargue with its saltwater lagoons and flocks of pink flamingoes retains its pale air of desolate mystery and the remote Cerdagne is still a botanist's paradise.

Because the region was for so long primarily agricultural and cut off from the north by the Massif Central, it has suffered little from industrialization or redevelopment. Fine cities with imposing cathedrals and magnificent bourgeois hôtels are still largely unspoilt; beetling châteaux and fortified towns may be in ruins or restored; and there are any number of beautiful small Romanesque churches with their graceful austerity and fanciful imagery scattered throughout. This vast amphitheatre sweeping round the Golfe du Lion is like an elliptical crown set with a few great jewels and many little semi-precious gems.

Geographically speaking Languedoc is the area – some three hundred kilometres wide – that runs from the Rhône to Roussillon, the French Catalan province in the lee of the Pyrenees, and from the Mediterranean seaboard to the plains of Aquitaine, the hills of Rouergue and the mountainous southern slopes of the Massif Central. In 1955 when the new regions were created, Bas and Haut Languedoc, both part of a province that had existed from the Middle Ages until the Revolution, were split up. The eastern and southern parts, Bas Languedoc, were merged with Roussillon to become Languedoc-Roussillon, while the north-western part, Haut Languedoc, became part of Midi-Pyrénées.

Despite these shifting boundaries, its many *pays* (small areas with their own distinct identities) and its proud, individualistic cities, Languedoc has enjoyed a cultural unity since the first century BC.

The Romans in 118 BC colonized Narbo Martius (Narbonne) and built the Via Domitia which led from the Rhône to the Pyrenees, and the two main Celtic tribes, the Volcae Arecomici and the Volcae Tectosages, were absorbed into the Provincia Narbonensis created in 27 BC. In 413 AD the Visigoths arrived from the eastern fringes of the Empire and, after the battle of Vouillé in 507 when they were defeated by the Franks and driven south of Toulouse, created the kingdom of Septimania (or Gothia) that was to last for two hundred years. Contrary to popular but now outdated belief, the Visigoths were far from barbaric; indeed in the sixth century a northern cleric begged the king not to appoint him to a bishopric in the south. As he was, he said, 'a simple man', he did not wish to submit 'to the boredom of having to listen to sophisticated arguments by old senatorial families who spend all their time discussing philosophical questions'.[1] During the eighth century Septimania was invaded and occupied by the Saracens for a brief period until the Franks from the north chased them out, and Charlemagne eventually incorporated the whole region into his empire. Some years after his death, with its dissolution, power passed into the hands of an emerging feudal nobility, of whom the counts of Toulouse and the counts of Barcelona became dominant in these southern lands.

Towns grew both in independence and prosperity, trading in wine, salt and, above all, cloth, and welcoming both Arabs and

Jews who brought with them their learning and their refined intellectualism. At the courts of the counts and their vassals the troubadours first sang of their love for women, creating from the speech of the Limousin and its variations a sort of common literary language, the *koiné*, properly described as the *langue d'oc*. (To call it *provençal* is wrong and *occitan* anachronistic, for the latter was a term not used until the nineteenth century.) North of the Loire and in the Ile de France Latin had persisted as the written language and *francien*, the spoken language, came to be known as the *lange d'oïl*. (*Oc* and *oïl* were the respective words for 'yes'.) It was this linguistic difference which led in the thirteenth century to the lands in which the *langue d'oc* was written being called Languedoc.

At the same time, in this part of the Midi, the established Catholic Church was in a state of decay, and reform was slow; and Catharism, a dualist religion with eastern European origins, easily took root. The papacy, determined to be rid of the heretics by any means, recruited an army from the north of France to stamp them out and the ensuing war, at the end of the first decade of the thirteenth century, came to be known as the Albigensian Crusade.

What had started as a local religious problem was quickly to turn into a political one. The Midi had been isolated from direct contact with the French crown since the tenth century but some hundred and fifty years later, the ruling dynasty of Capetians were beginning to cast covetous eyes on these southern lands. They had little time or energy to spare to do more than try to establish some sort of personal relationship with the vassals of the counts of Toulouse. They were too preoccupied in expanding their own territories nearer home around the Île de France, and attempting to contain the Plantagenets in the west. But they soon came to see that the Pope's crusade afforded them an opportunity they would be foolish to miss. The Albigensian Crusade served as a springboard for their acquisition of Languedoc which in fact accrued to them in 1271.

It has been said that this war was one between two civilizations and that at its conclusion the land of *oc* was absorbed into

'France'. In fact it accentuated a gulf which has never been bridged and perpetuated the divide between 'north' and 'south'. That this still exists may be seen from the relatively recent comment quoted by Fernand Braudel in *The Identity of France*: 'the old differences have not been wiped out. You must remember that the day you came through the Seuil de Naurouze [some 40 kilometres to the south of Toulouse] you left France; you are now in the land of *oc*, not in France anymore'.[2]

Similar feelings persist in Roussillon, which for a brief but glorious period from 1276 to 1344 was part of the independent Kingdom of Majorca and, until 1659, Spain, and where today there is a perceptible if not overtly aggressive desire for Catalan autonomy.

During the calamitous fourteenth century Languedoc, stricken by the Black Death like the rest of Europe, lost a third of its population, but in due course urban prosperity returned and the rural areas recovered, largely as a result of the cloth trade. The province was yet again fertile ground for new ideas, and the Reform movement was soon deeply entrenched. Indeed the Wars of Religion in Languedoc were as much a bid for independence from France as an expression of genuine theological differences. Emmanuel Le Roy Ladurie, who calls heresy 'the daughter of wool', asks if it was coincidental that both Catharism and Protestantism should have flourished in these largely wool-producing areas.

The seventeenth century was momentous: it was to see Roussillon attached to the French crown by the Treaty of the Pyrenees in 1659, and the creation of the Canal du Midi linking the Mediterranean to the navigable waters of the Garonne and thence to the Atlantic. But the Revocation of the Edict of Nantes in 1685 and the subsequent emigration of many Huguenots brought economic havoc in their trail. The predominantly Protestant population of the Cévennes, consisting almost exclusively of peasants and artisans, reacted to the draconian measures employed against them by taking to the hills and holding government troops at bay in 1702–4 during the Camisard uprising.

During the eighteenth century, Languedoc expanded its cloth trade, branching out from wool and silk into cotton, and developed its coal resources, though without any great degree of industrialization. Its days as a province were numbered and in 1791 it was carved up by the Revolutionary government into eight *départements*: Ardèche, Aude, Gard, Haute-Garonne, Haute-Loire, Hérault, Lozère and Tarn. There had been plans for one to be called the Hautes-Cévennes, but the Constituent Assembly gave in to the Catholics who thought it had too Protestant a ring about it, so it was called Lozère instead, and included areas of the Auvergne which had never been part of Languedoc.

After the Revolution, which was not marked by excessive terrorist zeal hereabouts, and with the slow decline in the cloth trade, Languedoc felt simultaneously abandoned by the central government in Paris and opposed to it. With the advent of the railway and tourists it gradually became less isolated, if not less isolationist. Its climate (despite the heat and the winds) and the quality of its air had always attracted visitors, and as Henry James said,

> Long before Mentone was discovered or Colorado invented, British invalids travelled down through France in the post-chaise or the public coach, to spend their winters in the wonderful place Montpellier which boasted both a climate and a faculty.[3]

The economy improved now that wine could be sent to the north of France in a day instead of a week. Increasing numbers of vineyards were planted to meet increasing demand, although the quality of the wine was not much better than it had been in the early eighteenth century when Jethro Tull complained that 'The dung'd Vineyards in Languedoc, produce nauseous Wine, from whence there is a proverb in that Country, That Poor People's Wine is best, because they carry no Dung to their Vineyards'.[4]

Over-production was, and still is, endemic. Vast quantities of wine were distilled into *eau-de-vie* and exported to northern Europe, and at one point the young were encouraged, by a propaganda campaign of which we would now disapprove, to drink more. Then the phylloxera louse struck and once the *vignerons* of the Corbières had recovered from that disaster, they were faced with competition from cheap Algerian imports; their discontent led to an outbreak of violent demonstrations in 1907.

Today, Corbières is still one of the largest wine-producing areas of France and strenuous efforts are being made to improve the quality of its wine. A number of delicious Vins Doux Naturels – sweet dessert wines – are also produced. They make a perfect aperitif, and can be drunk with *foie gras*, puddings or the delicious cherries, apricots and peaches produced in such profusion. The view from the tower of Narbonne cathedral afforded an English eighteenth-century traveller 'a pleasant prospect of a fruitful and most delicious Country, where human Industry has abundantly improv'd the natural Fertility and Beauty of the neighbouring Plains'.[5]

For Austin de Croze, a noted gastronomic writer, the food from this region of plenty was 'varied, eclectic, even bold; often admirable and always harmonious', and when one has tasted the fish and molluscs of the Mediterranean, the freshwater fish of the tumbling hill-rivers and the products of the sheep and the pig from the mountains, all cooked with skill and love, one cannot but agree with him.

Elizabeth David, lunching at Chez Nénette in Montpellier in the late fifties, made some comment about *provençal* food, only to be very mildly reproved: '*Ah, nous ne sommes pas en Provence, Madame, ici c'est le Languedoc.*' Some thirty years later nothing has changed. On a visit to the château of Tarascon on the eastern bank of the Rhône, the guide pointed west from its battlemented heights across the broad expanse of the mighty river: 'there', he said, 'is France'. While I knew about Breton and Basque and Catalan separatism, I was startled by the contempt in his voice. Next day, having crossed the river, I went into the tourist information office in Beaucaire, and could not resist asking if I was still in Provence, or in France. 'Neither,' replied the middle-aged woman behind the desk. 'You are in Languedoc.'

6

1

Rome and Romanys

*Beaucaire – Pont du Gard – Nîmes – Uzès –
St Gilles-du-Gard – Petite Camargue – Les Stes
Maries de la Mer – Aigues-Mortes*

BEAUCAIRE still stands sentinel on the west bank of the Rhône,
as it has for two thousand years, its importance deriving from its
strategic siting. Not only did it command the river, which was
for centuries the main north-south traffic artery, but it was also
at the intersection of two Roman roads; the Via Aurelia, which
ran from Rome to Lyon, and the Via Domitia, which ran from
Beaucaire to the Pyrenees and thence into Spain. Little remains
of the original Roman Ugernum, but the town is dominated by
its château, built in the thirteenth to fourteenth centuries on
Roman foundations and guarding the approach to the 'foreign'
territory that lay across the water on the east bank.

It is a pleasant walk up to the château through the luxuriant
garden established in the last century on the site of the defensive
ramparts razed by Louis XIII in 1632. There is a small restored
Romanesque chapel, with a simple tympanum and a cool
austere interior; a huge staircase, known as 'le Grand Degré';
a round tower and the 'triangular' tower, which is in fact
polygonal.

Beaucaire and its immediate surroundings do not in fact
differ much geographically from this contiguous part of
Provence, with its pale sun-baked soil, dark green cypresses and
silhouetted pines. From the summit of the château there is a
stupendous view of a vast panorama which sweeps from the
pays of the Argence in Languedoc, across the wide, swiftly

flowing Rhône, past the rival château of Tarascon on the far, east bank and on to the hazy blue lines of the Alpilles in Provence.

Aucassin, the hero of *Aucassin and Nicolette*, a thirteenth-century *cantefable*, lived in the château of Beaucaire. He was the son of the lord of Beaucaire, and the story tells of his devoted love for Nicolette, and hers for him, and their triumph over the trials and tribulations which befell them. The only copy of the manuscript, by an unknown author, was discovered in 1752. It was published in *Studies in The History of the Renaissance* by Walter Pater, and became quite the rage in the late 1880s.

The Musée municipal de la Vignasse, housed in one of the outbuildings near the top, contains some good furniture, documents of local interest and archaeological objects. The pride with which the museum attendants draw one's attention not only to treasures illustrating their own history but also to the rather more *outré* modern works that make up the temporary exhibitions is heart-warming. It is striking throughout Languedoc that although its denizens are proud of their past they are not locked into it. Having been asleep for so long, Languedoc is now wide awake and forward-looking.

In the twelfth century Beaucaire, according to a Limousin chronicler, was the scene of

> a foolish festival held by a multitude of local princes and celebrities . . . The count of Toulouse gave a knight, one Raymond Dagout, a hundred thousand shillings, which he immediately divided into a hundred times a thousand and gave a hundred knights each a thousand shillings . . . William Gros de Martel, who had three hundred knights with him, (there were about ten thousand knights at that court), had all their food cooked in the kitchen with wax candles and torches.[6]

It was perhaps this kind of luxury that excited the envy of the northern barons some forty years later and provoked them to ravage this countryside, but Beaucaire survived their passage. Its days of prosperity began in earnest in 1464 when Louis XI extended the town's trading concessions at its annual fair, an event which survived until the middle of the nineteenth century. The town started to decline at the time of the Revolution and as the effects of the Continental Blockade made themselves felt. The progressive silting-up of the bed of the Rhône, which made it difficult for heavily-laden barges to move, the construction of a viaduct across the river in 1852, and the arrival of the railway, between them spelled economic death.

But until then the fair of Ste Madeleine at Beaucaire was the most important in the Midi and attracted merchants from all over Europe and the Near East. The fine bourgeois houses still standing reflect this influx of wealth. It is difficult to imagine today what the town must have looked like with some hundred thousand people milling about its streets. Traders and dealers in every conceivable type of goods, bankers and money-changers, theatrical troupes who tried out their acts on a cosmopolitan audience, mountebanks and charlatans, thieves and prostitutes, all came to do business in the last week of July. The fair was held in a field at the foot of the château and the whole town was like a circus for several weeks. Many of the visitors left entertaining accounts of it; the Swiss, Felix and Thomas Platter were amongst the first to do so. Thomas was thirty-eight years younger than his stepbrother, through a quirk of his father's second marriage. Both were sent to study medicine in the late sixteenth century in Montpellier by their father, an illiterate herdsman who had risen to become a notable schoolmaster and the owner of a printing works in Basle. Both kept journals and their observations on the area are acute and funny. Thomas wrote of the fair that

> It is impossible to imagine the immense number of stalls that were set up in the town and round about. For this occasion all the avenues are covered with huts, and many of the houses too are turned into shops, where goods of all kinds are sold, especially pearls, precious stones, coral and *naturalia*. Great numbers of clever musicians also come to the town and various performers and exhibitors of curiosities of all kinds. A Burgundian, with his nose

weighed down by a pair of enormous spectacles, which served less to preserve his eyes, as he claimed, than to attract attention, exhibited performing fleas, which his daughter fed by putting them on her arm . . . The little creatures were delicately chained; one carried a tiny knight of silver, with his lance on his shoulder, others pulled a little chain of the same metal, as long as a finger and weighing a grain, which did not prevent them from hopping.[7]

The fleas, if not performing, were still hopping when Stendhal, on a visit in 1837, complained that it was

quite impossible to write; there was simply no room. One evening I resolved to cheat the fleas and the gnats and to get a good night's sleep, but had to go a couple of miles out of town to do so. The day I arrived at the Fair I was so stunned by the incredible din that it was really (I believe) several hours before I began to take it all in . . . such a mob, such a crush – in Paris you have never seen the like . . . The trip to Beaucaire is a holiday for everyone.[8]

Of the wide variety of goods on sale (and its trading figures had leapt from 8 million livres in 1728 to 47 million fifty years later), Stendhal noted in particular the booths of soap-merchants, grocers and drysalters from Marseille, the perfumiers from Grasse with their pomades, and those from Montpellier with their flagons of perfume – he bought some of 'Monsieur Durand's excellent *eau de Portugal*'. Not all his experiences were so pleasurable:

Continuing my walk, I found a number of huts full of dried figs, prunes, raisins and almonds. Then we were assailed by a powerful and rather disagreeable smell; we had strayed into a street whose thick, high walls were made up entirely of onions and cloves of garlic – we beat a hasty retreat.[9]

Felix Platter too had noticed the onion market on St Bartholomew's Day in Montpellier in 1533:

The onions are bound into strings with straw, and piled up like so many faggots, in piles two feet high. The whole square is covered with them, and only narrow passages are left for people to walk about. The onions are of all kinds, some very large and others white and sweet, but none of them are as strong as ours are.[10]

Beaucaire still has annual festivities, the first of which takes place at the beginning of June, and commemorates the 'Drac', a fabulous water beast who carried a laundrymaid from the banks of the Rhône to nurse his son in its watery depths. The other, in the last fortnight of July, includes such spectacles as bulls being run though the streets – bullfights in which, unlike Spanish *corridas*, the bull is not killed; wine tasting, and any number of good-humoured parties.

The town is certainly worth exploring. The monuments are well labelled and the tourist office map is unusually good, though the translation in the English language brochure is more amusing than informative. The buildings to look out for include the church of St Paul, a former Cordelier chapel with a sober exterior, a fourteenth-century nave and a fifteenth-century choir. The Estates of Languedoc, the provincial assembly, often held their sessions in this building and it was where Charles VII's financier, Jacques Coeur, was imprisoned, and from which he escaped to flee to Rome. Notre Dame des Pommiers is an altogether more elegant church, built in 1734–44 by Jean-Baptiste Franque and Guillaume Rollin. Embedded in the outer wall is a twelfth-century frieze with scenes from the Passion.

The only extant town gateway, the Porte Roquecourbe, is also the work of Franque. The Hôtel de Ville, built in 1679–83 by Jacques Cubizol and Alexis de la Feuille de Merville, is a harmonious classical edifice, with the Sun King's device and the town's coat-of-arms on its façade.

There are a number of seventeenth- and eighteenth-century houses of which the wide-arched openings on the ground floors show them to have been used as warehouses. Look out for the Hôtel des Roys de Lédignan; the Hôtel de Linages, built by Franque as an office for the royal tax collectors; the Hôtel de Margalier, with a fine set of caryatids supporting the balcony;

the Hôtel de Fermineau; the Hôtel de Clausonette; and a number of others. All have good doorways, beyond which the courageous and persistent will be rewarded by a glimpse of fine courtyards and staircases.

So much for the old at Beaucaire; the new is the development of a small pleasure port on the last stretch of the Rhône-Sète canal which runs right through the town.

The troglodytic abbey of St Roman l'Aiguille is a kilometre or so to the north on the road to the Pont du Gard. It can only be reached on foot, but the gentle climb up a stony winding road is well worth the effort. A fortified castle was superimposed on the abbey in 1538 and it was not until the demolition of the fort in 1850 that the original buildings were discovered. Its particularity lies in the fact that it was wholly constructed by excavating the limestone rock.

Despite theories that it was founded in the fifth century, there is no evidence that it existed before 1008 and as it has been quarried for centuries, there is no way of knowing the date of the remains that we see today. There are the outlines of a chapel enlarged from a natural cave, small enclaves used as cells, the abbot's seat with carved armrests, and a ledge for a wine press all dug out of the rock, and two huge vaulted rooms. The terrace above the abbey on the top of the hill served not only as the roof of a huge cistern which held 140,000 litres of rainwater, but also enclosed a cemetery. The graves, of which there are a hundred and fifty, are hewn in the rock and now lie, filled only with sparse vegetation, open to the sky and the magnificent view of the Rhône and the countryside beyond. There are no ghosts here: one feels that the monks' spirits have long since been freed.

The Roman conquest of this part of Gaul was relatively peaceful and was the work of Gnaeus Domitius Ahenobarbus, proconsul for the province of the Narbonensis. His main claim to enduring fame is that in 118 BC he inaugurated the Via Domitia, which started at Beaucaire and takes its name from him. The road traversed the entire length of Bas Languedoc to Ruscino (today Perpignan). There it forked, one branch continuing along the coast to the Col de Banyuls, the other leading up into the Pyrenees at Le Perthus on the present Spanish frontier. The road follows the route supposedly taken by Hercules when he went to collect the apples of the Hesperides from beyond the Pillars which bore his name (the Straits of Gibraltar). Certainly Hannibal used it when, in 218 BC, he set off from Spain with his thirty-four elephants to invade Italy.

Although the Via Domitia was built by the Romans primarily for military purposes, it rapidly became an important thoroughfare carrying a great deal of commercial traffic. Much the best-preserved section is the eight kilometres which run from the west of Beaucaire to Nîmes, where the continuation is irretrievably lost beneath that city's streets. Built solidly, with stout foundations and the Romans' usual attention to drainage, long stretches of the Via Domitia have survived and are at present being excavated. While it offers less dramatic views than those to be seen from Hadrian's Wall, this section makes a pleasant walk.

The Romans had halts every eight miles and posting-houses every thirty, and there are still some remains of small temples and dwelling-houses. Standing stones marked each mile and four groups of these milestones have been re-erected between Beaucaire and Nîmes. Some are now in the museum at Beaucaire and the archaeological museums at Nîmes, Béziers and Narbonne, but others have been incorporated within churches along the route. At St Laurent-de-Jonquières, a little to the north of Beaucaire, two serve as pillars, and at Maguelone, south of Montpellier, one has been embedded as the tympanum above the portal of the church.

Twenty-four kilometres north of Beaucaire, as the crow flies, is one of the most impressive monuments in Europe. The Romans needed water for their city of Nemausum (Nîmes) and the aqueduct they built to bring it down from the River Eure and the hills around Uzès is, by any standards, an incredible feat of engineering skill. The gradient of 18 metres dictated a length of 48 kilometres and, miraculously, a span of 273 metres across the River Gardon has been preserved.

The Pont du Gard is a three-tiered bridge, 49 metres high, still straddling the river like a colossus. The lower arches, of which there are six, rising to 24 metres above low water, support a second row of eleven smaller arches which in turn support a third row of thirty-five arches, across which runs the water conduit. The precision of the stonecutting cannot but excite our admiration, for neither mortar nor clamps were used to bond the blocks of masonry, some of which must weigh five tons. But over and above our admiration for the Romans' technical skill is a delight in the satisfying proportions and aesthetic balance of a great architectural work of art. Although Felix Platter phlegmatically recorded that 'it is of prodigious height, joining two mountains', Rabelais, who studied medicine in Montpellier at much the same time as Felix, is more whimsical. He says that Pantagruel built both the Pont du Gard and the amphitheatre at Nîmes in three hours, which, he continues, 'really sounds more like divine handiwork than human'. The young Rousseau, perhaps before he had become what Isaiah Berlin described as 'a militant lowbrow', had been advised to go and see the Pont du Gard:

> It was the first piece of Roman workmanship I had seen. I expected to see a monument worthy of the hands that had built it; but this time – I might say for the first time in my life – the reality exceeded my expectations. Only the Romans could have produced such an effect . . . I experienced a certain elevation of spirit; and asked myself, with a sigh, 'Why was I not born a Roman?' I remained there for several hours in rapt contemplation, from which I emerged listless and moody, and this mood was not well disposed to Mme de Larnage. She had taken care to warn me against the young women of Montpellier, but not against the Pont du Gard. One is never prepared for everything.[11]

Henry James, in the 1880s, was not altogether in agreement with Rousseau. Although he found

> the three tiers of the tremendous bridge . . . unspeakably impos-
> ing, and nothing could well be more Roman, [it had] a certain
> stupidity, a vague brutality. That element is rarely absent from
> great Roman work, which is wanting in the nice adaptation of the
> means to the end . . . It would be a great injustice however not to
> insist on its beauty – a kind of manly beauty.[12]

I will only add that it is worth paying the inflated price charged for a meal or a drink at the restaurant facing it in order to sit and gaze upon it. The meaner, or more adventurous and hard-headed, may care to get their thrills by walking along the uppermost level by the track of the watercourse.

The bridge and the aqueduct, which reached Nîmes at a building known as the *castellum* (which you can visit) carried enough drinking water to supply its citizens with 400 litres per head a day. Today the Nîmois each consume only about 320. The city, on the site of a healing spring and a settlement by the Celtic tribe of Volcae Arecomici, was named Nemausum for an old water god and built in about 28 BC by Roman veterans who had served in Egypt. The legionaries commemorated their victories there by minting coins, on the reverse of which they depicted a crocodile tied to a palm tree. The city adopted this image as its emblem in 1535 at François I's instigation, and now even the street drain-covers depict the reptile and his tree. There is also an imaginative modern fountain by Martial Raysse in the place du Marché, showing both. The fountain in the place d'Assas, also by Raysse, pays homage to Nîmes's water-gods and past worthies alike, and has vague Egyptian affinities.

Nîmes is the only city in Languedoc to have preserved any Roman buildings of consequence, although it was a much less important town than for example Narbonne, where virtually none still stand. The Arènes (amphitheatre), like its twin at

Arles and the Pont du Gard, was built towards the end of the
first century AD, also without mortar. There, within a perfect
ellipse surrounded by a hundred and twenty arcades rising in
two tiers, some twenty-five thousand people could watch
gladiatorial fights and other Roman entertainments. Seats for
such spectacles were reserved not only for the local dignitaries
as one would expect, but also for those vital members of the
community, the boatmen of the Rhône, Saône and Ardèche.

When Rousseau saw the amphitheatre, it was 'surrounded by
ugly little houses and filled with others even smaller and uglier';
and he could not resist a side-swipe at the French who 'have
absolutely no respect for their ancient monuments and take no
care of them. They are all afire for any new undertaking but
incapable of either completing or maintaining anything'.[13]

Arthur Young was more critical of the Romans than the
French, though he found it 'a prodigious work . . . which
shews how well the Romans had adapted these edifices to the
abominable uses to which they were erected'.[14]

Today, in summer, less sadistic though not perhaps always
less contentious theatrical and musical performances take place
in this most beautiful of settings. The weather, however, even
in the Midi, can be treacherous. Indeed some thirty-five years
ago, when I first saw the Arènes, its normally greyish-white
stone glistened pink in the aftermath of a terrifying electrical
storm. Now a roof designed by the architects Finn Geipel and
Nicolas Michelin has made it possible for performances to take
place in any conditions. It is an impressive piece of modern
technology; it can be erected in sixteen hours and consists of
two layers of material filled with warm air, supported on
stainless steel struts, and looks like a giant jellyfish.

The Maison Carrée is the other major Roman building of
Nîmes. Erected in the reign of Augustus as a temple, it is one of
the earliest monuments of the Roman ruler-cult in Europe. In
the course of its history it has been used as an assembly hall, a
dwelling-house, a stable, a church, a granary and the city's
préfecture. Louis XIV contemplated having it moved to Versailles, and Colbert forbade the Augustinian monks, who had

taken it over in 1670, from defacing the walls, and had drawn up plans for the blocks of stone to be numbered so that they could be reassembled. Thomas Jefferson, who spent whole hours gazing at it 'like a lover upon his mistress', as he wrote to Madame de Tessé, contented himself with copying it for the Capitol at Richmond, Virginia, rather than dismantling and re-erecting it, as some of his later compatriots would have done.

Fifteen very steep steps lead up to the open vestibule which has ten magnificent columns decorated with Corinthian capitals. There are another twenty columns embedded in the exterior side walls of the *cella* or chamber, where a museum is now housed, though in fact there are very few objects on display.

The Maison Carrée, manifestly not square, was referred to by Henry James as 'a little toy-temple' and he explained that 'the small "square house" [was] so called because it is much larger than it is broad'. The explanation given for its name by the attendant on duty is that the Romans called any right-angled edifice square. Arthur Young found it to have 'a magic harmony in the proportions that charms the eye. One can fix on no particular part of pre-eminent beauty; it is one perfect whole of symmetry and grace'.

Nîmes is also renowned for its gastronomic delights, amongst which are *choux de Nîmes*. They consist of lovely crisp round puffs of choux pastry filled with *brandade de morue*, topped by poached eggs and surrounded by a delicate pink prawn sauce. Alexandre Dumas credits the discovery of *brandade de morue*, a creamy emulsion of salt cod, olive oil and garlic, to Grimod de la Reynière, called 'the father of the gastronomic press' by Philip Hyman, and whom we shall meet at Béziers. Dumas, in his *Grand Dictionnaire de la Cuisine*, says that *brandade de morue* originated in Languedoc, though he does not name a specific town, and indeed Provence sometimes lays claim to having invented it. Dumas also explains that the word *brandade* came from *brandir*, to stir, shake or mix with force for a long time. The salted cod from which *brandade* is made must be thoroughly soaked before being mixed and cooked. Only in the market at Montpellier have I seen the cod lie shedding its salt in marble sinks under a running tap.

Although the Romans seem not to have eaten large quantities of fish, they were certainly interested in methods of fishing. Pliny has a charming tale of how fishermen in the region of Nîmes, closer to the sea then than now, would, if the wind was favourable, shout to bring dolphins to help them trap red mullet, for which the animals were rewarded by bread mash dipped in wine. The one fish that the Romans prized above all was red mullet (*rouget*), and indeed, for a time at the beginning of the first century AD, it enjoyed an extraordinary vogue. Cicero, Horace, Juvenal, Martial, Seneca and Suetonius all wrote about it. The Romans preferred large ones and would pay high prices for a sizeable specimen. Fresh red mullet are still expensive, though no one now thinks that size makes any difference to the taste. They appear frequently on Languedoc menus, sometimes cooked in white wine and sometimes wrapped in vine leaves and baked. Like woodcock, they should not be gutted.

A wall seven kilometres long surrounded the Roman city, but only the Porte Auguste and the Tour Magne are still standing. The Tour (which you can visit) has been in a ruinous state since 1601. In that year it was excavated by François Traucat, a nurseryman and amateur archaeologist. He was spurred on to do so by a prediction by Nostradamus that a gardener would discover hidden treasure there. Traucat found nothing, but deserves credit for having successfully propagated the mulberry tree, thereby at least contributing something positive to the economy of Nîmes.

The octagonal Tour Magne stands on the hill above the Jardins de la Fontaine and the ruins of the so-called Temple of Diana. At the end of the huge avenue Jean-Jaurès, so often filled with a monstrous funfair, the gardens are a peaceful spot where children and dogs play under the benevolent eye of sleepy gendarmes, and lovers come for a quiet stroll under the trees. Colette was entranced by 'the lovely garden and the lovely silence, broken only by the mild plashing of the water – by turns a haughty green, transparent, a sombre blue, or sparkling like the vivid scales of a dragon'.

The gardens are spacious and laid out in the formal French style with trees in rows punctuated by statues, balustraded walks, flights of steps winding their way through the different levels and water in pools and channels everywhere. They were designed, almost by chance, by Jean-Philippe Mareschal, the royal engineer and director of fortifications for Languedoc, in the mid-eighteenth century. He had been called in to deal with the pestilential waters of the city. Once the Roman aqueduct had fallen into disuse, the Nîmois relied on their spring waters and the River Agau not only for drinking and washing, but also for their textile industry. The waters, constantly recycled, became ever more polluted and a danger to the health of the citizens. Mareschal channelled the water from the underground spring of La Fontaine and built a series of ponds to act as reservoirs to take the water into the centre of the city by means of small canals. In so doing he created an elegant eighteenth-century urban garden.

The Nîmois had become, from the Middle Ages onwards, pre-eminent dyers. From wool they proceeded to silk, partly as a result of Traucat's mulberry trees, and from the 1740s to cotton too. The cloth they dyed was mostly destined for the cheap end of the market, and they thrived on exports to South America through their trade counter at Cadiz, and the Levant by way of Genoa. There is an intriguing piece of blue cotton in the departmental archives of the Hérault labelled *Nims, un drap façon Londres*. When large numbers of Huguenot clothworkers fled to London after the Revocation of the Edict of Nantes in 1685 – many Nîmois amongst them, for they were mostly Protestant – they took with them their own methods of both weaving and dyeing. It is thought that this sample is an early piece of what we call 'denim'. The Genoese made a similar blue cloth for their sailors, and the origin of the word 'jeans' may come from 'gin' for 'Genoese' or perhaps from an Anglo-Saxon mispronunciation of the dye 'bleu de "chine"'.

In the sixteenth century, *pastel* or *guède*, our woad, was the most common blue dyestuff but its production and use was a lengthy, smelly and expensive business. The importation of indigo from the east in the seventeenth century and chemical discoveries such as 'bleu de chine' in the late nineteenth century greatly reduced the cost of producing a good blue dye. Nîmes took advantage of this to market a sturdy cotton fabric with a white warp and a blue weft. Blue, a colour which had been worn by Cévenol peasants since the seventeenth century, was thereafter to become standard for workers' clothes – an example of what might be called the 'democratization of colour'. The mythology relates that blue jeans owe their origin in the United States to a Bavarian Jew named Levi Strauss. He arrived in San Francisco during the Gold Rush in 1853 with bolts of brown hemp cloth to make tents and awnings for the gold-diggers. He quickly saw that they needed hard-wearing trousers too, and his brother in New York sent him blue cloth to make them. Trousers almost certainly made from blue denim imported from Nîmes were on sale in New York by 1860.

The Musée du Vieux-Nîmes, housed in the elegant seventeenth-century bishop's palace, started in 1682–5 by Cubizol from plans by La Feuille de Merville, was not completed until the mid-eighteenth century. The museum has a fine collection of furniture; some paintings, of which the most interesting is of Liszt at the age of fifteen in 1826, when he gave three concerts in Nîmes; some pewter and faience; and a collection of pipes and smoking paraphernalia. Jean Nicot, who introduced tobacco to France, was born in Nîmes. He had been François II's ambassador to Lisbon and returned to France with a powdered preparation which he supplied in 1560 to Catherine de Médicis to cure her of migraine. For the rest of the sixteenth century, tobacco was known as the 'queen's herb', and used only for medicinal purposes.

The museum was recently damaged by both fire and water and the permanent collection is in the course of restoration and rearrangement. In the meantime there are temporary exhibitions showing the cloths, and clothes made from them, on which Nîmes' wealth was founded. The cloth trade declined in the nineteenth century because of a disease which attacked the silkworm and increasing British competition, but the opening of the railway line in 1841 to Montpellier saved Nîmes' fortunes as it became an important rail centre. A few years later the large square, now called the Esplanade de Gaulle, was laid out in front of the station. The central figure of its monumental fountain personifies Nîmes. Its sculptor was James Pradier, for whom his mistress, Juliette Drouet, served as model. She was an indifferent actress but owes her fame to having later become Victor Hugo's mistress. The figures surrounding her represent the Garonne, the Rhône, the Fontaine d'Eure and Nemausus.

A less successful nineteenth-century work is the cathedral of Notre Dame and St Castor, a fairly uninspired rebuilding of a much earlier church, the only remnant of which is a charming Romanesque frieze set into the outer wall. The other churches offer little of architectural interest, but the many bourgeois houses in the rues du Chapitre, des Marchands, de la Madeleine, de Bernis, Dorée and de l'Aspic are worth trotting round to see. (The *aspic* of the rue de l'Aspic is *aspique*, a variety of lavender, *lavandula spica*, which grows in the surrounding countryside.)

The Hôtel de Ville was designed by Charles-Augustin Daviler and put up by Cubizol in 1700–3, but was also re-fashioned in the nineteenth century. The Musée des Beaux-Arts is housed in an early twentieth-century building and has a moderate collection of paintings and sculptures. The former Hôpital Méjean, with its Jack popping out to strike the hours on the clock, is now called the Maison de Tartarin after Daudet's boastful provençal hero. Alphonse Daudet, the son of a silk merchant, was born at 20 boulevard Gambetta; Tartarin however was born in Tarascon but is sent to die in Beaucaire.

The last word on Nîmes should be left to Tobias Smollett. Writing in 1766 from Provence, he says, with his usual acerbity, that

the inns are not so good here as in Languedoc, and few of them are provided with a certain convenience which an English traveller can very ill dispense with. Those you find are generally on the tops of houses, exceedingly nasty; and so much exposed to the weather that a valetudinarian cannot use them without hazard of his life.

At Nismes, in Languedoc, where we found the temple of Cloacina in a most shocking condition, the servant maid told me her mistress had caused it to be made on purpose for English travellers; but now she was very sorry for what she had done, and all the French who frequented her house, instead of using the seat, left their offerings on the floor, which she was obliged to have cleaned three or four times a day. This is a degree of beastliness, which would appear detestable even in the capital of North Britain.[15]

The spring at Vergèze, for those interested at least in inner cleanliness, is a few kilometres to the south of Nîmes on the main road to Montpellier. Here the water rises from a single source and is naturally carbonated. Hannibal appears to have known of its existence, and in 1863 Napoleon III decreed that it should be bottled 'for the good of France'. In 1903 Lord Northcliffe's brother Sir John Harmsworth, recently down from Oxford, was in the area to perfect his French. He met a Dr Perrier who had been selling the spring water, in bottles in the shape of women's legs, to the French colonies. After one tasting, Sir John bought the spring, and gave it the name of the good doctor. Describing the water as the 'champagne of mineral waters', with great percipience he predicted that 'in fifty years' time there will be a revolution in our dining habits' and that 'mineral water will be found on every table'. He also changed the shape of the bottles to look like the Indian clubs with which he exercised. Two years later he had a royal warrant from Edward VII (who might, one supposes, have preferred the shape of the original bottles).

The sales figures speak, or spoke, for themselves. Until the benzene scare in early 1990, the French consumed 800 million bottles a year. In 1972, 20 million bottles were sold in the UK; in 1974 the *Financial Times* opined that Perrier water was only for 'cranks and foreigners', but by 1988, 130 million bottles were being sold. It will be interesting to see if Perrier regains its lead in the market. Some people took the opportunity to change, but by the end of 1990 Perrier had recovered 60 per cent of its sales.

Although Uzès is only 25 kilometres away from Nîmes, it seems to be in a different world. Indeed one of the characteristics that quickly becomes apparent when touring Languedoc is not just its physical diversity, but the sense one gets of a whole series of self-contained and, it must be said, self-regarding entities, as if each town were a mini-state unto itself, which was virtually true in the past. Neither motor-borne tourists nor the television has succeeded in reducing them to uniformity. It is one of Languedoc's many attractions.

'O little town of Uzès! Were you in Umbria, tourists from Paris would flock to visit you!' Alas, André Gide's apostrophe to the city in which he spent many of his school holidays is now no longer true; tourists come from further away than Paris. But Gide's reference to Umbria is not out of place. The surrounding countryside (which he described as 'the rough *garrigue*, blasted by the sun') and the Tour Fenestrelle (the round twelfth-century campanile with its rows of twin open-arched windows – unique in France) are unquestionably Italianate.

As a boy Gide stayed with his grandmother and his uncle Charles, a noted political economist. Their house was in the square next to the mildly Baroque church of St Étienne and a rectangular Romanesque tower with an incongruous pepper-mill perched above it. On rainy days when Gide was confined indoors, his time was largely spent chasing mosquitoes. But for a boy of his sensitivity, born in Paris and with a Norman mother, the outdoor world of the Midi was a revelation in more ways than one. There was the countryside itself so different from that of Normandy.

Clumps of purple or white cistus enlivened the rough brushwood, while lavender perfumed it. A dry, bracing wind blew across it, sweeping the road clear of dust which coated everything around. Our carriage wheels put up huge grasshoppers which, as they

23

leaped, suddenly displayed wings of blue, red or grey, becoming for an instant bright butterflies; then settled again a bit further on, colourless and blending with the rocks and undergrowth. On the banks of the Gardon asphodels grew; and an almost tropical flora on the river-bed itself, which was dry for most of its length.[16]

Then there were the inhabitants, again so unlike the northerners he had encountered. In *Si le grain ne meurt (If It Die . . .)*, in which he recalls these childhood memories, he tells of an encounter with a peasant 'whose turn of phrase was both picturesque and precise . . . What style, what liveliness, what distinction compared with our dull-witted agriculturists in Normandy.'

Not everyone however found Uzès to their taste. Two other writers, some eight hundred years apart, were confined there unwillingly. The first was the princess Dhuoda, who in 824 married Bernard of Septimania, the son of Guilhem de Gellone. After the birth of their sons, he sent her to his castle where she spent the rest of her life. She passed her time writing, under the protection of Bishop Eléphant, a manual on Christian behaviour for her elder son. The manual is remarkable not least because it was written by a woman, a rare feat at that date. It is valuable also for providing, amongst the homilies, a unique record of the intellectual preoccupations of an aristocratic lady in the ninth century and for details about her family and the vagaries of life. Her husband Bernard, chamberlain at the imperial court, over-fond of women and with outsize political ambitions, eventually found himself on the wrong side in the struggles for power and was executed in 844 by Charles the Bald. Dhuoda's elder son William was killed in Spain six years later and her second son, Bernard, went on to become a great magnate whose descendants became the counts of Toulouse.

Uzès subsequently became the centre of a virtually independent county which, in the eleventh century, was to pass into the suzerainty of the house of Toulouse. In 1565 Charles IX elevated Count Antoine Uzès de Crussol – the family name used from the fifteenth century – to a dukedom, and in 1572 made him a peer of France. When in 1632 Montmorency, until then the premier duke, was decapitated (see page 71), Uzès de Crussol took his place by virtue of his seniority. The head of the family is still the premier duke and peer of France, as the rather haphazard notice pinned above the entrance to the château, called the 'Duché', proudly proclaims.

Thomas Platter, who spent six months in Uzès in 1567–8, was present at the seven-year-old duke's ceremonial entry when he came to take up his inheritance. Amongst the festivities Platter described was a performance:

> Three young boys, very beautiful and dressed as women, but in different costumes, represented three nymphs speaking in turn to discuss which of them the duke would prefer. One represented France and spoke in French, the second spoke in Latin, and the third in the tongue of Uzès.[17]

The Edict of Villers-Cotterets of 1539, by which François I had sought to impose French as the official language throughout the kingdom, was clearly taking its time to be applied in Languedoc, for Platter remarks that the French nymph thought the Uzès nymph 'nothing but a foolish peasant'.

Although the dukes' motto was *Ferro non auro*, implying that they had won their renown by the sword rather than by gold, and that money was beneath them, they were certainly prepared to spend it, at any rate on building suitable accommodation for themselves in Uzès. The large square tower, the Tour Bermonde, is eleventh century (with some nineteenth-century modifications); the gateway and drawbridge by the round tower and the Tour de la Vigie were put up in the thirteenth century, as was much of the château and the building known as the Vicomté, with a small hexagonal tower. The chapel is Gothic, but was reworked in 1838. The first duke certainly did not despise *aurum*, for it was he who gave the main façade a Renaissance facelift (attributed to Philibert de l'Orme) and installed a monumental stairway to lead to a series of grand apartments. They are pleasantly furnished and one room is given over to a formidable recent duchess who, when widowed, devoted herself to fighting for the rights of women.

Thomas Platter, who enjoyed the chestnuts in Uzès and reckoned that the bread was the best in Languedoc, remarked on the wealth of the Uzétians and noted that many of them earned their living by weaving and dyeing, making the best serge but 'called Nîmes serge, because that town is better known'. Like so many towns dependent on the textile trade, it was staunchly Protestant, adhering to what the Catholics referred to as the 'Religion Prétendue Réformée', and in 1546 its bishop was deposed for his Calvinistic leanings. After the Revocation of the Edict of Nantes at least sixty of its cloth-workers and tradesmen fled. This spelt doom both for the local economy and for any semblance of intellectual activity, as Jean Racine was to discover.

The 22-year-old future poet and playwright hoped to acquire a benefice through the good offices of his uncle, Sconin, who was a canon there. He spent eighteen miserable months in the city from November 1661. His letters are full of grumbles: despite his pleasure in 'the fine days: the finest you will find anywhere', he found Uzès 'quite the most wretched place imaginable', though he thought the olives the best in the world and the women attractive. The natives were boring and uncouth: 'I'm exiled here with even less congenial company than Ovid by the Black Sea', and after having been shown some poems by the Uzétians, decided that he 'would sooner make love in honest prose than in bad verse'. The language was barbarous: 'in less than six months, I've all but forgotten the little good French I once knew. If ever I get back to Paris, no one will understand a word I say: how will you feel on finding that I've become the complete country bumpkin?' On top of it all, like so many others, he found the summer heat excessive: 'I should die if I went outside for an instant: it is like stepping into a bread oven'.[18]

Laurence Sterne, travelling through the area in 1762, echoes Racine's simile:

I never saw a cloud from Paris to Nismes half as broad as a twenty-four sols piece. Good God! We were toasted, roasted, grill'd stew'd, carbonaded on one side or other all the way – and being all done enough (*assez cuits*) in the day, we were eat up at night by bugs, and other unswept-out vermin, the legal inhabitants (if length of possession gives right) of every inn we lay at.[19]

Uzès did not recover from the exodus of its cloth workers and an official complaint in 1718 stated that the city would perish if her manufacture of serge was not re-established. Nevertheless there was no real renewal of economic activity though by the mid-eighteenth century the planting of vines and mulberry trees brought some temporary relief. Life in the city became ever more miserable throughout the nineteenth century; there was therefore little new building and precious little restoration, so that Uzès has retained many of its early monuments.

Above all it is conspicuous for its towers. In addition to the five already mentioned, there are the Tour du Roi and the Tour de l'Evêque or de l'Horloge, which still glower at each other, reminding us of the kings and counts and bishops who all owned different parts of towns and were endlessly at odds with each other. Today red and yellow diagonal-striped flags fly from them all, regardless of past rivalry.

Thomas Platter spoke of the galleries below the solidly built houses of dressed stone, 'so that one may walk in shelter in the street whatever the weather', and refers to the large square in the centre of the city where the markets and fairs were held. Both the galleries and the lovely peaceful square – the place aux Herbes – with its round stone fountain and pollarded plane trees casting a dappled light, are still there, as is the market.

Elizabeth David, shopping there one Saturday in February some five or six years ago, when the *mistral* was blowing so ferociously that she could hardly stand upright, found the produce remarkably varied, particularly for the time of year. She noted

the good creamy-fleshed firm potatoes . . . the little round, crisp, bronze-flecked, frilly lettuces, baskets of *mesclun* or mixed salad greens, great floppy bunches of chard, leaf artichokes, trombone-shaped pumpkins which make admirable soup, fat fleshy red peppers, new laid eggs, eight or nine varieties of olives in basins and barrels, thick honey and clear honey, in a variety of colours, in jars and in the comb, and honey soap in golden chunks, bouquets of mixed fresh flowers, tulips, dark purple anemones, marigolds. And then cheeses, cheeses.[20]

And so she goes on; it makes one want to rush there instantly.

There are a few Renaissance buildings still standing, the best of which is the Hôtel Dampmartin, thought to have been the birth place or at least the family home of Nicolas Froment who painted *Le Buisson Ardent* now in the cathedral at Aix-en-Provence. (Whatever the 'burning bush' really was, in autumn the countryside round about Uzès is filled with the flaming oranges and deep yellows of pyracantha.) There are rather more hôtels of the seventeenth and eighteenth centuries, town houses of the bourgeoisie as well as of local nobility, such as the Hôtel du Baron de Castille in the place de l'Evêché (see below). The beautiful Hôtel de Ville, dating from 1773, is intact, and although its northern façade was redone about 1900, that to the south is original. It has a pretty inner courtyard. The bishop's palace, large and lovely, has a dusty pink, rather crumbling exterior. It was begun in 1671 by one of Madame de Sévigné's relatives, who also completed the rebuilding of the cathedral.

Alas, the cathedral had a new façade in 1871 and new stained glass at much the same time. Inside there is a fine wrought-iron balustrade and a baldachino over the high altar, and the late seventeenth-century organ, restored in the 1960s, is quite special. Its silvery grey pipes are framed in cream and gold, colours repeated in the decoration of the shutters, which fly out in great wings like some huge bird.

Dedicated to St Théodorit, the cathedral stands on a terrace planted with chestnuts from which one has a splendid view.

A few kilometres to the west of Uzès at Arpaillargues there is a handsome château which is now a hotel and is named for one of its previous incumbents, Marie d'Agoult, the mistress of Liszt and mother of Cosima Wagner. To the south-east of Uzès is an altogether more bizarre set of buildings (which for a time belonged to Douglas Cooper). Gabriel Joseph de Froment, Baron de Castille was a splendid eccentric who, having seen Bernini's colonnade at St Peter's in Rome, became totally obsessed by columns. He appears to have erected two hundred of them hereabouts, although only some fifty have survived. When the Baron returned from Italy, where he had spent part of the revolutionary years, he not only added columns to the simple building of his hôtel in Uzès, he also set about rebuilding his family château at Argilliers between Uzès and Remoulins. Although it is not open to the public, you can get a good look at its exterior from the D981. The approach is flanked by a semicircle of columns topped by a balustrade and a straight drive also lined by columns; yet more columns decorate the façade of the château and a number of broken ones lie about in romantic disorder.

But the Baron did not stop there; he also built a number of strange little architectural fantasies of which the remains of only two are still to be seen. The circular *château d'eau*, on the lane to the east, has a cupola surmounted by an Islamic crescent, and buried in the woods beyond is a pyramid rather like the one at Vienne. There are also two chapels; one supposedly Roman-esque, and the other built by the Baron in neo-Classical style with a pillared portico. On the far side of the main road there are two mausoleums, both overgrown with lush vegetation. One, with monolithic pillars, was for his second wife; the other, consisting of three high pillars, was for his son, killed at the battle of Essling in 1809.

The Baron maintained a lengthy correspondence with the Countess of Albany about these follies, and when she visited him in October 1822 local society came to gawp at the lady billed as 'the Queen of England'. Louise de Stolberg had married Charles Edward Stuart, the Young Pretender, in 1772. She subsequently left him, and lived in Rome with the Italian poet, Vittorio Alfieri, as his common-law wife. After Alfieri's death, she took up with the French painter François-Xavier Fabre after whom the fine arts museum in Montpellier is named (see pages 47–8).

St Gilles-du-Gard, as it is properly called, some 45 kilometres to the south, is set in very different surroundings. It lies on the edge of the flat plain which leads down from the *garrigue* through the marshy lands of the Petite Camargue to the sea. In the early Middle Ages St Gilles was not only the site of a shrine to an eighth-century hermit which attracted pilgrims to it in its own right, but a vital staging post on the Voie Regordane (see pages 250–1). It has kept one monument of great historic importance – the portal of its abbey church.

Though many find the sculptures on it aesthetically pleasing, for me its prime interest lies in its purpose rather than its execution. Prosper Mérimée, who was responsible for saving and restoring so many medieval ruins in the middle of the last century, found the restoration 'rather dull and old-fashioned, clumsy in its workmanship and eccentric in its plan. It is a monument put together by second-rate antiquarians. Decidedly the το καλὸν (ideal perfection) of sculpture is only to be found in the centre of France'.[21]

A new abbey building was started in the late eleventh century and the high altar was consecrated by Urban II in 1096 when he was in Languedoc preaching the First Crusade. It was from here that the forces he raised set out for their first assault on the Holy Land. The reigning count of Toulouse, Raymond IV, known also as Raymond of St Gilles, responded to the call and took an oath that he would not return to his own territories until the Holy Land had been reconquered from the Saracens. But Raymond's absence, and subsequently that of his two sons who followed him to the Near East, and his death there in 1105, was the start of a slow, century-long decline of his house and left a vacuum of power which his vassals were only too ready to fill.

At the same time, the emergence of heretical sects in Languedoc in the early twelfth century had begun to worry churchmen and the papacy alike, not so much because their adherents criticized the clergy's way of life – though they did, and with reason – but more disturbingly because they challenged the very dogmas of the Catholic Church.

From 1119, when the Council of Toulouse first noted its appearance with alarm, the heresy rapidly spread in Languedoc. One heretic, an itinerant preacher called Pierre de Bruys, denied the Eucharist, questioned the value of prayers for the dead and the veneration of relics, and advocated the destruction of crucifixes. In 1136 he was put to the stake at St Gilles. But although Pierre de Bruys had no following, the beliefs of the sect known as the Cathars were gaining ground in the area. Neither Raymond V, Raymond IV's grandson who became count in 1148, nor his son Raymond VI did anything to halt the 'cancer', as the Council of Tours described it in 1163, eating away at the Toulousain.

Where better then for the Church to make a direct statement of its position than in the much-frequented town of St Gilles? The abbey portal was thus deliberately conceived as a statement, whose full theatricality would be instantly apparent and comprehensible to the many travellers passing through. It consists of three heavily arched and elaborately decorated doorways with statues and friezes whose shape and style show strong classical influence and borrowings from palaeo-Christian iconography on sarcophagi such as those at Arles. Scholars date the work variously from 1160 to 1180, and seem reasonably convinced that it was the work of five sculptors and was conceived as a whole.

The originality and importance of this story in stone lie in the subjects chosen. The days for a representation of the Last Judgement were past; topics more relevant to contemporary issues were necessary if the Church was to make architecture and sculpture fulfil its didactic purpose and combat the beliefs of the heretics, who denied Jesus's incarnation and doubted the value of the sacraments. Hence the depiction of the Apostles, not only as eye-witnesses to the events of Jesus's life and death, but also as the very pillars of the faith, stamping out the forces of evil; the events surrounding Christ's birth; His incarnation; Christ enthroned in glory; and the Last Supper, which stressed the significance of the Eucharist and the certainty of redemption.

If the past was presented so dramatically in the stones of the portal, there was soon to be a contemporary drama played out on the steps in front of it. It is one of history's ironies that the civil war that was to destroy the counts of Toulouse, and with them the independence of Languedoc, should have had its *casus* in St Gilles.

On 15 January 1208, one of the papal legates, Pierre de Castelnau, was murdered there by a member of Raymond VI's entourage. Raymond admitted responsibility and Innocent III chose the steps of the abbey church for his *coup de théâtre*. On 12 June 1209, clad only in breeches and a shirt, Raymond was bidden to St Gilles to make his *amende honorable*. The legate Milon gave him absolution, and wrapping his stole round the Count's neck, led him to the altar, beating him the while with birch rods. Barely five weeks later, on 21 July, the army of northern barons, recruited by the Pope to extirpate the heresy, was at the gates of Béziers, and the Albigensian Crusade was under way.

The subsequent war, the founding of a new port at Aigues-Mortes and the ravages of bands of mercenaries during the Hundred Years War all contributed to the decline of St Gilles. The only remains of the abbey, apart from the portal, is the crypt, an underground church of relatively little interest, and although it houses the tomb of St Gilles, the entry fee of 10 francs seems a high price to pay. Amidst the ruins there is a spiral staircase called 'the screw of St Gilles' which excited for technical reasons the admiration of medieval master masons. A fragment of a Last Judgement and ornithological and ethnological objects are to be seen in the nearby little museum, in the house called the Maison Romane, where Pope Clement IV was born.

*

The Petite Camargue, like the Camargue proper over to the east, is part of that huge strange area of marshland created by the deltas of the Rhône and the Petit Rhône. An isosceles triangle, covering some 60,000 hectares, half of which consists of saltwater lakes, the Camargue is an amphibian world of its own. If it is less desolate than it was in the past, with offers of 'safaris' in Range Rovers and children riding ponies and looking much as they do in the Home Counties in the school hols, nothing can really detract from the perennial beauty of this haunting countryside.

In the past, its inhabitants, who were for the most part fishermen and *chasseurs*, had a short life-expectancy, for the combination of evaporation and low rainfall produced stagnant waters, albeit salt, which bred mosquitoes in their millions. Swamp fever and malaria killed not only men but most of the fish and all but salt-loving plants. The marshland is still alive with wild iris, sea purslane, water mint, marsh samphire and sea lavender, while on the dunes tamarisk, blue thistle, mathiole lilies, wild marguerites and sea rocket find toeholds in the sand. The reeds were used to roof fishermen's huts and the sea bulrushes to plug coopers' barrels.

The creation of a protected area and a Natural Park, and the progressive disinfestation of the Camargue has turned it into a birdwatchers' paradise. Among the four hundred or so different species are egrets, avocets, gulls of every type, snipe, sand-pipers, bitterns, tern, teal, plovers, mallard, coot, larks and red-legged partridges. Less easy to spot is the barn owl, now so rare elsewhere. Here it is known as the *beuloli* from the belief that it consumed the oil in lamps and lanterns. But by far and away the most spectacular sight is of a colony of up to fifteen hundred pink flamingoes, especially at eventide with the reflection of the setting sun burning in the sea. There are also large flocks of purple herons which feed on the insects they pick off the black cattle and white horses.

Many of the human inhabitants of the area between the Etang d'Or, the region of Magueio and the Petit Rhône where the Camargue proper begins, earn their living and get their fun

from both the cattle and the horses. The cattle, in herds of
between one and two hundred, are raised on farms called
manades, by *manadiers*, and their branding at *ferrades* provides an occasion for general jollity. The bulls, who may live to
be as old as forty and are small with lyre-shaped horns, provide
good sport when they are run through the streets to the
amusement of the crowds. In the ring the bulls are neither
fought nor killed: a *cocarde* (favour) is fixed between the horns,
which are capped with small acorns held on by rubber bands. It
is a test of both the courage and the skill of the *razetteurs* to
remove them with a small hook and without injury. The
razetteurs operate on foot; the *manadiers* and the *gardiens* –
the 'cowboys' of the Camargue – seem almost to have been born
in the saddle.

There have been herds of wild horses here for centuries.
Sturdy animals, they know the terrain well and negotiate the
marshland sure-footedly and swim without fear. The foals are
born dun-coloured but when they are five acquire their characteristic grey-white coat. They do not at first take kindly to being
broken in at the age of about three, but once tamed serve their
masters well. The *gardiens*, a splendid sight in their wide-
brimmed felt hats and as often as not a coloured kerchief at their
neck, take the bulls to and from the arenas, and from April to
October the Camargue is alive with these festivities.

Les Stes Maries de la Mer, the only town in the Petite
Camargue, is a good place from which to see the bull-running
and these 'fights'. The exact identity of the saints for whom the
town was only named in 1838 is so uncertain that Marina
Warner dubs them a 'muddle of Marys' in her book about the
Virgin, *Alone of All Her Sex*. The Holy Marys are thought to be
Mary Jacobi, perhaps the Virgin's sister, and Mary Salome,
perhaps the mother of the apostles James the Greater and John.
Whoever they really were, the two of them together with Mary
Magdalene, her sister Martha and her brother Lazarus, and two
evangelists, Maximinius and Sidonius, were believed to have

been cast adrift on the sea in about 40 AD by the Jews of Jerusalem. Sara, their black servant, was left ashore, but Mary Salome threw her cloak on the sea and Sara walked across the water to the boat. This party, which had no means of propelling their craft, was eventually beached at Les Stes Maries de la Mer. Only Mary Jacobi, Mary Salome and Sara stayed there; the others went on to evangelize elsewhere, mainly in Provence. The relics they brought with them, the bones of the Holy Innocents and the head of St James the Less, were not however 'discovered' until the fifteenth century.

There has been a sanctuary at Les Stes Maries de la Mer from the sixth century and a small church was built on the site in the twelfth century. Fortified to keep the Moors at bay, it still stands, its crenellations and flat belltower golden against the deep blue sky. Inside, the stone has turned pink, and it is stiflingly hot at any time of year because a huge number of candles and night-lights burn constantly in the blackened crypt. Sara, to whom this crypt is dedicated, is the patron saint of the gypsies and is still a major cult figure for European Romanys. The 'sons of the wind', as they have been called, congregate here on 24 and 25 May each year. Hundreds of them gather from all over France, the women in their traditional clothes offering to tell one's fortune for a suitable remuneration. Figurines of Sara, shrouded in an elaborate lacy dress, and the two Marys, in pink and blue satin, are carried through the thronged streets.

Midnight mass on Christmas Eve is the other great occasion for the locals, when a procession of *gardiens*, fishermen, shepherds and their girls arrive with offerings for the church. They are the descendants of the amateur artists whose ex-votos hang on its walls, powerfully evocative and touching examples of faith.

The history of the Camargue and its traditions is displayed in the Musée Baroncelli, named for the Marquis Falco de Baroncelli, a *manadier* and poet whose tomb is on the seashore.

Vincent van Gogh, then living in Arles and nearing the end of his life, made an expedition by diligence to Les Stes Maries

35

where, as he wrote to his brother Theo, he found the Mediterranean to have

> the colours of mackerel – changeable, I mean. You don't always know if it is green or violet; you can't even say it's blue, because the next moment the changing light has taken on a tinge of rose colour or grey . . . You get better fried fish here than on the Seine . . .[22]

Van Gogh was certainly right about the fish. Amongst the souvenir and clothes shops to be found in any comparable seaside resort, restaurants, cafés and food stalls cater to the holidaymakers and day-trippers, offering many fish dishes and delicious 'finger-food' such as slices of pizza, variously topped with squid, octopus or anchovy, and sizzling batons of *pan bagna*. Elizabeth David notes that the origin of pizza, which we now think of as Italian, comes in fact from *pissaladière*, a French Mediterranean onion tart with anchovies and olives.

There are few roads across the salt marshes, but for those who like variety, there is the Bac du Sauvage, a free car ferry across the Petit Rhône. The strength of its current is by no means *petit*, since a restraining wire is required to prevent the ferry from being swept downstream. There are also pleasure boats which ply between Les Stes Maries de la Mer and the Bac; a peaceful excursion and a good way to see the wildlife.

Extraordinary mountains of salt, some eight hundred metres long, shining whiter than white like great piles of washing powder are a characteristic feature of this part of the coastline. The Compagnie des Salins du Midi was formed in 1856 and now controls all the *salins* (saltpans) on the Mediterranean coast. The salt is produced by letting seawater into large shallow basins where, dried by sun and wind alike, it slowly evaporates. As the summer progresses, the saltpans turn from a pale pink to a rusty red. The colour comes from the presence of two animalcules, a tiny shrimp (*Artemia salinae*) and a microscopic pink alga (*Dunaliella salina*). As the brine thickens, the

Artemia which live on the algae die and the algae increase so that their roseate hue accentuates.

Between March and September 45 million cubic metres of seawater are processed. Whereas the production of salt along the Atlantic coast is inevitably dependent on the tides, and the salt has therefore to be collected daily in summer in small quantities, along the tideless Mediterranean it is only collected once a year, nowadays by highly mechanized means. The salt, washed and now pure white, is stored in *camelles* (as the mounds are known) which in the past were covered with tiles to protect them from rain, but as this is a costly and laborious process they are now left uncovered. When it rains, the top layer dissolves and recrystallizes, with the sandy grit blown on to it, to form a protective shell. By 15 October 400,000 tonnes of salt are ready for packaging and sale, mostly for human or animal consumption.

Of the 14,000 hectares owned by the Salins du Midi in the Aigues-Mortes area alone, 10,800 produce salt. The remaining 3,200 are planted with vines. The root-stock here is unusual, for the phylloxera louse will not breed in sand. When in the mid-nineteenth century the rest of France was stricken and had to import new vine stocks from America, these vineyards were untouched. Even today the vines are largely ungrafted and on French stock. The Compagnie proudly advertises the 'natural' qualities of its wines which are made without recourse to chemicals or pasteurization. They are marketed as Listel Vins de Pays des Sables du Golfe du Lion. There is also a special *gris de gris* where the grape juice has only had the briefest contact with the skins. All are good value, light and dry, and the rosés go particularly well with fish.

However stagnant the waters or malaria-infested the coast I wonder that any town should, from its inception, have been given so accurate but so discouraging a name as Aigues-Mortes – 'Dead Waters'. 'Its inhabitants more than once forcefully besought St Louis to rename their town "the Good", but to no avail – they had to resign themselves to the inauspicious label attached to it from its foundation'.[23]

Once the French crown had acquired a toehold in Languedoc in 1229, Louis IX gained access to the Mediterranean and was able to build a port on his property. He chose the site of Aigues-Mortes, for although today, because of progressive silting up, it is five kilometres away from the sea, it was then right on the coast. He bought the land from the monks of the abbey of Psalmodi in 1240 on which to build a *bastide*, and offered the usual attractive terms to prospective citizens willing to settle there. *Bastides* were in effect new towns and were almost invariably laid out to the same geometrical plan within an enclosing wall. The streets conformed to a strict grid pattern and the houses, set close together to minimize fire hazards, were all the same shape and size.

Much of the stone for Aigues-Mortes was brought downstream from the limestone quarries near Beaucaire, but to speed up its construction Louis authorized the use of stones from the abbey at Maguelone. Some of his contemporaries thought that it was sacrilegious to remove materials from churches and that the failure of the Eighth Crusade and Louis' death in Tunis in 1270 was attributable to this theft. Nevertheless the town had been sufficiently advanced for him to have assembled his thirty-five thousand men and their horses there some twenty-two years earlier, when he set sail for the Seventh Crusade.

One of the first buildings to be erected was the Tour du Roi, later called the Tour de Constance in posthumous honour of Louis VII's sister, who had married Count Raymond V of Toulouse. The tower is a massive round building standing outside the ramparts, with a curved parapet added in the sixteenth century and a smaller tower which served as a lighthouse on its roof. The austerity of the exterior, built primarily for defence, gives no hint of the elegance of the decoration inside the two superimposed circular rooms with their thin Gothic ribs and carved bosses.

The greater part of the town, including the ramparts, was built by Louis' successors over the next forty years and the whole of the fortified wall, together with its fifteen towers and gateways, is still standing. Although there was a population of about fifteen thousand until the fourteenth century, as the sand encroached the town became less important even as a trading-post. The acquisition of Marseille by the French crown in 1481 and the creation of the port at Sète in 1666 ended all semblance of viable economic life at Aigues-Mortes.

The Tour de Constance became a prison in 1686 for recalci-trant Protestant land poachers. John Locke, who was in Mont-pellier in 1675–9 seeking a mild climate on account of his health, kept a journal during his travels in the surrounding countryside:

> We saw aboundance of partridges, and they say there are plenty of hares & other games preserved there by the strict order and severity of the marquis de Vards [the governor] who, not long since, clapt a towns man up in a little hole in Constance's Tower, wher he had just roome to stand upright, but could not sit or ly down, & kept him there 3 days for committing some small trespasse on his game.[24]

The tower subsequently housed many of the Huguenots from the Cévennes, though their leader, Abraham Mazel, and six-teen fellow-prisoners managed to escape by the age-old ruse of knotting their sheets and clambering down them. Marie Durand, the daughter of a Protestant pastor from the Vivarais, was less fortunate: she spent thirty-eight years imprisoned there, and still had the strength to engrave 'résister' on the wall of her cell.

The centre of the town is its main square fringed by cafés and dominated by a statue (1849) of St Louis by Pradier, said by Henry James to have been 'almost as bad as the breakfast I had at the inn that bears the name of that pious monarch'.

Two of the perquisites that Louis offered to prospective inhabitants at Aigues-Mortes was exemption from the salt tax (*gabelle*) and freedom to help themselves to salt from the *salins* at Peccais, which were owned by the abbey of Psalmodi (of which little trace remains). At that time these produced about one-seventh of the total *gabelle* in the whole of France.

The fort of Peccais, built during the Wars of Religion and restored in the eighteenth century, was thereafter maintained to keep watch over the saltpans and the transport of salt along the Canal de Bourgibou to Aigues-Mortes. It served no military purpose after the Peace of Alais (Alès) in 1629 removed the Huguenots' political privileges and their right to strongholds. Thereafter it was taken over by the customs men who found their lonely residence slowly becoming marooned in a saltwater lagoon. Smuggling was a common occupation for which the punishment was the galleys. Finding the ruins of the fort today entails something of a search. From Aigues-Mortes, it is eight kilometres to the east of the Mas de Bousquet in the direction of the Mas de Mourgue.

The Tour Carbonnière is easier to find. This medieval watch-tower guarded the only land approach to Aigues-Mortes, three kilometres to the north, at the head of the bridge crossing the River Vistre. When the Vistre was diverted to prolong the Rhône-Sète Canal, the Tour Carbonnière equally served no further purpose. The same can no longer be said of Aigues-Mortes itself, for thanks to tourists and the wine trade, it presents today a less melancholic aspect than it did when Chateaubriand thought 'when seen as a whole, with its towers and ramparts, it seems like a high-prowed ship stranded on the sand by St Louis, time and the sea'.

2

Monks, Montpellier and Molière

Maguelone – Montpellier – St Martin-de-Londres –
Aniane – St Guilhem-le-Désert – Lodève – Clermont
l'Hérault – Villeneuvette – Lamalou-les-Bains

Tɪᴍᴇ and the sea had not only made the Camargue both insalubrious and inhospitable, but the littoral beyond it to the west has been infested with millions of mosquitoes ever since the inhabitants complained to the authorities in 1635 that they were being driven to desperation by them. When in the 1960s it was decided that economic life in Languedoc had to be resuscitated and that one way to do so was by creating coastal resorts which, with luck and good judgement, might come to rival those of the Côte d'Azur, 'démoustification' was one of the first priorities. Rather than develop the existing small fishing ports, a number of towns were built from scratch. It was a major undertaking in this waterlogged terrain, but thirty years of effort have paid off: the new resorts, surrounded by plants and groves of trees, look as if they have been there for ever.

The first, at La Grande-Motte, where the Rivers Hérault and Gard meet, was started in 1966 and designed by the architect Jean Balladur. His apartment blocks, whatever one may think of them, were novel in design and, commendably, not pastiche; the pyramidal shapes lend an element of fantasy and relief to these endless flatlands. La Grande-Motte offers a marina, tennis, mini-golf and surfboarding, and is spotlessly clean. The other resorts are Le Grau-du-Roi, Port Camargue and Palavas-les-Flots, and between them they attract more than three million tourists in July and August alone. Despite this influx, and although pollution remains a problem, the 300-kilometre shore that stretches all the way to the Spanish border is claimed to be the cleanest of the entire Mediterranean.

There is, thankfully, no intention of turning Maguelone into a resort, though it may be fanciful to wonder if the eleventh-century bridge which connected it with the mainland might be restored. A new bridge would certainly make the approach to Maguelone more attractive. The only means of access is along an unlovely narrow road from Palavas-les-Flots across one of those spits of land that lie precariously between the sea and the saltwater lagoons.

The island of Maguelone was a Christian settlement in early days, though why a site so far from the Via Domitia and without natural harbour facilities should have been chosen remains a mystery. The first church was built in the sixth century and was the seat of a bishopric until 1536, when the see was transferred to Montpellier. Taken by Moors and damaged in the eighth century by Charles Martel, the original church remained unoccupied until the eleventh century when a new one was built. St Pierre was consecrated in 1054 and, together with its dependencies and two rows of fortified walls, was built in stages throughout the twelfth century, when it came to resemble nothing so much as a miniature city.

The church is all that now remains of this large medieval ecclesiastical complex, solitary and austere in a green enclave of pine and eucalyptus and wild flowers, surrounded by the blue sea and the white seabirds. Chateaubriand's description of Aigues-Mortes as a 'stranded ship' could equally well be applied here. The local seigneur had in the ninth century acquired not only the land but the bishopric too, and in 1085 the reigning count offered his territories to the Holy See in return for the Pope's protection. Urban II gladly accepted them and made a point of visiting the cathedral when he was in Languedoc in 1096. Thenceforward the papacy took a special interest in Maguelone. Indeed, over the next decades it came to be a refuge for the popes when the going got rough for them in Rome. Suger, Abbot of St Denis, who was responsible for one of the first and grandest of the Gothic cathedrals in the Île de France, visited Maguelone in 1118 and found it 'small and poverty-stricken [on] a narrow island inhabited only by the bishop, his clerics and a small retinue'.

It certainly did not remain either small or poverty-stricken, as it accumulated revenues from the production of salt, from letting out the rights to fish in its lagoons, and from the tolls it imposed on the *graus* (an occitanian word for a canal draining water from a lagoon into the sea). Work went ahead in fits and starts under the aegis of two particularly active and ambitious bishops. It comes as no surprise to learn that by the end of the twelfth century, Maguelone had become a citadel of orthodoxy, nor that Innocent III should choose its archdeacon, Pierre de Castelnau, as one of his legates to negotiate with Raymond VI of Toulouse over his protection of heretics.

But by the middle of the thirteenth century, the days of Maguelone's glory were over and, as we have seen, it was pillaged to build Aigues-Mortes. Worse was to follow: the whole enclave was sacked by the Protestants in 1562 and the last fortifications were dismantled by Richelieu in 1632. The final indignity was when more of its stones were removed in 1708 to serve as foundations for the Rhône–Sète Canal dug out through the Etang de Pérols. A *cathédrale engloutie* indeed.

The church and its surrounding land were bought and restored to life in the nineteenth century by Frédéric Fabrèges. The agricultural outbuildings he erected are now used to house and train the mentally handicapped for reintegration into the local community. Fabrèges also restored the church, a simple but sturdy structure. The portal, between two towers, is an odd amalgam of disparate objects. The lintel is one of those reused Roman milestones and has been embellished with a scroll of acanthus leaves, signed and dated 1178 by one Bernard de

Tréviers. One of the lovely sixth-century sarcophagi inside the church, with a pattern of intertwined acanthus and vine leaves, is reputed to have been that of 'la belle Maguelonne', the heroine of a story attributed to Bernard. The bas-reliefs on either side of the door depicting St Paul and St Peter, and the white marble tympanum, showing a massive and rather clumsy Christ sitting in majesty and surrounded by the four evangelists, were later additions.

The interior of the church is also massive but far from clumsy, and has a splendid architectural unity. There is just the huge single nave with a tribune, added in the thirteenth century, over the first two bays. The semicircular apse is unadorned save for three small windows with marble colonnettes set high in the wall. The Romanesque church dedicated to St Etienne at Villeneuve-lès-Maguelone on the 'mainland' is also worth visiting and the village has some charming sixteenth-century houses.

One of the reasons for the decline of Maguelone was the growth of Montpellier, though by the standards of other cities in Languedoc, Montpellier is *arriviste*, a newcomer born in the tenth century, with no Phocean or Greek or Roman or even early Christian antecedents. But it has never let this hold it back. It rapidly became a prosperous and cosmopolitan town, welcoming Arabs and Jews, both of whom were instrumental in developing its commerce and its reputation for medical studies.

Its counts, nearly all called Guilhem (in much the same way that the counts of Toulouse were called Raymond) ruled there from the eleventh century. They were particularly adept at making good marriages for their enormous number of children and Marie, the last direct heir, wed as her third husband Pedro of Aragon in 1204. She took Montpellier with her and it was to remain under Aragonese sovereignty until 1349 when the French king bought it for 120,000 golden *écus*.

Although the fifth Guilhem of Montpellier had gone on crusade under the banner of Raymond IV of Toulouse, his

44

descendants were to become rivals to the later counts of Toulouse. This may seem of mere academic interest, but the long-standing conflict between Toulouse and Montpellier persists to this day. Until recently each vied with the other for precedence as the capital of Languedoc. Toulouse, the once-proud seat of the province's high court, lost. It is no longer even within the region of Languedoc-Roussillon, though it can console itself with being the capital of the new region of Midi-Pyrénées, a name invented by bureaucrats and bereft of all historical connotations.

The main (perhaps the only) drawback to Montpellier is getting either into or out of it in a motorcar. The one-way road system and the eccentric signposting, which seems intent on sending one only to the Cité Universitaire, are daunting. If it doesn't suit you to arrive or depart by train (the SNCF station is conveniently near the centre of the city), find somewhere safe to leave the car (preferably empty), and take to your feet, or use the excellent bus service. That said, and one way or another it is advice that applies to all the other Languedoc towns, Montpellier is a treat to be savoured slowly. There is so much to see and all of it is so enjoyable that it would be a pity to be in a hurry.

Except for the rare occasions when it rains, the sky over Montpellier is invariably blue; the absence of cloud is due to one of the three prevailing winds, the *mistral*, the *tramontane* and the *marin*, which blow most of the time. These winds are a conspicuous feature throughout Languedoc; you have only to climb a few yards up from a breathless plain to find yourself almost blown away.

Although Montpellier survived the Albigensian Crusade intact, virtually all its pre-Renaissance buildings were destroyed by the Huguenots in the Wars of Religion. Religious feeling has always run high in the Midi, and even today there seems to be a greater degree of religious commitment – whether Catholic or Protestant – here than in other parts of France. A Montpellier friend (Catholic) told me that the son of one of his colleagues (Protestant) had fallen in love with his daughter. It was quickly pointed out to him that under no circumstances would the Protestant son be allowed to marry the Catholic girl. And this was only ten years ago.

Whatever their religious convictions, the Montpellerians have never been averse to making money. They became extremely prosperous from the middle of the thirteenth century, deriving their income from money-changing, spice-trading and dyeing cloth – red in their case, just as the Nîmois specialized in blue.

Felix Platter had noted growing hereabouts 'a kind of oak; its berries give a scarlet dye, or cramoisy. The last name comes from the berry, which is called *kermes*, it contains little worms, which give the tincture, and if the berries are not gathered in time, the worms grow wings and fly out of the shell'. Actually there were two scale-insects of the *Coccidae* family, both parasitic on two evergreen Mediterranean oaks (the kermes oak, *Quercus coccifera* and the holm oak, *Quercus ilex*); and it was these which, killed, crushed and mixed with water produced the scarlet dye. Other red dyes came from madder (*garance*) and mulberries (murrey), until about 1560 when imported cochineal displaced them all.

The citizens of Montpellier made a great deal of money from their monopoly in red dye, as they did from a virtual monopoly of the Ferme-Générale (the tax-raising body). As a result, there are some hundred or so beautiful aristocratic and bourgeois hôtels mostly in the old part of the city. All are worth looking at, but those which may be singled out for their grandiose architecture or historical connections are the Hôtel des Trésoriers de la Bourse; the Hôtel de Montcalm from which Louis-Joseph de Montcalm set out as head of the French army for Canada in 1756; and that of the Trésoriers de France in which Jacques Coeur lived. He became the King's personal financier in 1438 and in 1441 was one of the royal commissioners charged with raising subsidies from the Estates of Languedoc. He based himself in Montpellier and directed his commercial undertakings throughout the Mediterranean from this house until his arrest in 1451. It is now used by the Société Archéologique as a museum, though not, as its name would imply, devoted only to archaeology. It contains fragments of sculpture from the churches of St Guilhem-le-Désert, and the abbeys of St Pons-de-Thomières and Fontfroide; and some good examples of Montpellier faience. Faience vessels were first produced there to serve as pharmacy jars but by the early eighteenth century Montpellier was manufacturing domestic tableware under semi-industrial conditions. Though perhaps provincial in execution, its rich egg-yolk-yellow ground decorated with blue flowers and motifs makes it particularly attractive.

The fine Hôtel de Varennes houses two museums: that on the second floor is the private Musée Fougau (with very capricious opening hours), devoted to popular arts and crafts; and on the ground floor is the Musée du Vieux-Montpellier. Here there is some furniture, pictures of bishops and a display of ecclesiastical vestments, a few poor lithographs – though an interesting one showing the greenhouses in the Jardin des Plantes in its heyday – and a fascinating set of mallets used for playing pall mall (*mail*) displayed on a wall and looking at first sight like the spokes of a wheel. Locke noted shortly after his arrival in Montpellier that 'all the highways are fild with gamesters at mall, soe that Walkers are in some danger of knocks'.[25] The French passion for *boules* or *pétanque* played in public places obviously stems from their love of *Mail*. Alas it is no longer possible to play in the streets of Montpellier, even where pedestrianized.

It is a short walk to the 'new' church of Notre Dame des Tables, which takes its name from an earlier church on whose forecourt the moneychangers' tables were set up. (Only the crypt of the original church remains, a damp-smelling basement adorned with some rather feeble photos purporting to tell the history of Montpellier. It is in the place Jean-Jaurès, near the market.) The new church, by the side of the former Jesuit convent, has a sober, classical façade and was designed by Jean-Antoine Giral. Nearby is the Musée Fabre founded by François-Xavier Fabre. Henry James reckoned him to be 'a bad French painter, whose productions bear the stamp of a cold mediocrity'. Stendhal had met Fabre, whom he called 'that celebrated Gascon' with the Countess of Albany in Florence.

> People said that his presence there had driven the morose Alfieri to die of a broken heart. But Alfieri was bound to die broken-hearted over something or other, even though his former mistress had never passed him over for another man.[26]

Fabre left his own collection of Italian and French pictures to the city, as did Alfred Bruyas, another wealthy collector, who gave the museum fine works by Courbet, Delacroix, Géricault and Corot amongst others. It is fitting that there should be a whole room of portraits of him by the artists he patronized, including *Bonjour, Monsieur Courbet*, in which Courbet and his red-headed friend are greeting each other. There are a number of paintings by Frédéric Bazille, who was born in Montpellier and who was killed at a tragically early age at the end of the Franco-Prussian War.

The museum also has its share of nineteenth-century horrors, including some sentimental works by Jean-Baptiste Greuze and Alexandre Cabanel, whose erotic *Phèdre* brought tears to the eyes of the viewers when it was first exhibited at the Paris Salon, having won the Prix de Rome in 1845. Nevertheless, the Fabre has one of the best collections of works of art outside Paris. Nearly all are displayed in natural light, and are well hung. The Musée Sabatier-d'Espeyran-Cabrières is in a side-turning by the Musée Fabre. A Second Empire house, it contains nineteenth and early twentieth-century furniture displayed in its original surroundings.

The social heart of the city is the nearby place de la Comédie from which all traffic except buses has been banned. It is familiarly known as 'l'Oeuf' from its original egg-shape, which has been traced in red marble on the paving. What could be more agreeable than to watch the world go by from one of the cafés or restaurants on its perimeter, in sight of the fountain of the Three Graces, and the opera house. This latter was rebuilt in 1888 by J. M. Cassien-Bernard who had worked at the Paris Opéra, with which it has affinities.

The Hôtel St Côme, built for the Academy of Surgery as an anatomy theatre by Jean-Antoine Giral in 1752–7, is in a very different architectural style, exuding eighteenth-century rationality. The amphitheatre, surmounted by a circular dome, is elegant, in spite of the modern glass in the windows; the building is now in use by the chamber of commerce.

The covered market in the centre of the city is everything one could hope for. There is a huge choice of all kinds of provender, and Elizabeth David found it just as satisfying in 1960:

> Plenty of tourists spend their mornings in museums and picture galleries and cathedrals, and nobody would quarrel with them for that. But the stomach of a city is also not without its importance. And then, I wouldn't be too sure that the food market of a big city shouldn't be counted as part of its artistic tradition . . .
>
> How has a Montpellier fishwife so mastered the art of composition that with her basket of fish for the *bouillabaisse* she is presenting a picture of such splendour that instead of going to look at the famous collection of paintings in the Musée Fabre you drive off as fast as possible to the coast to order a dish cooked with just such fish?[27]

One of the city's specialities, which goes particularly well with fish, is Montpellier butter or its variant Languedoc butter, both highly flavoured green sauces made with herbs, capers, anchovies and eggs. Another is *oreillettes*, one of the many *douceurs* (sweetmeats) to be found here. These 'little pillows' are round, flattish sort of waffles, scented with bergamot or lemon and sprinkled with icing sugar.

The Préfecture is in the little place Chabaneau near the market, in the Hôtel de Ganges, built in 1686 by Cardinal Bonzi for his mistress, Jeanne de Gévaudan. Pierre de Bonzi, whom we shall encounter frequently, was a member of a powerful family of Italian prelates who dominated the ecclesiastical life of western Languedoc for the better part of half a century and five members of which were bishops of Béziers. Pierre himself, who subsequently became a cardinal and archbishop of both Toulouse and Narbonne, was notorious for his worldliness, and his affairs with women were the talk of Versailles. The Duc de Saint-Simon says that 'he was long a virtual king by the authority of his office, his influence at court, and his love for the province'.

A short walk leads to the place de la Canourgue, with its fountain playing in the shade of *micocouliers* (nettle trees), and on to one of the few pre-Renaissance buildings in Montpellier. The cathedral announces itself by two huge stone conical towers holding up a fourteenth-century canopy, all of which look as if they have been dreamed up for Disneyland. St Pierre started as a modest chapel in 1364 but was enlarged in 1536 when it achieved cathedral status, and has undergone endless transformations ever since. There are some pleasing pictures and sculptures in the chapels round the nave, including works by two native artists, Sébastien Bourdon and Jean de Troy (more of whose works are in the Musée Fabre). The mausoleum of Cardinal de Cabrières by Jean-Marie-Joseph Magrou, with its bas-relief showing him welcoming the delegation of *vignerons* whose revolt in 1907 he supported, is of interest as are the altar of beaten copper, the ambo in the chancel and a second altar and tabernacle door, all recent works by Philippe Koeppelin.

The cathedral struck Henry James as 'quite the weakest' he had seen. The town he found 'agreeable as certain women are agreeable who are neither beautiful nor clever'. He was there in

the days when Montpellier was still accounted a fine winter residence for people with weak lungs; and this rather melancholy tradition, together with the former celebrity of the school of medicine still existing there, but from which the glory has departed, helped to account for its combination of high antiquity and vast proportions.[28]

Montpellier had been famed from the early thirteenth century not only for its large number of hospitals but more especially for this faculty of medicine, founded in 1220. Rabelais, who subsequently became an eminent physician, took his degree there in 1530 though he could not resist a dig at his alma mater.

> Thence came he [Pantagruel] to Montpellier where he found fine Mirevaux wines and merry company; and took a fancy to study medicine, but then reflected that the profession was an exceeding troublesome one, melancholy too, and that the doctors stank of clysters, like the very Devil. None the less, he had a mind to study law, but seeing that there was no more than a scurvy bunch of jurists in that place he took his leave.[29]

Thomas Wentworth, another of those indefatigable English travellers, visited the faculty in 1612 and was told of the never-to-be forgotten day when Rabelais, going up to the podium in his red gown to receive his degree, 'voluntary fell downe with his nose upon the stare, arising kepte a snorting; the reason asked, saide he felt the smel of many an asse that had gone thear before him'.[30]

Rousseau too spent some time in Montpellier, lodging with an Irish doctor called Fitzmorris, who he says was a great *mail* player and under whom he took a course in anatomy which he abandoned 'owing to the horrible odour of the corpses they dissected, which I was unable to endure'. Amongst the physicians he saw was the famous Dr Fizes whom Sterne also consulted in 1764:

> I am preparing, my dear Mrs. F., to leave France, for I am heartily tired of it – That insipidity there is in French characters has disgusted your friend Yorick – I have been dangerously ill, and cannot think that the sharp air of Montpellier has been of service to me – and so my physicians told me when they had me under their hands for above a month – if you stay any longer here, Sir, it will be fatal to you . . .
>
> P.S. My physicians have almost poisoned me with what they call *bouillons refraishissants* – 'tis a cock flead alive and boiled with poppy seeds, then pounded in a mortar, afterwards pass'd thro' a sieve – There is to be one crawfish in it, and I was gravely told that it must be a male one – a female would do me more hurt than good.[31]

A later visitor was Joseph Conrad who spent the winters of 1906 and 1908 in Montpellier, on account of his wife and son's ill health, and wrote part of *The Secret Agent* there.

The Faculté de Médecine is housed in a former Benedictine convent in the rebuilding of which Jean Giral, Jean-Antoine's uncle, had a hand. It contains the Musée Atger, which has a collection of drawings, and the Musée d'Anatomie, but both are shut during university holidays.

John Ray, a naturalist who visited Montpellier in the late seventeenth century, was struck by finding a hundred and thirty pharmacies, much as Thomas Platter had been amazed to find eight in Uzès some hundred years earlier. Stendhal too found them worthy of comment:

> I went out to look for a tolerable café, but could find only chemists. It is a fact that Montpellier is full of doctors, and, in consequence, of wealthy invalids. Gloomy consumptive Englishmen come here in shoals to die.[32]

The teaching of botany had become an official part of the university's functions in 1550 and one of its exponents was Guillaume Rondelet, a friend of Rabelais and chancellor of the university in 1556–66, whose methods of teaching were revolutionary for the times. He actually took his pupils out into the countryside and solemn young men were to be seen roaming the fields and woods, gathering flowers to which no one had previously paid the least attention.

The Jardin des Plantes, the first botanical garden in Europe, was founded by Henri IV in 1593. The great Swiss botanist Augustin-Pyrame de Candolle evolved his natural system of botanical classification there and made the study of plants into a discipline in its own right. The physic garden has been justly famous since its foundation, but now it is ghostly and rather sad. Only twenty years ago one was entranced by being sprinkled at regular intervals in the greenhouses where the tropical plants were kept. Today wild flowers push their way up to the sun through the broken glass and the rotting slatted wooden blinds. The severe winter of 1986 caused irreversible damage to the plants (in general Montpellier has more frequent and sharper frosts than London), and clearly not enough money is available to look after it properly.

Curiously enough, the garden provided the vine cuttings which were the start of the wine industry in Australia, having been shipped out there by James Bushy in 1832. With the recent arrival in Languedoc of a contingent of Australians trying to buy large vineyards, the wheel has come full circle. The *Midi Libre* newspaper however calls this antipodean invasion 'scandalous' and the local *vignerons* are doing their best to repulse it.

A short climb from the Jardin des Plantes leads up to the Peyrou. At the end of the seventeenth century Montpellier was still bedevilled by narrow smelly streets and in 1688 it was proposed to build a fine new esplanade outside the walls which could also serve as an exercise ground for the army. It was to be linked to the city by a triumphal arch like that at the Porte St Denis in Paris, where the victories of Louis XIV over both the enemy abroad and the enemy within – in this case the Huguenots – would be made manifest to the people of Languedoc. The arch was built by Daviler and it makes a fine statement, though the sculpture on the decorative panels by Philippe Bertrand is rather feeble.

It was also thought that the town should sport a monumental statue of the Sun King, and the Intendant, Basville, thought that it would look well – indeed that it 'would be the best placed in the whole kingdom' – on the new esplanade. Everyone else was horrified:

The notion of placing an equestrian statue of the King in such an exposed position, virtually in open country, and this in a Huguenot region on the threshold of the Cévennes, strikes all sensible people as outlandish and hazardous – and furthermore, seems to people of good sense quite contrary to established practice, which has always enclosed the statue of French kings safely within town walls.[33]

But there was no immediate cause for alarm; in the first place there was trouble with the statue itself. It was not cast until 1692, and it then had to be taken from Paris to Le Havre, by boat to Bordeaux, and thence along the Garonne, into which it fell. Recovered, it was transported along the new Canal du Midi as far as Frontignan whence a new channel had to be dug to get it as far as Montpellier. It was not erected on the Peyrou until 1718. (The statue was destroyed in the Revolution and a copy made in 1838 now stands in its place.)

The Peyrou itself was not making much progress either. Arguments about what form it should take proliferated and centred round money; nothing happened until mid-century when the need to construct a new aqueduct, which was to imitate the Pont du Gard, meant that the whole plan for the Peyrou had to be reconsidered. Jean-Antoine Giral won the competition for its design and in 1774 he transformed what might have been only a parade ground for the military into a sort of 'Babylonian ziggurat' (as one critic called it), where terraces on different levels rise in a crescendo to a little eighteenth-century temple disguising the reservoir, the *château d'eau* beneath.

At the foot of the Peyrou, on the far side of the triumphal arch, is a temple of a different kind. The neo-Greek Palais de Justice (law courts) by Charles Aubric was completed in 1856. Montpellier's contemporary urban redevelopments in the eastern part of the city are far from Babylonian; indeed they are aggressively modernistic and quite different from those at Nîmes. There are two new complexes called 'Antigone' and 'Polygone'. Antigone is what in the circumstances one can only describe as a neo-neo-Greek housing estate, designed by Ricardo Bofill, a Catalan architect, for low-income families who must find the mammoth fluted pillars and broken pediments novel to say the least. Polygone is a commercial centre with shopping arcades and smart boutiques. At least you can park there.

*

There are a number of attractions in the immediate environs of Montpellier. The site of the *oppidum* of Ambrussum has recently been excavated. It was occupied from the fourth century BC and the Romans took it over when they built the Via Domitia. Now one can see some 200 metres of the paved road, the ruins of a large public edifice and a number of dwellings. Alas, of the eleven-arched Roman bridge which carried the Via Domitia across the Vidourle, only a solitary one remains. In 1850 when Courbet painted it (Musée Fabre, Montpellier), there were still two.

Three kilometres to the south is Lunel. Whether or not it is true that it was founded by a colony of Jews after the fall of Jericho in 68 AD, it is certain that by the twelfth century there was an important Jewish school there. The town lost its château in 1632 when it was dismantled by Richelieu, but the medieval arcaded streets (the arcades are called *caladons*) remain. The church of Notre Dame du Lac was rebuilt between 1686 and 1699 and given a Baroque façade; the organ was started in 1856 by Aristide Cavaillé-Coll, many of whose works we shall encounter, but he left this one unfinished. Lunel is a lively little agricultural centre, and produces palatable red and rosé wines, and a sweet muscat Vin Doux Naturel.

There are also a number of châteaux charmingly described as 'follies' in the local tourist literature. Three lie to the west of the city. The château d'O, of which only the gardens may be visited; the château de Mosson, attributed to Jean Giral, where the very grand house may be visited; and the château de l'Engerran, gardens only, but beautiful. To the east, the château de la Mogère, also attributed to Jean Giral, has another fine garden and good pictures and furniture. The nearby château de Flaugergues, built in 1690, looks rather like an Italian villa and has an impressive interior. The château has its own vineyard and sells its wine.

The château at Castries (confusingly pronounced Castres), some ten kilometres to the north-west of Montpellier, could not in any circumstances be described as a folly. It is a typical Renaissance château, though with some later modifications, erected round a large courtyard and still inhabited by the family which built it. There are fine examples of furniture and paintings, and a charming collection of baby clothes.

The château de Marsaillargues, with a small museum of arts and crafts, is a well-proportioned seventeenth-century building in the process of restoration; that at nearby Teillan has two different attractions: seven Roman milestones, which have been there since 1621, and an enormous dovecote, with sufficient room for fifteen hundred nests, built in 1605 to keep travellers to Aigues-Mortes supplied with edible pigeons.

Throughout Languedoc and Roussillon one is far more likely to come across early Romanesque churches, like the one at St Martin-de-Londres, than these commodious country houses of the aristocracy and bourgeoisie. All the churches are very beautiful; some are perfectly restored but many are in a parlous state of decay. In the early decades of the eleventh century an enormous number of churches were built throughout Europe. 'Although', said Ranulph Glaber, a monk writing about 1048, 'most of the existing churches are of sturdy construction, and not in need of replacement, each Christian community was moved by a spirit of competition to have one that would be grander than that of their neighbours'.[34]

The Midi was no exception and in the Mediterranean areas of Languedoc and Roussillon, round about the year 1000, novel techniques and stylistic innovations began to make their appearance. The new style, which has no parallel in either Provence or the Toulousain, is described by architectural historians as the 'first' Romanesque. It is characterized by the use of small split stones laid in regular courses with thick mortar joints. The walls were rarely pierced by windows and virtually the only decorative element on the exterior was a row of small blind arcades high under the eaves resting on pilasters known as *lésènes*. This form of decoration had appeared in northern Italy in the ninth century and seems to have been brought thence to Languedoc by itinerant masons, which is why it is known as 'lombard arcading'.

The churches were simple in plan, and more often than not had a nave roofed in wood, with a vaulted chancel supported by raised semicircular arches resting on solid pillars with plain block capitals. As long as the walls were made of small stones which could not carry much weight, it was impossible to vault the entire nave. But slowly a row of semicircular transverse arches was inserted to support the vaulting. The weight of stone was carried in the interior on cruciform pillars linked by arches, and on the outside by buttresses. Square chevets were replaced by three semicircular apses. The addition of transepts and a dome were other new features. Almost the only decoration in the interiors was the use of a black basaltic stone in the window-surrounds in the apses, and a few simple sculptures in flat relief on the capitals.

The 'second' Romanesque period, of the twelfth century, shows that masons had by then acquired the skills needed to dress larger blocks of stone, held together by smaller joints. Lombard arcades, though, continued into the twelfth and even the thirteenth centuries. The plan remained much the same, with a single nave, by now vaulted without difficulty. The supporting pillars, often cruciform, became less crude, and the capitals decorated more skilfully in high relief.

The church of St Martin-de-Londres, like those at Quarante and St Guilhem-le-Désert, by whose monks it was built at the end of the eleventh century, is a fine example of the 'first' Romanesque style. Its exterior is harmonious, with one huge semicircular apse, flanked by two smaller ones like embryonic transepts, forming an unusual trefoil pattern, and surmounted by an octagonal tower, all with lombard arcades. The interior has been less kindly served by time, for in the nineteenth century much of the church was demolished and poor restoration in 1932 did not improve matters.

The village has vestiges of two fortified medieval walls, and some seventeenth- and eighteenth-century houses. St Martin-de-Londres derives its name from the occitanian word for marsh, for until the valley was drained in the Middle Ages it was marshland. It is now an attractive place, surrounded by hills covered in holm oaks.

St Benoît d'Aniane – whom we shall meet on several occasions – was a Goth. Named Witiza at birth, he was the son of Aigulf de Maguelone and was sent as a young man to the Frankish court. But in 774, after a narrow escape from drowning in Italy on campaign with Charlemagne, he took vows as a monk at St Seine, near Dijon. Being both puritanical and self-righteous, he soon became dissatisfied with conditions there and retired to a cell by the River Aniane where, as Edward James says, he founded a monastery

> on his own ancestral land – a disastrous experiment, because the rule he imposed was so severe that all his monks deserted. Around 787 he built a new monastery, larger and with the luxury and decoration he had hitherto despised. It was probably then that he adopted the more humane Benedictine rule and changed his name.[35]

His exposition of the rule of the great St Benedict (Benoît) of Nursia which advocated a combination of prayer, study and manual labour, in his *Concordia Regularum* (A Harmony of Rules) was to become one of the greatest influences on western monasticism.

Aniane, the small town where St Benoît was born, lies in a flat plain surrounded by fields and ringed by low hills and has some fifteen hundred inhabitants. It is wonderfully homogenous in colour, pale yellow and pink with its Roman tiles, and blissfully free of tourists.

Although Charlemagne authorized the use of columns and capitals from the Arènes at Nîmes for St Benoît to build his church (it is a wonder that any ancient buildings at all survive), both it and the original abbey buildings were razed by a Huguenot member of the Crussol d'Uzès family in 1562. A new church dedicated to St Sauveur was built in 1661 under the auspices of the congregation of St Maur, a reforming order founded to restore the morale of the monastic clergy and their buildings after both had been destroyed by the Wars of Religion. It is a sober Baroque building with an attractive façade, and the interior is much enlivened by an almost excessive number of cherubim. Their appearance, an Italianate feature, may perhaps be attributed to their abbots, who from 1615 to 1703 were members of the Bonzi family.

The church of St John the Baptist, with a thirteenth-century nave, stands on the site of another of St Benoît's churches. The eighteenth-century Mairie has a good façade, and the monumental gate to the cemetery is thought to be by an architect inspired by that Revolutionary fantasist, Claude-Nicolas Ledoux.

The road which links Aniane and St Guilhem-le-Désert (formerly Gellone) crosses a narrow eleventh-century bridge known as the Pont du Diable, for it was here that St Guilhem threw the devil into the Hérault. The road winds its perilous way up through a gorge of great majesty to what was described by one of St Benoît's contemporaries as

> so secluded a spot that any lover of solitude is bound to feel at home there. One is entirely surrounded by high mountains fringed with clouds: it is hard to imagine a place better suited to contemplation – no one would seek out such a retreat for purposes other than prayer and meditation.[36]

The site is certainly idyllic, catching the sun and protected by a dramatic backdrop of towering cliffs.

Guillaume (Guilhem in occitan) de Gellone, a Frank, was the grandson of Charles Martel and the son of Thierry, perhaps Count of Autun. Known as both Guillaume d'Orange and Court-Nez, he fought with distinction in Charlemagne's army, earning a reputation as a mighty warrior, and his exploits were exalted in a *chanson de geste*. He was rewarded for his faithful service in 788 with the county of Toulouse and in 793 with the duchy of Aquitaine. At this time he re-encountered Witiza–Benoît, his childhood friend and neighbour. It seems likely that it was Benoît's influence that led him to found and endow the monastery in the tree-studded valley of Gellone. In 806 Guilhem took the habit there himself and ended his days six years later in the community he had created. The village was renamed for him in the tenth century.

One of the treasures he had taken to Gellone with him was a fragment of the True Cross which he had been given by Charlemagne. This relic, together with Guilhem's reputation for saintliness and some effective propaganda by the monks, soon attracted flocks of pilgrims to the church, situated as it was on one of the routes to Santiago de Compostela. In the twelfth century the monks at Gellone compiled the *Vita Sancti Willelmi*, a hagiographical work which bore little resemblance to the *Geste de Guillaume d'Orange* and which claims he sought solitary confinement in despair over his wife's death.

St Guilhem-le-Désert remains a peaceful village in spite of the crowds of rightly curious visitors, and the church is one of quite exceptional beauty. The decorated portal leads into a narthex over which in the fifteenth century a defensive tower was built, and serves today as the belltower. A nave and two narrower aisles carry the eyes inexorably to the central apse at the far end, flooded by a golden light. They, and the two smaller apses of unequal size and shape, were built at the end of the eleventh century; all are perfectly proportioned and of a singular austerity. The church contrives to exude, even for non-believers, an unmistakable aura of holiness; its very simplicity and homogeneity concentrate the mind wonderfully. St Guilhem's tomb is in the crypt, and his relics and the fragment of the True Cross are taken in procession in May.

Harmony and balance are also evident in the exterior of the church, insofar as one can see the whole, for houses are built by its side. The restored refectory has a collection of stone remains, but little is left of the chapter house and dormitory.

Unfortunately the cloister is no longer intact since some of it was sold at the beginning of this century to The Cloisters, part of the Metropolitan Museum of Art in New York. The remaining two galleries, of a pinky-grey stone, enclose a garden with a huge plane tree underplanted with roses and lavender round a pond, which makes 'désert' seem a misnomer, though 'désert' in this context is derived from the northern French *essarter* meaning deforestation. It is curious that the southern word *artiguer* was not used.

It is a thrilling drive from St Guilhem-le-Désert across the limestone plateaux known as *causses* where the colours of the rocks range from white to red and grey to violet to black, running almost the whole gamut of the geological spectrum. Limestone follows schist and sandstone follows basalt. It is no wonder that the area is riddled with caves, of which the most striking is the Grotte de Clamoux, nor that there should be so many menhirs and dolmens.

The inhabitants of Usclas-du-Bosc, a small village at the foot of the *causse*, discovered that these rocks could be put to good use, and for centuries they fabricated sharpening and polishing stones of an exceptional abrasive quality, not only supplying local needs but also exporting them to Carrara for finishing the marble. The quarry-workers' corporation was only disbanded in 1934.

The château at Usclas was built in the twelfth century and soon became a Templar hospice, and as this village was also on the route to Santiago de Compostella, growing numbers of pilgrims stopped there. Pilgrims who died on their travels had the right to be buried in a marked grave, and fifty-two round tombstones, known as discoid stelae, have been found in the cemetery at Usclas. (They are now in the Musée Fleury at Lodève.) Some have a pedestal like a short neck sloping down to the shoulders and virtually all are decorated, more often than not with a Greek cross – the symbol of eternal life. (The Latin cross, the tau, stood for Christ's death. When both are used together, as in the cross of Lorraine, they symbolize the resurrection overcoming death.) Attempts have been made to prove that the stelae, which date from the twelfth to the fifteenth centuries, were peculiar to the Cathars, but it is more probable that they just mark the passage of pilgrims to the next world.

The priory of St Michel-de-Grandmont between Usclas-du-Bosc and Lodève is now in private hands. It belonged to the order of Grandmont founded in 1076 by a Limousin, St Etienne de Muret, as a congregation dedicated to poverty. This priory was one of its first houses, most of which were in the Midi, and the simple twelfth-century church, some conventual buildings and a cloister remain. The church is undecorated but mullioned windows have rather incongruously been let into its side.

The landscape of the Lodèvois is less dramatic, domesticated as it were by the fields of vines and olive trees planted on the *garrigue*, which, with their paler colours, stand out against the dark evergreen oaks and darker still pine forests.

Lodève lies at the confluence of the Lergue and Soulondre between the summer pasture lands of the Causse de Larzac and the vineyards of Languedoc. It has prospered from wool since the twelfth century, and by the end of the eighteenth there were four thousand clothworkers living in the town and outlying districts. While the numbers have dropped catastrophically since then, it is satisfying to know not only that textiles are still produced, but that since 1962 the Gobelins have had a tapestry workshop there, staffed by forty Algerian women with their nimble fingers.

Cardinal Fleury, Louis XV's minister and the third of the powerful cardinals who ruled France, was a native of the town and in 1730 granted it the monopoly of supplying cloth to the army. The house he lived in has been turned into a museum. It contains, in addition to the stelae from Usclas-du-Bosc, geological specimens, fossil remains of reptiles and dinosaurs found when prospecting for uranium in the nearby Montagne de Grèze, prehistoric tools, Gallo-Roman pots, textiles and examples of local folk arts, paintings and sculpture. An example of the last is a model for the truly dreadful sculpture of Cro-Magnon man that lowers over the village of Les Eyzies in the Dordogne. It is by Paul Dardé who was born nearby, and who was also responsible for the Monument aux Morts in the garden behind the Hôtel de Ville.

The cathedral is dedicated to St Fulcran, a tenth-century bishop whose mummified corpse was displayed on the high altar once a year, with an arm held aloft in blessing. As if that were not grisly enough, in 1573 the Protestants dragged the body to the butchers' quarter and had it dismembered. What remains is taken on procession in its reliquary on the Sunday before Ascension.

The cathedral was started in 1280 and has been added to subsequently. It is in the northern Gothic style rather than in what is invariably referred to in Languedoc as the 'meridional' Gothic. The art historian Emile Mâle summed up the differences between the two by saying that while northern Gothic churches soar to heaven, those in the Midi inhabit the earth. In the north height and light were paramount desiderata. To achieve both, the walls, pierced by large expanses of stained glass, had to be supported by the construction of aisles and reinforced by external flying buttresses. But in Languedoc the Gothic style was more conservative and was a development of the Romanesque rather than a break with it. Neither height nor light were deemed to be important, though size was. A wide single nave without aisles is the most characteristic feature of the meridional Gothic and its vaulting was supported by interior buttresses between which chapels were occasionally inserted. These plain large naves were relatively cheap to build and they enabled the clergy to communicate easily with their flock. Since light was not a problem in the south, the windows were high and narrow or round, when they are known as *oculi*. Occasionally a rose window with unexceptional stained glass is to be found inserted in the façade. These meridional Gothic churches as a whole have a dignity that comes from their simplicity.

St Fulcran, then, remains resolutely northern, with a good Gothic doorway and a huge rose window, an elegant eighteenth-century iron balustrade along an upper balcony, a belltower and a small cloister. There is a pleasing monumental cross in the place de l'Evêché where the old bishopric, an eighteenth-century building, is now the Hôtel de Ville, its roof gaily decorated with shiny polychromatic tiles rather in the Burgundian manner. There are agreeable if not remarkable houses (in one of which Georges Auric, a member of the early twentieth-century French group of composers who called themselves Les Six, was born). The streets are lined with placid restaurants in which one can sample the local specialities. Inevitably they come mainly from the sheep, and apart from more usual cuts, you may find yourself offered tripe, trotters (*fraisettes*) and stewed head, the brains having been used for sauces; *cabassol*, a cheese made from ewe's milk, and *flaunes* or *flauzonnes*, a kind of cheese cake made from flour, eggs and *cabassols*.

Clermont l'Hérault is another wool town and, like Lodève, specialized in cloth for the army. It is also known for the production of table grapes, and there is a good view of the surrounding countryside with its covering of vines from the huge twelfth-century château which dominates the town. Its ramparts, gates and towers are among the best preserved in Languedoc. The church of St Paul is an imposing example of northern Gothic with powerful flying buttresses. It was built from 1276 onwards on Romanesque foundations, was fortified in the fifteenth century and has a particularly fine rose window. Most of the other churches of interest are closed but can be admired from the outside, as can the Louis XIV façade of the Hôtel de Martin.

*

A kilometre or two to the west, up through a double row of venerable plane trees, is a 'new town' of a rather unusual kind. In 1553 François I agreed to supply fine woollen cloth to the Ottoman empire in return for spices, dyes, silks and cotton. But by the seventeenth century both the English and the Dutch were competing with lighter, finer, and above all, cheaper cloth. Colbert therefore persuaded some Parisian and Montpellerian financiers to put up the money to create a number of textile workshops and a trading company to sell their products exclusively to the Near East. A new complex was built in the countryside outside Clermont, where water from the River Dourbie provided the driving force for the fulling mills. The walled village included both a cloth factory and living quarters for the workers. In 1677 it became a Manufacture Royale, which entitled it to special subsidies and favourable treatment in terms of taxation, and with the right to a 'woolmark' incorporating three fleur-de-lys to indicate that the cloth conformed to the required standards. By 1681 sixty-six dwelling houses had been put up and specialists from the Netherlands were brought in to teach the weavers the latest techniques. The fabric produced was known as *londrins seconds* and was a fine light cloth woven, dyed and finished at Villeneuvette. The workers and their families did not have to pay for their housing and were provided with shops and a sort of model farm on which they could work in times of unemployment.

The village prospered into the early years of the eighteenth century and by 1729 there were ninety looms and eight hundred employees working for the manufactory. By the end of the century, with changed economic conditions, the cloth trade was less remunerative and the financiers were replaced as owners by a Montpellerian family of entrepreneurs. Joseph Maistre, whose descendants still own the village, took it over in 1803, and put it back on its feet by producing cloth for both army and school uniforms, soutanes and cloaks for priests, and upholstery for railway coaches, on machinery he bought in England and Belgium. It was one of his descendants who had 'HONNEUR AU TRAVAIL' carved in huge insensitive capital letters over the main gateway, thereby ruining an elegant classical portal.

Even if one jibs at the sort of paternalistic Christian socialism that the message implies, the neat little houses with their own gardens, arranged in serried rows, would surely have been the latest thing in mod. con. and a cut above what the workers might have expected elsewhere. They were also well looked after in social terms; doctors were on hand and evening classes on offer. Perhaps the price for this was high, since it entailed subjection to lectures on the merits of 'early to rise and early to bed'.

The manufactory stayed in business until 1954, and since then the industrial buildings and the houses themselves have fallen into decay. In 1968 the sole proprietor, Camille Maistre, started selling individual houses in an attempt to save the village from complete collapse. The municipality has helped with sewerage, lighting and paving, and one must hope that the whole village will eventually be restored. In the meantime, there is a pretty hotel with a swimming pool to dissipate the gentle melancholy of a ghost town, a fig tree sprouting in the main street, the roots of the plane trees pushing up the cobbles, and luxuriant weeds and secret overgrown gardens all accompanied by the gentle plash of the village fountain.

Although monasteries were founded primarily to enable their incumbents to escape from the world, worldly necessities, not least an income, pressed in on them. Perhaps they had more in common with this workers' village than seems apparent. Certainly the abbey of Valmagne, in the plain to the south-west, depended on the vines which have now come to be the mainstay of the area around Villeneuvette. The abbey was founded in 1138 by the Viscount of Béziers and was affiliated in 1145 to Cîteaux. The refectory and chapter house were built from 1145 to 1179, and though the church and cloister were started in 1252, all underwent subsequent modification. The church itself is huge, of cathedral-like proportions, its façade flanked by two towers and its walls supported by massive flying buttresses. In 1477 an aristocratic Cévenol became commendatory abbot, an office he held for an astonishing eighty-six years. He was succeeded first by a cousin, who was there for a mere fifty, who in turn was followed by a nephew. Inspired perhaps by the beautiful fountain his predecessor had installed in the cloister in 1635, he set about turning the monastery into a sort of rural palace where he entertained lavishly, welcoming amongst others Louis XIV's grandson, the little Duc d'Anjou on his way to become king of Spain.

Bédarieux is a pleasant enough town but with nothing remarkable to detain one. Alas, there are few remains of the Benedictine abbey at Villemagne l'Argentière, though it is worth strolling round to see its vestiges, two churches and a late thirteenth-century mint, which made coins from the local silver-bearing lead. A visit to Hérépian is another matter, for here, in normal working hours, one can see one of the four bell foundries in France. The technique of making moulds and casting has barely changed over the centuries, though the founders, who have been in the iron business for four hundred years, nowadays run to compressed air to help them fan the flames of the furnace. Although they make many sizes of bell (and you can buy the small ones), it is thrilling to see one of the really large ones taking shape and to envisage it hanging in some ancient belfry and ringing for centuries to come.

It is very easy to miss the church of St Pierre-de-Rhèdes, despite being on the main road just by the turning to Lamalou-les-Bains. Although it is on a slight hill, it hides rather modestly behind the cemetery wall and one has to wend one's way through a forest of tombs and mausoleums, garishly gay with bunches of ceramic flowers and photographs of long-dead ancestors in dusty cracked frames. It is a very beautiful example of the first Romanesque style with especially fine lombard arcading, and the two doors to the church (which is not often open) have black basalt decorations of great simplicity and effectiveness. Inside, there is a single nave ending in a trefoil which is not apparent from the outside and, most unusually, the bays are separated by engaged twin columns, a feature more characteristic of the northern French style.

Lamalou-les-Bains has all the marks of a spa town with a Grand Hotel, a theatre and a casino, but on a small scale. The healing properties of the hot springs were first discovered in the mid-seventeenth century and were progressively developed over the next two hundred years until, by the end of the nineteenth, three separate sources were being exploited. Largely because the great Dr Jean Charcot recommended Lamalou, it became very fashionable with *curistes* during the Belle Epoque, when villas and public buildings were put up to cater for them.

Gide was taken there as a child in 1881 and has much to say about his sensations in the 'opaque and rust-coloured' water, in which 'myriads of tiny bubbles formed to tease you, stinging, mingling with the coolness of the water a mysterious warmth which relaxed the congested nerve-centres . . . you came out of the bath with skin flaming and bones frozen'. For Léon Daudet, Alphonse's son, it had rather different memories:

> There are few spots so beautiful, so sombre, so bleak and yet so touching as the spa of Lamalou . . . My father had plans for a book about this watering place, to be entitled *Le Doulou*, but died leaving it unwritten. It was Charcot who brought prosperity to the spa, sending to it his numerous clientele, drawn from every country. Where custom led, science had the good sense to follow, although the therapeutic outcomes were variable . . .
>
> Opium was the great palliative. Morphine was all the rage at Lamalou and the pin-pricks of euphoric poison were as common as mosquito bites. When people had exhausted the topic of their ailments – their location, their severity and the choice of treatments – they would move on to their doses of the drug; a spirit of rivalry would emerge as though in a competitive parade of suffering.
>
> 'I, madam, am on one gram a day.'
>
> 'Why, that's not much! I for my part am on one gram and a half.'[37]

68

3

Greeks and Heretics

Pézenas – Sète – Etang du Thau – Agde – Béziers –
Fonséranes – Ensérune – Minervois

WHILE Pézenas has much in common with Montpellier in that
it abounds in grand sixteenth- and seventeenth-century town
houses of a similar style, there the similarity ends. Montpellier
is unquestionably a thriving, go-ahead modern city, with no
hint of provinciality, while Pézenas is a sleepy, small town
suspended in its past.

It is also much older than Montpellier, having been founded
probably in the sixth century BC by the inhabitants of the
oppidum of St Siméon once they abandoned their hilltop for the
plain. It was well placed on the route to Agde and the valley of
the Peyne which led to the copper, iron and lead mines. By the
beginning of the first century AD it had become a wool-
producing town; Pliny says that its wool was of excellent
quality, rivalling the best, which came from Spain and Egypt.

During the early Middle Ages the town appears to have been
passed like a parcel from the viscounts of Albi and Nîmes and
the bishops of Agde and Béziers, until in 1209 it was bought by
Simon de Montfort. But as he needed cash for the siege of
Minerve, he quickly sold it in 1211 to Raymond Salvignac, a
rich Caorsin moneylender who lived in Montpellier.

When Louis VIII visited the town in 1226, so the story goes,
he left one of his mares who was unwell in charge of the
municipality. By the time he returned, she had foaled and, to
commemorate the event, the King asked that a wooden foal be
made and be used in all the town's festivities, which were fairly

frequent, for five great annual trading fairs were held there. By the seventeeth century the wooden horse carried on its back two manikins, known as Estieinou and Estieinetto. This time the explanation is that during Louis XIII's visit to the town, one of his courtiers rescued a stranded peasant and rode into town with her on his crupper. To this day, a wooden horse, carried by six porters, parades through the streets of Pézenas on Shrove Tuesday, accompanied by its citizens celebrating the last day of carnival, and eating the *pâtés de Pézenas* of which they are so proud. These are little pastry chimneypots with crenellations, like mini-pork pies, filled with candied fruits, minced lamb and a little suet. They originated, we were told by one *pâtissier*, with a Scot who stopped at Pézenas with his Hindu servants. In fact they really do seem to have been introduced by Lord Clive of all people, who for reasons of health spent the winter of 1766 in Pézenas, travelling with his Indian servants. Not bad for folk memory.

In 1261 Louis IX bought the town and it became 'royal'; the town's arms still proudly consist of a dolphin and three fleur-de-lys. The Estates of Languedoc first met in Pézenas in 1456 and thereafter the town acquired considerable political importance as well as maintaining its commercial role. As a result, an enormous number of very grand houses, in warm yellow stone, were built. Most of them are still untouched, even by the usual layer of rendering. Many of the streets too seem unchanged and are lined with beautiful façades, pretty loggias, small towers and wrought-iron balconies. Impressive courtyards and monumental staircases lie behind the great carriage doors. All the hôtels and the other buildings and quarters such as the former ghetto are exceptionally well labelled and you have only to follow the arrows for an agreeable promenade.

In 1563 Henri I de Montmorency became governor of Languedoc (a post which had been created in 1337) and Henri IV gave him the county of Pézenas. Montmorency completed the building of the Grange aux Prés on the outskirts of Pézenas in 1593, the same year that the town became the seat of the provincial government. Montmorency's son became governor in his turn, but when in 1632 Richelieu, determined to end provincial autonomy, removed the Estates' rights to levy their own taxes, Henri II de Montmorency led a revolt which aimed to re-establish Languedoc's independence. With Montmorency's capture and execution in 1632, Languedoc lost not only its governor but its financial autonomy. The powers of the Estates were considerably curtailed, and Pézenas suffered a loss of status, though not before it had one last burst of glory.

The post of governor, albeit honorific, was reinstated and given to Armand de Bourbon, Prince de Conti, whose mother Charlotte was the decapitated Montmorency's sister. Conti, a Prince of the Blood and married to one of Mazarin's nieces, transformed his court at Pézenas for a short and brilliant period into a mini-Versailles. By great good fortune for them both, Jean-Baptiste Poquelin, who called himself Molière, and his troupe were playing in the region. The imaginatively named 'Marquise' Thérèse de Gorle, who had married a jolly actor whose stage name was Duparc, had joined the troupe in 1654, and was thenceforward known as 'La Duparc'. She counted, amongst others, La Fontaine and Racine as her admirers. Her beauty and her success on the casting coach ensured that Molière's company was chosen to become the 'Comédiens des Etats du Languedoc et de SAR le Prince de Conti'.

They gave some performances in the Hôtel d'Alfonse, a grand building which is still to be seen, though most performances were given in the Grange aux Prés. The Prince de Conti, who later turned into a pious old bigot, died there in 1666 and the palace was sold and used as barracks before its demolition. A copy of Molière's bust by Jean-Antoine Houdon stands by the existing building and a statue of him by Jean-Antoine Injalbert is to be found in the place du 14 Juillet.

Although it is sometimes claimed, without any hard evidence, that Molière wrote *Les Précieuses Ridicules* while in the town, he certainly found plenty of good copy in Pézenas; some of it perhaps at the Bât d'Argent where he lodged, and in Gély's barber's shop, where he appears to have spent much of his time, and which is now the tourist office.

71

The Musée de Vuillod-St-Germain, in a sixteenth-century hôtel restored in the nineteenth century, is full of local furniture, faience and Aubusson tapestries. Amongst the Molière memorabilia is a curious miniature of him depicted as St John the Baptist, wearing a wig and holding a copy of his *Don Juan*, for whose hero Conti is thought to have been the original (obviously before he was overcome by religious scruples). As Marcel Pagnol said, 'Jean-Baptiste Poquelin was born in Paris; Molière was born in Pézenas'.

The aptness of Pagnol's *bon mot* is obvious: to call Sète 'the capital of the French Florida' is simply perverse and to dub it the 'Venice of Languedoc' because it consists of a series of small islands and canals, is to make a false comparison. Sète is Sète (or it has been since 1928 when the spelling was changed from Cette) and a picturesque town in its own right. Surrounded by water, with the Etang du Thau to the north and the sea to the south, it lives by water, and is the largest French fishing port on the Mediterranean. It also has a large commercial port, now more dependent on petroleum products from the refinery at Frontignan than on the wine trade, though that is still enormous, and a harbour from which ferries ply their way to Majorca, Ibiza, Valencia, Oran and Tangier.

One of the attractions of Sète is its wonderful beach with 12 kilometres of golden sands stretching away south along the coast lapped by the blue sea –

> a happy smiling nymph – a Venus undefiled. The sky is white, with sparkling and streaming light. All the most beautiful notions of the Greeks recur to the mind – the weddings of the gods; their limbs of marble couched among the reeds; the waves kissing the goddesses with their foam.[38]

Hippolyte Taine, who succeeded Viollet-le-Duc as professor of Aesthetics and of the History of Art at the Ecole des Beaux-Arts in Paris, could not resist the classical allusion, though Sète was not, like Agde, founded by the Phoceans. Little is known about its early settlement but Charlemagne gave the land on which it is built to St Benoît d'Aniane. It was only a small fishing port until the late seventeenth century when it became the obvious place for the Canal du Midi to join the sea. The port installations were built by Cévenols and Provençals attracted by the pay, and many of them stayed on to work in the exporting of wine and *eau-de-vie* that became the commercial staples once the port was operational. The opening of the railway from Montpellier in 1839 increased the traffic considerably, and with French colonial expansion in Algeria, Sète became a port for troops embarking overseas. By 1878, with a population of thirty thousand, it was the fifth most important port in France.

Although one is offered a large number of fish dishes throughout Languedoc and especially of course on the coast, Sète is the place *par excellence* to eat shellfish and the fishy molluscs – cuttlefish, squid and octopus. The last three may not taste all that different from each other, and certainly at table they tend to look similar, but their varying shapes and sizes are obvious as they lie in glistening pink and grey array on the fishmongers' slabs.

Alan Davidson, whose *Mediterranean Seafood* is much to be recommended, identifies them: cuttle (or ink) fish is *seiche*, a smaller version is *sépiole*; squid is *encornet*; flying squid is *calmar*; octopus is *pieuvre* or *poulpe*, and curled octopus is *eledone*. Many of them are served with the fiery mayonnaise called *rouille* which also comes along with fish soup, another great speciality. This rust-coloured sauce accords ill, at least aesthetically, with *encornets* when they are served stuffed with an astonishing luminescent pink sausage-meat.

It is only too easy in one of the canalside restaurants to be tempted by a five-course meal for under 100 francs and to have the lot in one go. An error; much better to have only one course at a time or try a rather more expensive restaurant where, with luck, you might be served black noodles (made with the ink) and a sprinkling of tender cuttlefish lightly fried in a garlicky sauce.

The fishermen go out daily in their *chaluts* and, in season, at night with their lights lit up (*pêche au lamparo*) to attract a catch. They fish in the sea for tunny, sardines and anchovies and in the lagoon for sea bass (*loup*), bream (*daurade*), grey mullet (*muge*), eels and shellfish. When the boats return the fish is sold by auction conducted electronically. It may well claim to be the world's fastest auction, clearing between two and three thousand lots in a four-hour session – or a sale every five to seven seconds. There are a hundred seats for buyers, linked electronically to a central console. Each lot is displayed with its opening price, which is then automatically reduced in steps of ten centimes until one of the buyers presses his button, and the sale is made. Working at full speed, the system can handle a new lot every two seconds. The grateful fishermen celebrate their patron saint's day, usually on the first Sunday in July, with a procession through the town and down to the shore where a service is held to bless the sea.

Water tournaments are another of the jollier entertainments that take place at Sète and at many of the other eastern Languedocian ports such as Le Grau-du-Roi, Palavas-les-Flots, Port-la-Nouvelle, Frontignan, Balaruc, Marseillan and Mèze. They are thought to have originated in the days when the bored troops at Aigues-Mortes amused themselves while waiting to embark for the Holy Land. Certainly the jousters treat their boats as if they were horses and use their lances to topple their opponents. The boats have a long wooden protuberance (*tintaine*) at the stern on which the jousters stand, lance in one hand and shield in the other, rocking the craft which the oarsmen have to manoeuvre to their best advantage. The combatants belong to clubs with their own colours of blue or red and, like rugby teams, have supporters who, together with musicians playing for dear life, make the whole event noisy as well as colourful. The marina is a lot quieter.

Sète is criss-crossed by canals (making for yet another one-way system of some complexity) and has an animated atmosphere which makes it stimulating to walk round, but it has few buildings of any great architectural interest. On its southern extremity, perched up on a hill, is the Cimetière Marin, less melancholy than it might be because of the view. Here Paul Valéry is buried. He remained deeply attached to his home town throughout his life, and aware that

> to the port of my birth, I owe my mind's first impressions, a passion for the Latin sea and for the incomparable civilizations which mingle along its shores. I feel that my whole work bears the stamp of my first origins.[39]

Valéry, a friend of Gide, was much concerned with philosophical and metaphysical problems, and some of his poetry is rather obscure. It is not immediately obvious that the long and evocative poem he wrote called 'Le Cimetière Marin' is a soliloquy on the theme of death.

> Temple of time, within a brief sigh bounded,
> To this rare height inured I climb, surrounded
> By the horizons of a sea-girt eye.
> And, like my supreme offering of the gods,
> That peaceful corsucation only breeds
> A loftier indifference on the sky.
>
> Even as a fruit's absorbed in the enjoying,
> Even as within the mouth its body dying
> Changes into delight through dissolution,
> So to my melted soul the heavens declare
> All bounds transfigured into a boundless air,
> And I breathe now my future's emancipation.[40]

Next to the cemetery is a small museum named after Valéry, one of whose rooms is devoted to the singer and lyricist Georges Brassens, another Sétois. While Brassens' meaning is always transparent, he uses a vocabulary all his own, a bar to comprehension compounded by the thick Midi accent with which his lyrics are sung. His 'Prayer to be buried on the sand of Sète' is redolent of his habitual wit and mockery. He wanted to be buried 'by the edge of the sea . . . in a small niche in the sand, near his childhood friends, the dolphins'. He hoped that

Valéry, whose poems he said were better than his, would forgive 'the humble troubadour' as he called himself, for being buried nearer to the lapping blue waves. His prayer was not answered for he is buried in the nearby cemetery of Py.

On the far side of the Etang du Thau and along its shore are a number of charming small villages: Bouzigues with its Musée de la Conchyculture and, a few kilometres away, Balaruc-le-Vieux and Balaruc-les-Bains. Thomas Platter did not think much of the spa in the latter in 1595:

> The baths . . . are a gunshot from the inn at which we were staying, which was once a monastery. The bathing establishment is no more than a wretched shelter . . . This does not prevent crowds of fashionable people from visiting this spa; they come from Montpellier, from Nimes, from Toulouse, and from other places and have to be content with that miserable shack.[41]

One of the fashionable people who visited it a century later to cure his gout was the Marquis de Grignan, but he too may have been uncomfortable, for a permanent spa building was not erected until 1712. The present Pavillon Sévigné is so named because although Grignan's mother-in-law Madame de Sévigné did not visit Balaruc, it is she who has the greater cachet. Nowadays the cure is effected by mud rather than water-baths.

Mèze is a charming small village with its seafront and fishing boats and pleasure port. It has an agreeable square, overlooked by the gay balconies of its not-quite-seedy houses, and its church, with a square tower, sports one of those decorative open wrought-iron belltowers (*girouettes*) that are common in these parts.

Little shacks selling freshly gathered oysters, clams and mussels line the road running along the north-west edge of the Étang du Thau. These molluscs are bred in large quantities in the lagoon and the stakes of the oyster-beds break up the smoothness of the water making a myriad of ripples.

Marseillan is another small, civilized, old-fashioned fishing port. It is quiet, neither developed nor too run down, though its theatre is derelict. Noilly Prat, which does such signal service by turning low-grade wine into aromatic vermouth, has its *chai* on one of the quaysides. Two of the local wines are left for nearly a year to age in vats of Canadian oak; the wines are then transferred to new casks and stored in the open in all weathers, and the tiny amount which evaporates is delicately referred to as the 'angels' share'. After another year the wines are mixed with *mistelle* (a natural grape juice), fruit alcohol and herbs. The amber liquid with its unique flavour is then ready to go to be bottled in Marseille, or to be tasted and bought on the spot.

Cap d'Agde is a small-scale resort round a wonderful natural harbour with low-lying neat but not gaudy houses painted pink or ochre and surrounded by oleanders. The Musée d'Archéologie Sous-marin et Sub-aquatique of Mas de la Clape is to be found there and is well worth a visit not only for the *Ephèbe*, an exquisite Hellenistic bronze statue of the fourth century BC. It is by far the most important object to have been recovered from the underwater excavations and was found in the bed of the Hérault in Agde.

Cap d'Agde also has the largest 'naturist reserve' in Europe, a fate rather different from the one which Richelieu had in mind for it. The end of this spit of dune seemed to him to be an obvious place on which to build a military fort, but he died before even the jetty was completed and work stopped then and there. A fort had however been built just across the water on the Ilot de Brescou in the sixteenth century and, improved under the aegis of that great engineer, Sébastien le Prestre, seigneur de Vauban, became a prison in 1693 which it remained until 1852. A small boat ferries visitors across to it.

Agde, through which the River Hérault runs, is a totally unspoilt and picturesque city built mostly from basalt, a blackish spongey volcanic rock which comes from Mont St Loup and weathers better than limestone. The cathedral of St Etienne, with a square keep, is a rather forbidding black fortress with crenellations, and was restored in the nineteenth century, though part of the Romanesque cloister is still extant. Inside is a fine seventeenth-century painted reredos and an eighteenth-century pulpit. St Etienne backs on to the Hérault, a stark contrast to the neighbouring limestone houses and enticing restaurants on the quay, all sunny yellow with boats bobbing at their feet.

Agde was founded as a port in about 500 BC by Phoceans, already installed and trading at Marseille. It was called Agathe Tyche (meaning good fortune) and its main trade was in wine and olives. Many of the amphorae that the wine travelled in have been brought up from the seabed and are to be seen not only in the museum at Cap d'Agde but also here in the Musée Agathois, Agathois being the delightful adjective for Agde. Sometimes called 'Escolo dau Sarrat', the museum is housed in a late seventeenth-century hôtel which was built as a charitable institution. It also contains, amongst other things, a splendid display of the wooden shields brandished by the Agathois jousters, and a notice boasting that the first-ever water tournament was held here on 31 May 1601. The lack of proper descriptive labels is tiresome, but at least they are not necessary for the lovely women's and babies' clothes and lace, all beautifully laundered, the kashmir shawls and bonnets, and a bad but informative painting of the different headdresses worn by women of the *département* of the Hérault all speak for themselves.

A surprise in the last room is the collection of Indo-Chinese furniture, clothes and so on, bought when the 1931 Colonial Exhibition closed in Paris. The exhibition was immensely successful and represented for its organizer, Maréchal Lyautey, as he said, the apotheosis of his career. For a seasoned colonial administrator, it is odd that he should have added that he did not feel at home in nearby Béziers.

Before we reach Béziers, we must consider the Cathars. They appear repeatedly throughout the towns and countryside hereabouts, and as we go west to Toulouse and Albi. At first sight this mysterious group of medieval heretics may seem of remote interest, but their rise and fall was closely connected with the history of the huge province that came to be known as Languedoc in the thirteenth century, and today they are seen as martyrs in the struggle which ended the independence of the Midi. Their presence here is pervasive: one is invited to make the round of 'Cathar châteaux' (with some of which they had no connections at all) and one can hardly be unaware of the huge obtrusive statues by Jacques Tissinier in one of the bleaker stretches of the Corbières by the side of the *autoroute*.

While there is no argument about the word 'heretic' deriving from the Greek, meaning someone who chooses, there seems to be some confusion about the word Cathar. According to Steven Runciman

> this name is clearly the Greek word Καθαροί and was probably in origin the heretics' own name for their Elect or purified class, and thus gradually came to be applied to the whole church. It is first used by Eckbert in Germany in the mid-twelfth century . . . In Germany as 'Ketzer' it became the regular word for any heretic.[42]

It is generally agreed that the Cathars derived their beliefs from the dualist Manichaeism which had travelled from Persia to Constantinople with the Bogomils, and thence via Bulgaria (Bosnia) to the south of France. The Crusades and renewed trade in the Mediterranean had opened the west to eastern ideas. The heretics believed that all matter was the creation of Satan, and that only the spirit, which came from God, was pure. Everything physical, including the human body, was a manifestation of evil: 'the soul was a point of light trapped in the darkness of the body'.

There were two categories of Cathar. The 'Parfaits', also known as the 'pure' or the 'goodmen' (*bonshommes*), who formed the priesthood and organized the structure of their church, were chosen by the flock, the 'Croyants' (believers), and after a long apprenticeship they were consecrated by the *consolamentum*. This sacrament, also commonly called 'heretication', was given to the rank-and-file Croyants only on their deathbed, in order finally to free the spirit.

The Parfaits, and Parfaites (for there were many women members), whose lifestyle was a direct consequence of these beliefs, were dedicated to austerity but not necessarily to poverty, and they had *questores* looking after their financial affairs. Their income came from gifts or legacies of money and in kind, and we shall find at Fourquevaux in the Lauragais a château belonging to one of their bankers. They also lent money (since all matter was sinful, what difference did it make?), and this was a bitter subject of complaint by the Church, opposed as it was to usury.

The Parfaits were committed to chastity, and because copulation and everything that resulted from it was evil, would not eat meat, milk or eggs. Their diet consisted of bread, vegetables, fruit, some fish and oil, though no wine. It does not seem unduly meagre, especially in the climate of the Midi. The Croyants were not subject to these restraints, so inevitably they were accused of loose living and even unnatural practices, often being referred to as 'bougres' (buggers) or, according to a recent English guidebook, 'as living a life . . . apparently of licentious and wild promiscuity (one reason, no doubt, for the sect's popular appeal)'.

In fact one of the greatest strengths and attractions of the Parfaits was their patent sincerity, and they endeared themselves to all and sundry by their preaching throughout the countryside. They dressed in sombre black clothes and, having no Latin, spoke in a language that all could understand. Both their clothes and their use of the demotic were to be emulated later by the Dominicans whose job it became to convert them.

Just why the Cathars had so many followers in this particular region is not clear. There is no doubt that anti-clericalism was rife in the Midi, just as it had been at the end of the eleventh century before the Gregorian reforms, and while some bishops may have been men of probity, two of them had had to be removed from their sees. The temporal ambitions of the epis-copacy, combined with the spiritual poverty and moral laxity of the lower clergy, who of course resented attempts to persuade them back to both celibacy and the tonsure, certainly made for an atmosphere in which heresy might flourish. Neither they, nor the monks, who might have upheld orthodox views more forcefully but had withdrawn into the seclusion of their convents, did anything to reassure or give hope to people who, knowing themselves to be damned, wanted to save their souls. If the Pope could refer to his own priesthood as 'blind men, mute dogs who no longer know how to bark . . . who absolve the rich, [and] condemn the poor', it is not surprising that in this atmosphere of justified and openly-voiced criticism the Cathars, who advocated and appeared to live a life of Christian simplicity, should have been so well received.

Moreover they appealed to all classes of society. The seigneurs protected them and even welcomed them to their courts, where troubadours such as Peire Cardenal and Guilhem Montanhagol were singing of the delights of the ladies and erotic love – neither of them topics popular with the Church. But more importantly, the seigneurs had become accustomed to taking for themselves the tithe on agricultural revenue that was due to the Church, and were not best pleased when the Church reclaimed it, so that to tolerate or even defend the Cathars was in their own financial interest. Certainly there was a whiff of laicism in the air blowing across town and countryside alike.

There was a simultaneous movement towards independence from the towns. However, to claim that Catharism gave impetus to anything that could be called democracy is going too far. The citizens of these southern towns, like the nobility, showed marked religious toleration and in the larger ones there was a sizeable if not enormous Cathar population, spinners and weavers figuring conspicuously – a point to be borne in mind when we come to the woolworkers of the Cévennes, who were the staunchest of the Huguenots some five hundred years later. Many of the towns had both Arab and Jewish communities living alongside them amicably enough and in Béziers, for example, the Jews were allowed to have their synagogue outside the ghetto.

The regular clergy often adopted a passive attitude to the Cathars, as did some of their secular brothers; it was the bishops, and then the popes, who wanted to be rid of them. Support for the Cathars thus came from all sections of society, from the nobility and peasants, the merchants and urban artisans. There was no one of any standing anxious to be rid of them, until the papacy, with a pressing need to unite the whole of Christendom if it was to succeed in ejecting the infidel from the Holy Land, came to see the movement as a genuine alternative to Catholicism and a serious rival to the established Church. Few French historians or writers, whether Catholic or Protestant, are objective about the Cathars or the part they played in the war that broke out in the early thirteenth century. There is no agreement either about the part they played in the movement towards self-government in the larger towns where they were popular.

'According to the accepted view' (and what on earth might that be?)

> the Crusade unleashed fire and the sword upon a peaceful land where freedom and brotherhood reigned, where gentle manners, tolerance and respect for the individual allowed all to live in peace and tranquillity . . . Quite the contrary: Languedoc, from a political and social standpoint, was a country in perpetual unrest and disturbance, ravaged both by external wars and internal feuds. Even its vaunted liberty turned to license . . .[43]

From the early eleventh century the heresy had gained ground in this western part of Bas Languedoc, Quercy, the Agenais and Périgord, and as the century progressed so did the heresy, putting down firm roots in the triangular area covered by the Carcassès, Razès, Lauragais, Minervois, Albigeois and Toulousain. Several heretics had been put to death in Toulouse as early as 1022 and we have seen Pierre de Bruys burnt at the stake in St Gilles a century later. Though neither he nor his disciple, 'Heretic Henri' of Lausanne, were Cathars, both were violently anti-clerical.

In 1147 the Pope decided to ask no less a person than St

Bernard of Clairvaux to lead a mission against the heretics. St Bernard was appalled by the number he found in Toulouse but even his forceful oratory had little lasting effect. It was then thought that a solution might be to hold *colloques*, those public discussions so loved by medieval schoolmen, whereby the truth would emerge from the logic of the arguments. One such took place in 1165 at Lombers, near Albi, between the Catholics and the Cathars, but did nothing to convince the latter of their errors, and two years later they openly held a council of their own at St Félix-de-Caraman.

Innocent III, who became pope in 1198, tried to involve Philip Augustus, who succeeded to the French throne in 1180, in his campaign to dislodge the Cathars. He started by tempting him to 'replace the dispossessed heretics' whom he had excommunicated, 'with Catholics who would be content to serve God under his (the King's) government and his orthodox faith'. He went on to ask the King to appoint 'an energetic, discreet and loyal commander to lead the champions of the Holy Cause under his banner'. Uncertain of the King's response, he also wrote in 1207 to the great barons of the north asking for their help. Philip Augustus counselled prudence, but eventually he gave permission for five hundred knights from Burgundy and the Nivernais to go south.

How attractive the prospect must have seemed for the northern barons and their mercenaries as they set off, without having to cross the sea, for the exotic surroundings of the south where the living was easy. Not only would they be given remission for their sins for forty days, and pardoned for their debts, but they would also be guaranteed a place in heaven, for practising what, after all, was their profession. Their souls would be saved while they played a splendid war-game.

The terms used by the Pope and the anti-Cathar chroniclers to justify the Albigensian Crusade were, as usual in such cases, extreme. The Cathars themselves left no histories or chronicles (if they ever produced any) so we have to rely on Catholic historiographers. The main sources for the early period are Pierre des Vaux-de-Cernay, a Cistercian monk; Guillaume de

Puylaurens, a secular priest, employed by both the Bishop and the Count of Toulouse; and the *Chanson de la Croisade contre les Albigeois* written by two poets in the *langue d'oc*. The first, Guillaume of Tudela, tells a rattling good tale, while the second, a rather better poet, whose name is not known, defended the southerners, since he saw the Crusade as an exercise in land hunger and greed on the northerners' part.

The size of the crusading army astonished Guillaume of Tudela:

> In all my life, never have I seen so great an army as the one then mustered against the heretics . . . I will not even attempt to describe how they were armed and equipped, mounted upon horses cased in steel or caparisoned with coats-of-arms.[44]

He estimated their numbers at 20,000 knights and 200,000 foot soldiers; this is obviously an exaggeration, a figure of 5,000 –8,000 plus hangers-on seems more likely. Germans, Poitevins, Gascons, Rouergats and Santongeais as well as Provençals and even locals were there together with the Duke of Burgundy, the Count of St Pol, the Count of Nevers, and a minor baron from the Île de France, Simon de Montfort, who at this juncture held only a subordinate position. Led by the Abbot of Cîteaux, Arnaud Amalric, it assembled on 24 June at Lyon and marched though Valence and Montelimar, stopping briefly at Montpellier, a resolutely Catholic town. On 21 July 1209 this host was at the gates of Béziers.

The city, which thought itself impregnable, was taken after only one day. A number of people were herded into the church of Ste Madeleine which was then fired. There is a scorch mark supposedly still to be seen on one of its pillars. The cynical instruction, attributed to Arnaud Amalric, 'to kill them all, God will recognize his own' (*Caedite eos, novit enim Dominus qui sunt eius*)[45] actually appears for the first time in the work of a much later German chronicler, Caesar of Heisterbach, and is a distortion if not an untruth.

These hyperboles, alas, persist and current guidebooks are liable to repeat them. It is reasonably certain that only a few hundred people were butchered, though that was bad enough, and the scale and savagery were quite unusual for the times. Guillaume de Puylaurens thought that Béziers was punished for its pride in refusing to obey the Pope's demand to hand over such heretics as there were. They said they would rather drown themselves in the Dead Sea than alter by one iota their method of governing themselves. Béziers was to serve as an object-lesson for anyone else foolish enough to resist.

Béziers in fact survived, and today glitters golden in the sun or pearly in the rain, perched on the top of a plateau rising above the River Orb, which sends back its dancing reflection. It still occupies the site of the pre-Roman *oppidum* which is something of a rarity, though nothing remains of the Roman occupation that followed. Driving up to the town, at least in summer and on market days, is rather like trying to get to the top of Brueghel's *Tower of Babel*. You spiral up, round and round, and round and round, and down again if you are not careful, without ever finding a place to stop or to park. But forewarned, a cool head and a town plan will take you to the summit where the church of St Nazaire (formerly the cathedral, for Béziers ceased to be a bishopric in 1789) looms over the town. The view is splendid, with the fertile Biterrois plain lying beyond the River Orb and reaching across to the Pyrenees.

St Nazaire has a solid, complex air from the outside. Its dour western façade is enlivened by a fine rose window above a decorated porch and flanked by two rather flat fourteenth-century towers. There are a few good twelfth-century capitals and some of the chapels have fourteenth-century frescoes; the choir was reworked in the eighteenth century. The sacristy, dating from 1444, is an excellent example of what we would call Flamboyant Gothic and it is well worth the effort of finding the sacristan who has the key. There is little left of the mid-fourteenth century cloister which has been turned into a small garden.

Béziers, however, is primarily a commercial town, having made its wealth from wine, and its heart lies in the Allées

Paul-Riquet, a large busy esplanade straddled by four magnificent rows of pollarded planes and surrounded by any number of grandiose private dwellings. The Allées are named for Béziers's most famous son, the creator of the Canal du Midi, and the town is proud of its statue of him by Pierre-Jean David d'Angers, for which the money was raised by subscription in 1835. David d'Angers was also employed to decorate the façade of the pretty little theatre, which was built in 1842–4. There plaques commemorate Sophocles and Molière, the performances of the latter in the town some two centuries earlier constituting a source of rivalry between Béziers and Pézenas.

Béziers rather goes in for statues. One much venerated, of Roman origin, called Pépézut, a very battered fellow, is to be found in the rue Française. Another, which now stands outside the elegant classical building used as the Palais de Justice by the far side of the church of St Nazaire, is in much better shape, even though shorn of a life-sized bronze female figure who wept by its side. She was melted down by the Vichy authorities in 1941. It commemorates Casimir Péret, mayor of the town and deported to Cayenne (where he died) for his part in opposing the 1851 *coup d'état* that put Louis-Napoleon in power. At the base of a short column is a cameo of Péret, and on its summit is perched a 'Marianne', the embodiment of the République Française. The monument is by Jean-Antoine Injalbert, many of whose statues are to be seen in museums throughout Languedoc and in the two Musées des Beaux-Arts in Béziers itself. Injalbert's Marianne was to remain the official emblem of the French Republic until 1933. (Subsequent models for this honour have been Brigitte Bardot and, since 1985, Catherine Deneuve.)

Statues of Marianne are a feature in many Languedoc towns, and indeed Languedoc makes some claim to have invented her as an affectionate personification of the Republic. Various explanations have been given for her name. It would seem most likely that it simply derives from Marie, the mother of Christ, and Anne, her mother. She was first mentioned in a song by Guillaume Lavabre, born in Puylaurens in 1756, and was rapidly popularized for, once the monarchy was abolished, the king's portrait could hardly serve as a symbol for the state. Successive governments were exercised to find a satisfactory substitute. Liberty was consistently shown as a young girl, breasts bare and dressed in white with or without the Phrygian bonnet, but the Gallic cock for 'La Patrie', oak leaves for 'La Gloire', an urn to denote the arrival of universal suffrage, the lictors' fasces or even trees of liberty were all too abstract both in concept and execution to make much impact. Marianne was not too abstract and at least in song rapidly became and stayed a symbol of republican sentiments. By 1840 she had become the embodiment of democratic and socialist ideals. After 1848 when such seditious symbols were proscribed, Marianne went underground, not to resurface until the word 'republic' was authorized once more in 1875. The first statue to her in the Midi appeared in 1878 at Marseillan in the Hérault, and over the next thirty years or so others proliferated. They are to be seen at Montignargues, Réalmont, Puisserguier, St Pons-de-Thomières, Maureillan, Lautrec, Puechabon, Aniane, Albi, Puylaurens and Arles-sur-Tech.

There are other works by Injalbert in Béziers; his overpowering *Titan* towers above a grotto in the plateau des Poètes, a garden at the far end of the Allées from the theatre, where his *Child with the Fish* and Monument aux Morts are also to be found. There too is a statue of Jean Moulin, another of Béziers' native sons and the greatest hero of the Resistance. Marcel Cordier has chosen to portray him in the nude as a young Roman soldier.

Some examples of Jean Moulin's own work are to be seen in one of the two Musées des Beaux-Arts where there are four of his drawings, amusing in an Osbert Lancasterish sort of way, done for Paris magazine covers and signed 'Romanin'. The museum, in the fine Hôtel Fabregat, has other works of local interest, some good paintings and Greek vases. The Hôtel Fayet nearby houses the remainder of the collection. There is a splendid new museum, the Musée St Jacques, in the former barracks built in 1695 by Daviler, up by the church of the same name.

This church, mostly rebuilt in the early eighteenth century, is ringed by great clumps of acanthus growing at its feet and is surrounded by a rather unkempt garden from which you get a good view of the River Orb again, and five bridges: the medieval Pont Vieux, which followed the line of the Via Domitia; the nineteenth-century Pont Neuf; the Pont Canal, built in 1857, which carries the Canal du Midi over the river; the railway bridge; and a new one serving the *autoroute*.

Béziers, unlike some of the other towns in Languedoc which were ruined by the arrival of the railway in 1857, thrived as never before. It enabled the wine merchants to send their product, of which at the time they were making enormous quantities, cheaply and quickly all over France. One of their number, Castelbon de Beaux-Hostes, made so much money that he endowed opera in 'Apéritivopolis', as one wag dubbed Béziers, and enabled another to claim that 'here wine turns into song'. He sponsored the first performance of the incidental music for *Déjanire*, an opera by Camille Saint-Säens which was given in 1892 in the newly-built Arènes. *Héliogable*, by Marie-Joseph-Alexandre Déodat de Séverac, also had its première there in August 1910, when fifteen thousand people heard it.

The Biterrois seem particularly fond of spectacles: they hold real bullfights in the Arènes; they, like the other inhabitants of Languedoc only more so, are passionately addicted to rugby football, having founded in 1911 the Association Sportive de Rugby de Béziers, known to all its fans as 'ASB' and which has won more cups than any other French rugby team; they hold water tournaments on the Canal – and they have their camel.

For an obscure saint, St Aphrodise seems to have given rise to a remarkable number of legends. It seems that when he arrived with his camel to bring the gospel to Béziers he was not altogether welcome, and indeed was decapitated in short order. His head was thrown into a well, whereupon the water boiled and brought it up to the surface. Aphrodise picked it up and walked off with it. So the Biterrois strewed his path with snails, but he went on his merry way, head in hands, without crushing them. These miracles, amongst many others, seem to have converted the populace to Christianity, and to a sense of responsibility towards the camel. In order to ensure that the animal would not lack food, a fief was created to support it, and on its death, the revenues were to go to the poor. Since then, and to this day, festivities have been enlivened by the appearance of a huge wooden camel (rather like the horse at Pézenas), covered with a huge and gaudily patterned cloth and its jaws champing away. Burnt during the Wars of Religion, refashioned and burnt again at the Revolution, the poor old camel was nevertheless added to the list of *émigrés*, so that its income could be sequestrated as a *bien national*.

The Romanesque church dedicated to the saint is nothing like so decorative, but worth seeing, especially for its early crypt, a fine third-century sarcophagus and its restored refectory, which is now used for exhibitions.

Béziers has remained faithful to its snails, too, if the restaurants which serve them and the recipes for snails *à la biterroise* are anything to go by. There are almost as many recipes for cooking these gastropods as there are towns in Languedoc, with garlic and herbs, with anchovies, with raw ham, with almonds or walnuts or with cherry brandy. The combination of raw ham and walnuts with an unctuous herby sauce are the ingredients which supposedly differentiate Béziers' speciality from the other fifteen or sixteen recipes for *cagaraulo* (*cargolada* in Roussillon), and as a final touch, the snails are stewed in the local wine and flambéed in the *eau-de-vie* for which the town is famous.

Three kinds of snail, collected mostly by peasants and children, are on sale in the fine covered market in the centre of the town: the *petit gris* (*cagarols*) found almost everywhere in the surrounding countryside; the *mourguettes*, which are smaller than the *petit gris*, cling to vines and abound in the *garrigue*, with their pretty mother-of-pearl-coloured shells; and the even smaller *cagaraoulettes*, pale biscuit-coloured with stripes, which live on the bushes in dried-up riverbeds. They are so small you have to pick them by the handful.

If the English are still dubious about eating snails, it is some consolation to learn that not until the last century did the French take to them in a big way. They do not for example figure at all in the work of Alexandre Balthasar Grimod de la Reynière. Grimod, to whom we owe that first reference to *brandade de morue*, spent six years in Béziers and wrote glowingly of the meals he had there, in spite of saying that 'life is a progress from one indigestion to another – the only illness Béziers knows'. His grandfather was a pork butcher, a fact of which he was deeply ashamed, who had actually died of indigestion brought on by gluttony. His father rose to become a Fermier-Général and set the boy to study law, but he made few appearances in court, and by dint of his rackety exploits was confined in a monastery near Nevers. When he was freed in 1788 he disappeared from view for a time to surface later as the proprietor of a grocery business in Béziers. He certainly enjoyed the food there, to judge from his description of a meal at which he was served

the most succulent fish, quails the size of chickens, partridges which should be eaten on one's knees, rabbits raised on aromatic herbs, heavenly melons, exquisite aubergines, muscat grapes of which you can only form a notion on the spot and, finally, roquefort cheeses fit to be served to a reigning monarch.[46]

On Grimod's father's death he went back to Paris and lived at No. 1 rue des Champs-Elysées (today the US embassy) where he held open house – and table. In 1803 he published the *Almanach des Gourmands* and five years later, his celebrated *Manuel des Amphitryons*, almost a textbook for the generation to come. Again according to Dumas, it was 'at one and the same time a brilliant innovation and a veritable course of instruction for the newly-rich, by a survivor who had known the *douceur de vivre*'.[47]

Amongst Béziers' other specialities today are little sweatmeat pies similar to those produced in Pézenas – another source of rivalry between the two towns – and *oreillettes*.

In 1787 Arthur Young visited Béziers, and found it 'becoming, they say, a favourite resort for the English, preferring the air to that of Montpellier'. When he expressed a wish to meet the Abbé Rozier, the celebrated editor of the *Journal Physique* who was publishing a dictionary of husbandry, he was told that the Abbé had left Béziers two years previously. He asked why.

> They gave me a curious anecdote of the bishop of Béziers cutting a road through the Abbé's farm, at the expence of the province, to lead to the house of his (the bishop's) mistress, which occasioned such a quarrel that Mons. Rozier could stay no longer in the country. This is a pretty feature of a government: that a man is to be forced to sell his estate, and driven out of a country, because bishops make love. – I suppose to their neighbours' wives, as no other love is fashionable in France. Which of my neighbours' wives will tempt the bishop of Norwich to make a road through my farm, and drive me to sell Bradfield?[48]

This Abbé, for one, does not appear to have been related to the Bonzi.

If you are driving round the Biterrois countryside, particularly in the spring or early summer, before the leaves are out, you may catch a glimpse of a number of grand slate-tiled houses at anchor in their sea of vineyards, some of which are surrounded by 'English' gardens. About forty of them were built in the last two decades of the nineteenth century, and they display a bewildering variety of styles, ranging from 'Loire Renaissance' to 'Balmoral Gothic'. They were mainly by two architects, Louis Garros and René Hodé, and are not just pastiche. Their eclecticism represents the social and financial aspirations of the *nouveaux riches* who cashed in on the wine boom at the time. Look out for Roueyre, near Quarante, now a sort of holiday home, Grézan, near Laurens, and La Gardie, near Vias.

At Fonséranes, immediately to the south-west of Béziers, by way of a bumpy road lined by shady-looking garages offering car-body repairs, is a series of contiguous locks constituting a sort of monumental water stairway. They were built in the seventeenth century to bring the water from the Canal du Midi down by 25 metres to join the River Orb. Today there are only seven locks, but originally there were nine, spanning 312 metres, and they were the crowning glory of the man who had conceived and constructed the whole waterway that was designed 'to unite the two Languedocs'.

It was sad that Pierre-Paul Riquet did not live to see either the completion of his life's ambition or the ceremonies held to mark its opening. A glittering party of bishops, *parlementaires* and any number of other notables, members of Riquet's family, a host of kitchen staff, supplies of food, and a band were taken all the way in some thirty barges from Toulouse to Béziers, a journey which lasted for ten days. The rear was brought up by thirteen barges laden with French, Dutch and English goods destined for the fair at Beaucaire, with none other than the Cardinal-Archbishop Bonzi at its head.

Locke who, like Arthur Young some hundred years later, seemed bemused by French clerics' mistresses, recorded seeing Bonzi as ex-officio president at a meeting of the Estates of Languedoc:

> The Cardinall sat uppermost, nearest the altar & had a velvet quishon, richly laced with broad silver & gold lace; the bishops had none at all. He also had his book and repeated his office apart very genteelly with an unconcearned look, talking every now and then & laughing with the bishops next him. He keeps a very fine mistress in the town, which some of the very papists complain of, and hath some very fine boys in his train.[49]

The *oppidum* at Ensérune, unquestionably one of the most important remaining pre-Roman sites of the Mediterranean Midi, was founded on an escarpment above the lake of Montady. During the Middle Ages the lake started to dry out, so in 1248 it was completely drained by means of cutting rows of dykes from a central point, making a spoke-like pattern. The result is a number of wedge-shaped fields, which produces a most unusual piece of landscape where the different crops planted by the numerous owners make it look as if it has been coloured in by a child wanting to use all his paints.

In 1914, Félix Mouret, a rich local landowner, was plant-hunting in the area, looking in particular for the rare *Anagria fetida*. He found it, and at the same time discovered the ruins of an early settlement atop the triangular-shaped plateau which rises some 120 metres sheer out of the plain just to the south of Montady.

Although you can park at its foot and enjoy the stony climb up through cypresses and pines to the top, don't. Smart alecs, presumably on Mobylettes or some such, knowing that you will be gone for an hour or more, totally engrossed in the view, the site and the museum, have ample time to rifle through your car and make off with whatever they have been able to excavate. Drive the car up to the top and leave it there. The view on the way up and from the summit is breathtakingly beautiful; the vast panorama stretches to the pass of Le Perthus 97 kilometres away to the west, and sweeps round from the peak of the Canigou down to the sea and back all the way to the Cévennes.

The excavations, which started in 1915, reveal Ensérune to have been inhabited continuously from the sixth century BC to the first AD. During the earliest period, up to about 500 BC, there were just simple wattle-and-daub huts scattered around, but gradually an upper town emerged with a rampart and dry-stone houses, and the grain silos were replaced by *dolia* (terracotta jars) which were sunk into the foundations of each house. During the second phase of occupation, some hundred and fifty years later (between 300 and 240 BC), it was transformed as its people came in contact with the Celts. It was greatly expanded, with new cisterns and silos, the hillsides were terraced and beyond the new rampart a necropolis was built over towards the west. More than five hundred tombs have been found there and excavated. A final phase, around 225 BC, saw almost the whole of the plateau covered, approached from the east by an access road which ran through a vast terrace, pierced by silos and serving as a sort of storehouse. There were several dozen cisterns, each of about 20 cubic metres, which ensured a constant water-supply brought up from the lake of Montady.

The whole complex was destroyed, probably by Hannibal, at

93

the end of the third century BC, by which time its population had reached between 8,000 and 10,000. It was reconstructed by the Romans in 118 BC at the same time as they colonized Narbonne, and it found renewed life and prosperity. New cisterns were built, the drainage and sewers renovated, the walls of the houses were painted and the floors cemented. During the first century AD, by which time the Romans had made it safe to live in the plain, Ensérune was abandoned.

All the archaeological finds have been assembled in the museum on the site itself. Among the pottery, weapons, coins and jewellery, there are interesting small domestic objects such as spindle-shanks, dice, tweezers, and so on, and even an egg found intact in one of the tombs. All are well labelled and really do make it possible to envisage the kind of life these people led. Their artefacts, home-made or imported, show that they were culturally influenced by, and did business with, the Catalans on the far side of the Pyrenees, the Celts to the north and the Greeks and Romans who traded along the shores of the Mediterranean.

On the way up to or down from the *oppidum*, call in at Nissan-lès-Ensérune and look at the fourteenth-century church, by the porch of which stands a thirteenth-century funerary stone inscribed in the *langue d'oc*. There is a small museum there too.

From Ensérune and Montady one can make a leisurely but roundabout tour of some of the villages and churches to be found in the Minervois. The roads are narrow and there is little traffic save for that of the farmers and their tractors, especially at the time of the *vendange*. The *pays* of the Minervois is split between two *départements* – the Hérault and the Aude – an administrative distinction which reflects its geographical differences. To the north, on the slopes of the Montagne Noire, its bleak wildness with bare granitic outcrops and scrub-covered ravines is forbidding; in the south it becomes a smiling and friendly plain as it slopes down to the Canal du Midi.

Ste Marie at Fontcaude is set in the *garrigue* amidst the vineyards of St Chinian and takes its name from a hot spring on the site. The Premonstratensians, an order founded by St Norbert in 1120 at Prémontré near Laôn, started work on the abbey of Ste Marie in 1154, but it was badly pillaged during both the Wars of Religion and the Revolution, and all that now remains are three apses and a transept dating from 1180 to 1202, a chapter house and a dormitory. The cloister has totally disappeared, which is a pity because it was unusual for the region in that its arcading was ogival, but an arch has been reconstructed to give an impression of what it was like. In 1969 the abbey was bought and restored by the Association des Amis de Fontcaude, and a Gregorian choir was founded in 1986 to give performances which take advantage of its fine acoustic properties. Remains of an early bell foundry have been discovered and part of its furnace may be seen. Some seventeenth- and eighteenth-century ecclesiastical vestments are on display in the former scriptorium.

Not far away is the village of Quarante, which legend says takes its name from a site on which forty Christians were martyred and on whose tomb Charlemagne founded a church later dedicated to Ste Marie. The more likely explanation is that it was called after a local river which the Celts called Caranta, meaning a sandy place. There was certainly an abbey here from the tenth century but what we see today is the eleventh-century building erected on its foundations. It is one of the earliest Romanesque churches in Languedoc and has all the characteristics of the 'first' style: the use of small stones, lombard arcading and bands of black basalt inset as the only interior decorations. Its slightly fortress-like appearance is the result of much later additions.

There are two exceptionally fine white marble altars, also dating from the eleventh century. They are flat slabs with a simple but highly decorative pattern incised in low relief. The huge third-century sarcophagus, which at first sight one thinks dates from the Renaissance, is also magnificent and, in the treasury, there is a moving life-size bust of John the

Baptist, a silver reliquary made in 1440 by Jacques Morel of Montpellier.

The approach to the village of Minerve is most dramatic. The surrounding limestone countryside is bleached white and drained, even in the sun, of all the rich colours one has come to expect. Little grows here but for the holm oak and the vines. Minerve itself is perched on a bluff above the confluence of the Cesse, which runs through a rocky gorge, and the Brian, both of which are dry for much of the year. The area abounds in caves and underground channels and some of the huge rocks have made natural bridges across the river beds. There are also a number of Bronze Age dolmens in the area and as usual one wonders at the strength and skill of the people who heaved them into position.

The little village, with its 112 inhabitants, ruined château and church of St Etienne (which contains a mid-fifth-century altar table – one of the earliest in the region) is certainly pretty, though now rather too big for its boots, since it has been over-advertised for its Cathar connections and attracts thousands of visitors in season.

Simon de Montfort, who financed his siege of the village by selling Pézenas, as we have seen, took seven weeks in high summer to bring about its surrender. These weeks must have been as ghastly for the attacking troops, a body of about a thousand men, as for the defenders in the heat and the parched inhospitable surroundings. When Minerve finally surrendered, the Cathars, who were given the option of renouncing their faith and becoming Catholics or being sent to the stake, chose the latter, the women amongst them apparently being the most obdurate. One hundred and forty of them (or a hundred and fifty or a hundred and eighty, depending on who you read) were burnt in one huge holocaust.

At Caunes-Minervois, a little further to the west, it appears that only the Cathar bishop of Carcassès, Pierre Izarn, was sent to the stake. This village, guarding the passage to the Montagne Noire, and originally surrounded by a wall with six gates, lurches down the sides of a very steep hill, its precipitous and narrow roads better avoided in the car. They are lined with a number of hôtels, of which the best are the medieval Hôtel Sicard, the Renaissance Hôtel Alibert, which is in fact a pleasant little *auberge*, and the seventeenth-century Hôtel Tapié with its striking window on the corner of the street.

At the foot of the village, on the banks of the Argent-Double, nestles its abbey, dedicated to St Peter and St Paul, whose 1200th anniversary fell in 1991. The exterior, in lovely honey-coloured stone, is a good example of both the 'first' and the 'second' Romanesque styles, for the lower part of the chevet typifies the former, with its small stones in regular courses and its engaged columns, while the upper part, made of larger dressed stone with nine semicircular arcades, is characteristic of the latter. The interior is full of red marble looking like the very best bathroom suites; the altar is made from both local and Carrara marble, and there is a fine lectern and a monumental candlestick to match.

The red marble, which comes from the nearby quarries, enjoyed a great vogue in the seventeenth and eighteenth centuries, and remained a good source of income for the village for another hundred years. Though production had fallen steadily, the quarries were still worked up to June 1988, exporting the marble far and wide, but especially to Italy, where it and others from the locality were known as variously as 'Incarnat de Languedoc' and 'Rosa di Francia'. Marble from Caunes was used for both the Grand and the Petit Trianons at Versailles, at Marly, and later, for the Paris Opéra.

As you drive west on through this countryside, which has now become a sea of vines punctuated by the silvery green of ancient olive trees, you come to Rieux-Minervois. It does nothing to announce itself and you might well be out the other side without knowing that it contained a real gem. The village is fairly scruffy, and uncomprehending and incomprehensible old men sit about on the benches in the square deeply puzzled to see a foreign car parked or to be asked where the church of Ste Marie is actually to be found.

It is tucked away off the main street and not immediately

obvious since houses have been built into the sides of its walls. It has a sturdy heptagonal belltower, of which the lower storey is Romanesque and the upper Gothic. The porch, which originally opened into the chapel where the organ is now to be found, is surmounted by a board on which 'République Française – Liberté, Egalité, Fraternité' has been rather crudely painted. Do not be put off.

Because you have not been able to see the exterior as a whole you do not know what to expect inside. Ste Marie – unique in Languedoc – is a circular sanctuary surrounded by a fourteen-sided regular polygon. The dome over the sanctuary is supported by four square pillars and three round columns, a building convention perhaps inspired by Proverbs 9, i, which says 'Wisdom has built her house and has set up her seven columns', and where wisdom may be equated with the Virgin, and therefore the Church itself. Outside these pillars and columns which are joined by arches, is an ambulatory, originally hexagonal and out of which chapels were later built.

Although the leaflet in the church tells you it is an eleventh-century building, it was in fact erected in the latter part of the twelfth century, on earlier foundations and, despite later alterations, much of the Romanesque original is in evidence. Apart from its curiosity value, the church also contains some exceptional capitals, attributed to the workshop, if not the hand, of the Maître de Cabestany. The most remarkable is that of the Assumption of the Virgin, probably by the Maître himself, where a doe-eyed Mary is set apart in a clearly defined mandorla held by four angels and surrounded by the apostles. There is also a fine fifteenth-century polychromatic Burgundian Entombment and another of those grand red marble altar tables.

A detour to Lastours for those who like ruined châteaux is worthwhile. The name of the present village, which was only established in the early nineteenth century, comes from the presence of four châteaux – Cabaret, Surdespine (or Fleur d'Espine), Quertinheux and Tour Régine – which lie cheek by jowl 300 metres above the River Orbiel. There is evidence of the site being inhabited from the Bronze Age, for there was gold and copper to be mined in these hills. Cabaret was attacked by Simon de Montfort but he failed to take it; walls and towers remain. Of Surdespine only the walls still stand. Tour Régine and Quertinheux were both built in the middle of the thirteenth century and have no Cathar connections; each has a round tower and some vestiges of the walls.

It is said that Simon de Montfort, having taken Bram, put out the eyes, cut off the noses and top lips of one hundred of its garrison and told them to march to Cabaret in the hope that the mere sight of them would result in its surrender. History does not relate if the men ever arrived there.

To the south of this last outcrop of the Montagne Noire lie the Minervois vineyards. Although Minervois wine was accorded an Appellation d'Origine Contrôlée in 1985 it has, to use a current in-phrase, no pretensions. The red, white and rosé from the vines on the hills are better than from those grown in the plain, though all are fruity and fresh, just right for gulping down, preferably on the spot. The area also produces Muscat de St Jean de Minervois, a Vin Doux Naturel.

There is a good museum devoted to viticulture at Lézignan-Corbières, where the old town nestles behind its ring of boulevards with a nice enough church, and where one reaches the boundary line between the Minervois and the Corbières.

The Corbières, an extensive range of hills, occupy most of the hinterland to the south-west of Narbonne. Much of it is deserted tree-covered *garrigue* where the holm oak still grows amongst the pines and cedars, but a quarter of the area, especially over to the east and round Limoux, is one vast vineyard. As one drives through mile after mile of fields wholly devoted to vines in their serried ranks, one is only too well aware that the Corbières is one of the major contributors to the 'wine lake'. In fact the concentration on viticulture to the exclusion of other crops, which started in the nineteenth century, brought to this part of western Languedoc a host of social problems from which the area has not wholly recovered even now.

4

Wine, Women and Song

Narbonne – Montagne de la Clape – Fontfroide –
Lagrasse – Cathar country – the Fenouillèdes

STRANGE as it may seem to us now, wine has not been the staple product of Bas Languedoc for very long. At the end of the eighteenth century Haut Languedoc, and the Lauragais in particular, had become one of the largest grain-producing areas in France. Wheat was the main crop, though there was a certain amount of maize and pulses, and even cattle-raising, but the farmers worked with outdated equipment and had a poor understanding of the virtues of manure and fertilizers. The land rapidly became exhausted and production declined so that the price of grain fell by nearly a third between 1818 and 1824, not least because it could be imported more cheaply from . . . Russia! By mid-century there was a massive flight from the land, and those landowners who remained enlarged their holdings, creating a sort of new seigneurial society as stratified as it had been in feudal times. To lessen their dependency on wheat, they also introduced a greater variety of crops, including vines, and increased the number of cattle.

Bas Languedoc until the beginning of the nineteenth century had more varied crops and now began to devote itself to the commercial production of wine on a big scale, and by about 1850 the vine had taken over. The arrival of the railways meant that wine could be easily transported and with the expansion of the industrial towns in the north of France, consumption increased dramatically. At the same time, the producers of olives found themselves facing competition from imports of cheap groundnut oil from Senegal, and the supply of silk was badly hit when the worms were attacked by disease. Desperate peasants and greedy landowners reacted by planting yet more vines.

From 1840 to 1850 wine sold for nine francs a hectolitre but in the ten years from 1856 to 1866 it shot up to thirty-five francs. By then Sète was sending 800,000 hectolitres abroad, mostly to Algeria, and the area covered by vineyards in the Hérault alone doubled between 1850 and 1874. Although the phylloxera louse first struck in 1863 and was laying waste the Gard vineyards five years later, it did not appear in the Hérault until 1875. The area round Béziers was the last to be affected, and with wine selling there for forty francs a hectolitre in 1880, it is no wonder that all those grand houses were built.

The owners of the larger vineyards, who were as often as not lawyers from Montpellier or chemists from Nîmes who had invested in them as both a speculation and a hobby, could afford to take preventative measures and import the American root-stocks that were immune to the louse. They did not lose their livelihoods, but for the small producers it was a disaster and many of them emigrated to Algeria, only for their descendants to return some sixty years later. By then, ironically in the circumstances, wine was being imported from Algeria to supply the ever-increasing demand and to support the colony.

A new breed of middlemen saw that money was to be made, aided by the government which had, in 1903, under pressure from the beet-growers of the north, reduced the tax on sugar and permitted its addition to wine to increase its alcoholic content. This led to a series of fraudulent practices, such as colourings, acids and sugar being added to water and sold as wine. By 1900 the genuine article from Languedoc was fetching only six francs a hectolitre.

The crisis in the Midi came to a head in 1907. Marcellin Albert, a *vigneron* from Argilliers in the Narbonnais, had become the leader and spokesman of the discontented vine-growers, and on 11 March 1907 he put their case to a government commission of enquiry at Narbonne. It had little effect, and demonstrations, which began in a minor way, escalated. On 5 May some 60,000–80,000 people were on the streets of Narbonne where they had the support of the socialist mayor. The unrest spread rapidly through the Hérault, Roussillon and even the Gard. On 12 May at Béziers 120,000–160,000 people demonstrated; 170,000 on 19 May at Perpignan; 250,000 on 26 May at Carcassonne; 300,000 on 2 June at Nîmes and at least 600,000 on 10 June at Montpellier. Clemenceau, then President of the Council, called the troops in to Narbonne on 19 June, but they were mostly men of the 17th Territorial Regiment stationed in Agde, many of them sons of the *viticulteurs*. They mutinied and refused to fire on their fathers and brothers. Even so, five people were killed and many more injured. Despite the immunity promised by Clemenceau, some five hundred mutineers were later deported to Gafsa in southern Tunisia.

The government did however bring in new legislation on 29 June which reduced the tension and led to a restoration of order. The price of wine from Languedoc climbed back up, increasing steadily during the First World War, partly because a tot was issued to every serving man. Even so the Midi was left with a bitter taste in its mouth and a dislike for both the central government in Paris and the Parisian wine merchants. By 1935 increased competition from Algerian imports led to more trouble, and even as recently as 1978 there were demonstrations near Narbonne, where the police used tear gas and were fired on by the enraged *vignerons*. Two people were killed and some forty injured at Pont de Mondredon. The wine crisis of 1907 at least made the rest of France aware of the problems in Languedoc, vividly brought to its attention in the press by headlines such as 'LE MIDI BOUGE' and 'LE MIDI ROUGE'.

The description of nineteenth-century Narbonne as 'a little Babylon' – a term of derogation obviously dear to generations of critics – seems absurd, and never more so than today when one might complain that it is too quiet. The mid-town hotels grumble that they have few tourists, for those who do come are passing through or staying somewhere out in the countryside. This seems a pity, for although Narbonne has not the immediate allure of some of the other Languedoc towns, it is agreeable, spacious and has its fair share of good buildings. Curiously, it does not have a very southern feel about it – not even the cathedral is in the meridional style – nor indeed does it display any evidence of the Spanish influence that impressed Stendhal, who found it 'as gay as Carcassonne is sad'. Perhaps Narbonne is simply resting, exhausted by its prestigious past.

Narbo Martius, founded in 118 BC, was the first Roman colony outside Italy, and by 27 BC it had given its name to a huge province which stretched from the Pyrenees to the Alps. In 45 BC Caesar settled veterans of the Xth legion there and it grew steadily, exporting oil, linen, wool, hemp, dyes and aromatic plants to Italy, and importing marble and pottery. Pliny, at the beginning of the first century AD, wrote that Narbonne was 'in one word, not a province, but Italy itself', and Strabo, at much the same time, said it was the most populous city in Gaul with 30,000–40,000 people; it now has 42,657.

Narbonne remained a large and important town for centuries, its wealth derived from its trading activities throughout the Mediterranean. Ausonius, writing at the end of the fourth century, spoke of its 'glory':

> The province bearing thy name, in extent a mighty kingdom, brought many peoples under its sway. The land where the Allobrogi mingle with the Sequani, those where the Alpine peaks mark the boundaries of Italy, where the snow-capped Pyrenees border Spain, where Lake Leman gives birth to the Rhône's headlong current, where the Cevennes enclose and confine the plains of Aquitaine to the lands where the Tectosages still keep their ancient name of Volcae . . . Narbo, all these were thine.[50]

Although Roman Narbonne had all the usual buildings associated with a town of its size – a forum, capitol, amphitheatre,

theatre, baths and mausoleum – none except the Horreum is extant. This is an underground storehouse which serviced the market at street level above and was only discovered in 1838. An intrepid abbé exploring its corridors soon found himself in the sewers of the houses which had been built over them in the intervening period. Because the houses (and presumably the sewers too) are still there today, only part of the Horreum has been excavated, but the two galleries, with their carefully organized alcoves and air vents, remain impressive as an example of the Romans' skill in keeping their food supplies as fresh as possible. It is inevitably a bit bleak but a few pieces of sculpted and engraved stone have been affixed to the walls to give some atmosphere. The most intriguing is of two friendly-looking bears watching their trainers bathing in tubs.

The Musée Archéologique, in the Palais Neuf, has a good collection of antique fragments, including the oldest inscribed milestone to have been found in Gaul, dating from the city's foundation and the creation of the Via Domitia. There might perhaps have been more if François I, 'that protector of the arts', as Mérimée quite correctly described him, had not encouraged the use of classical debris as building material when the city's ramparts were enlarged, though at least, he says, 'the town walls are like an open-air museum, for along their whole length they display a series of bas-relief inscriptions and antique fragments'.[51]

There are also a number of funerary stelae in the museum, many of them rescued when the ramparts were demolished in 1868. One shows merchants loading a boat for their trading post at Ostia, three days' sailing away, where the Horrea Epagathania is one of the few surviving grain stores. The museum is well laid out and organized on thematic lines, which makes its collection of prehistoric and protohistoric fragments of more than passing interest, if still a bit specialized.

After the sack of Rome in 410, Narbonne became the capital of the Visigoths, and recently the public authorities have taken to referring to their city as the 'Capital of Septimania'. Its history was summarized by Stendhal pretty sketchily:

Visigoths and Saracens took possession of Narbonne. Charlemagne reigned there, and after him the Normans. The title of viscount of Narbonne was made hereditary around 1180, after which that city was drenched in blood during the Albigensian Crusade. Since the days of Louis XII, Narbonne has belonged to France.[52]

There is more classical sculpture, and some medieval, in the Musée Lapidaire housed in the disaffected church of Notre Dame de Lamourguier, a meridional Gothic building which seems not to be open very often.

The cathedral of St Just and St Pasteur, or such of it as there is, is by contrast wholly northern Gothic in style. The first stone, decorated with a golden cross sent from Rome by Pope Clement IV, born Gui Foulques at St Gilles, and archbishop of Narbonne in 1259, was laid on 3 April 1272. In 1286 Jean Deschamps, who also worked on the cathedral at Toulouse and in Clermont-Ferrand, Limoges and Rodez, became *maître d'oeuvre*. But the money ran out, and the choir was not completed until 1354. There the building stopped, so that all that was achieved is a curiously truncated edifice. Though it has magnificent flying buttresses, crenellations and soaring towers, its exterior is nevertheless somewhat unsatisfactory as an architectural entity.

The interior, where one is less conscious of it being un-finished, is another matter. Stendhal put it well when he talked of 'the choir vault of a prodigious height, pillars of admirable simplicity and elegance, column-clusters like bundles of asparagus'.[53]

The 40-metre-high nave is certainly prodigious and is only surpassed in height by those in the cathedrals of Metz, Amiens and Beauvais. Like them too, the cathedral has huge windows, with good fourteenth and fifteenth-century stained glass; it is also full of treasures, amongst which are a number of splendid tombs. That of Cardinal Pierre de la Jugie, Archbishop of Narbonne, 1347–75, is a masterpiece of Flamboyant sculpture, and it is sad that the sides of the tomb are still in the Musée des Augustins in Toulouse. Cardinal Briçonnet lies under a Renaissance canopy with lugubrious mourners and grisly death's head beneath. 'A pretty monument to a monstrously ugly knight' was how Stendhal described that of Jean Seigneuret de la Borde, who was Henri IV's Trésorier-Général. There are also some fine Aubusson and Gobelins tapestries, and the elaborate red marble high altar is surmounted by a colonnaded canopy made after drawings by Jules-Hardouin Mansart.

Perhaps the most beautiful and certainly one of the most original statues of the Virgin and Child is to be found here. Known as Notre Dame de Bethléem, it is one of the finest examples of fourteenth-century Languedoc sculpture. A serene young woman, clad in richly flowing draperies about her person and her head, holds aloft a bouncing, confident Child. Unusually, she wears a large brooch at her neck with a complicated design showing her coronation, and a ring on her left hand. The iconographic significance of these details is that they depict the Virgin simultaneously as the Church, as wife and as mother, a conflation of roles which the Church was anxious to encourage, to combat the rather different image of women portrayed by the troubadours.

The statue was kept for years in a niche in the central chapel of the choir, which had been clad in marble panelling in the early eighteenth century. Not until 1981, when the statue was removed to be sent to the exhibition 'Les Fastes du Gothique' in Paris, were the fourteenth- and fifteenth-century polychrome sculptures representing, for the most part, hell, and some wall paintings, discovered.

The chapel of the Annunciation, reached by a spiral staircase, is a little round brick-vaulted chamber with acoustic properties akin to those in the Whispering Gallery at St Paul's, and houses reliquaries and ecclesiastical objects.

Sadly what might have been Narbonne's pride and joy, Raphael's *Transfiguration* – 'the most celebrated picture in the world' according to Augustus Hare – never reached the city. Although Cardinal Giulio de Medici, in his capacity as archbishop of Narbonne commissioned it for the cathedral,

Raphael died before the work was finished and the painting never left Rome. However, in 1520 the Cardinal sent *The Raising of Lazarus* by Sebastiano del Piombo to Narbonne in its place. It was acquired in the early eighteenth century by the Regent, the Duc d'Orléans, sold during the Revolution and bought in 1798 by John Julius Angerstein, on the advice of Sir Thomas Lawrence. In 1824 it was bought by the National Gallery, London as its first picture and is still No. 1 in the catalogue.

Only vestiges remain of the cloister from which steps on the far side lead into the passage de l'Ancre, so named from the anchor embedded in the wall to signify that the rights to the local coastal navigation belonged to the archbishops. Stendhal found it a draughty little corridor, where the wind was so strong that he was afraid of being blown over.

The passage runs between the Palais Vieux and the Palais Neuf. To the right, abutting the cloister, is the thirteenth-century Palais Vieux and the Tour de la Madeleine set round an elegant courtyard, and to the left, the Palais Neuf, the archbishop's palace, built in the fourteenth and modified in the nineteenth century. Today it houses, on the ground floor, the former kitchen, a high vaulted room in which medieval sculpture is sometimes to be seen, and the huge halls known as the Salle des Consuls and the Salle des Synodes of which if you are lucky you might catch a glimpse, for they are not often open to the public.

The Musée d'Art et d'Histoire, reached by a magnificent staircase, is on the first floor. The rooms themselves, in which both Louis XIII and Louis XIV slept, and which were redecorated in the eighteenth century, are perhaps more impressive than the paintings, many of which appear to be on loan from the reserves of the Louvre. The Narbonnais seem not to have been great patrons of art, discouraged perhaps after their experience with *The Raising of Lazarus*. A more likely explanation though is poverty, for from the thirteenth century Narbonne went into a long, slow decline. Its position as a maritime city of wealth and importance ended when the Aude changed course and the port became silted up. The expulsion of the Jews and the sporadic fighting during the Hundred Years War only depressed it further, although it continued to produce cloth, the *draps de Narbonne*, which sold well at the fairs of Pézenas.

Even when the city decided in the seventeenth century, when Riquet was busy with the Canal du Midi, that it too wanted a canal, and work started on one in 1688, it did not progress far or fast. The Canal de la Robine, which runs from Port-la-Nouvelle through the city along an old riverbed which had long since been dry, was not operational until 1787. Today its banks are a favourite place for an evening promenade or for a meal.

To the south of the canal is a most beautiful church dedicated to St Paul Serge, who evangelized Narbonne, and who may have been a friend of St Aphrodise of Béziers. The church was rebuilt in the twelfth century on much earlier foundations, in a mixture of styles which marry well. The ogival vaulting in the interior is thought to be the first of its kind in the Midi and though basically northern Gothic in style, it has a half-hearted air, as if its architect had been reluctant to dispense wholly with more familiar local traditions. There are some Romanesque capitals in the nave, and the choir, dating from 1229, is huge and airy.

Just inside the south door of the church is a sixteenth-century white marble baptismal font containing a carved frog in it. The frog was made by the father (or grandfather – no one is quite sure which) of the Surrealist poet Pierre Reverdy, and is not of any great antiquity. (There is another frog in the font at Fontfroide, where it is part of an unidentified coat-of-arms dating from the Renaissance.) There are the usual legendary explanations connecting St Paul Serge with the frog, many of them along the lines of St Aphrodise and his snails. Can it be coincidence that Narbonne has frogs while Béziers specializes in snails, or is it just a manifestation of a long-standing gastronomic rivalry? On the other hand it must be said that the only time I have eaten *haute cuisine* snails was at Le Réverbère in Narbonne, where they serve *pâtés d'escargots aux pommes de terre avec ses trois huiles macérées aux herbes fraîches*, a delicious couple of mouthfuls.

It is worth trying to get into the crypt to see six early sarcophagi and, more difficult, to the sacristy where there is a remarkable tympanum, now embedded in the wall of the sad remains of the cloister. In white marble, it shows in low relief in the somewhat crude style characteristic of the eleventh century, two figures assumed to be archbishops because they are larger than the eight bishops who are beside them.

The Renaissance house round the corner from St Paul Serge is known as the Maison des Trois Nourrices, from the full-busted caryatids (of whom there are actually five) on its façade, and is imposing in a rather heavy way. It was here that Cinq-Mars and de Thou were lodging in 1642 when Richelieu had them arrested.

Henri Coiffier de Ruzé, Marquis de Cinq-Mars, was a dashing and spoiled youth who had replaced Mademoiselle de Hautfort in Louis XIII's affections some four years earlier. He was a handsome boy of eighteen, of somewhat dissolute habits, though almost certainly not homosexual, and Richelieu thought he would serve well both as a spy and, in his own words, 'as a toy' for his sovereign. Cinq-Mars was rapidly promoted and soon became Grand Ecuyer de France, which led to him being known as 'Monsieur le Grand'. But he quickly became too grand, with political ambitions which inevitably brought him into conflict with Richelieu. According to that unreliable arch-gossip, Tallemant des Réaux, Louis XIII loved him 'to distraction'. When finally the Cardinal was able to produce incontrovertible evidence of his treacherous dealings with the Spaniards with whom France was at war, the King abandoned his former favourite.

After his arrest, Richelieu, who was by now dying, accompanied Cinq-Mars and his fellow-conspirator and friend, François-Auguste de Thou, to Lyon for their trial and be-heading. Cinq-Mars, courageous enough to refuse a blindfold but arrogant to the last, objected to sharing a scaffold with a mere commoner. The King, who is said to have been playing chess at the time of the execution, looked up at the clock and mumbled, 'Aha, at this very moment our dear friend is having a bad time'.[54]

From the early eighteenth century Narbonne slid even farther into economic and intellectual decline, so that by the time of the Revolution there were only a few thousand inhabitants and it even ceased to be an archbishopric. Nevertheless, it was filled with churches and convents, and dominated by its clergy, who thought they had money enough to ask Viollet-le-Duc to design a new façade for the cathedral and, indeed, to complete the whole unfinished edifice. The idea was rapidly abandoned but Viollet-le-Duc was employed in 1846 by the municipality to transform the old archbishop's palace into a new town hall. Although the work was done, he quarrelled with his employers because he objected to the municipality's choice of supervisor. The Hôtel de Ville, which links the keep of St Martial on the right of the Palais Neuf and that of Archbishop Gilles Aycelin on the left, is an unhappy example of Viollet-le-Duc's own style, uneasily combining Gothic in the lower storeys with Flemish Flamboyant above.

It took the wine boom of the nineteenth century to restore some of Narbonne's former animation, though Victor Hugo, in a rather fanciful piece, thought the Narbonnais was a typical Languedocian who 'was one of that tribe who . . . makes the sign of the cross in intricate Spanish style; drinks wine straight from the goat-skin, sucking from the bottle; scrapes a ham to the bone; goes down on his knees to blaspheme'.[55]

Henry James, visiting in the 1880s, was very unhappy there in what he called 'a *sale petite ville* in all the force of that term', and his distaste increased after he had breakfasted in his hotel dining-room:

It was very hot, and there were swarms of flies; the viands had the strongest odour; there was in particular a horrible mixture known as *gras-double* [tripe], a light grey, glutinous, nauseating mess, which my companions devoured in large quantities. A man opposite me had the dirtiest fingers I ever saw; a collection of fingers which in England would have excluded him from a farmers' ordinary.[56]

While Narbonne has unquestionably cleaned itself up, it seems to have done little in the way of beautifying itself in recent years, and the only contemporary work to be advertised is a very indifferent mural in the place Bistan. You pass it on the way to the church of St Sebastian which is difficult to get into but has some fifteenth-century retables and a painting of *Le Couronnement de Ste Thérèse* attributed to Pierre Mignard. The Maison Vigneronne, an old gunpowder store, has now been turned into a gallery for temporary exhibitions and sells local wines.

If Narbonne has never excelled in the visual arts, it was, in the twelfth century, a centre famed for its troubadours. Ermengarde, who combined valour with a love of learning, ruled her viscounty for over fifty years and made her court into one of the most illustrious in the Midi.

The emergence of the troubadours at the courts of the southern nobility was contemporaneous with the rise of the Cathars. The reasons for their appearance at the same time and in the same area are as obscure. In early feudal days the *chansons de geste* glorified martial valour and heroic achievement in a society that lived by conquest. These epics were recited by *jongleurs*, both at court and in the market-place. The poetry of the troubadours was of a markedly different kind and was aimed at a purely aristocratic audience. Indeed, the first troubadour, Guillaume IX de Poitou, Eleanor of Aquitaine's grandfather, was a noble of the highest rank. The majority of the troubadours however came from the lower echelons of society and they quite literally sang for their supper at the courts, of which Narbonne and Toulouse were the richest and largest.

The theme of their verse was love, a novel subject for

contemporary literature, and almost invariably love for a married woman of higher rank than themselves. The feudal structure was less rigid in the Midi than in the more densely populated north, and class divisions were less inflexible. Homage of this kind, paid to the wife of the local seigneur, has been seen as a form of social climbing, whereby the merchants or even the sons of newly-enfranchised serfs could aspire to a higher status.

Love, defined as 'fin amor', was a pure passion rooted in service. The fact that it was adulterous, and sometimes expressed in frankly erotic language, was irrelevant. No wonder the ladies encouraged the troubadours, and especially at a time when the Church, in an attempt to make the clergy celibate again, was thundering against women.

The most renowned troubadours were Peire Rogier, who worked at the courts of both Raymond V of Toulouse and Alfonso III of Aragon; Cercamon; Marcabru and Jauffre Rudel; Peire Vidal, reputed to be one of Ermengarde of Narbonne's lovers; Peire Cardenal, who lived to be nearly a hundred and who performed at the courts of both Raymond VI and Raymond VII of Toulouse and those of Foix and Aragon; and Guilhem Montanhagol. Their lyrical style ranged from transparent simplicity to the most complicated and, later, even tortured forms of versification.

Amongst others familiar at Ermengarde's court were Clara d'Anduze and Azalais of Porcairages (now Portiragnes, a few kilometres from Béziers), two *trobairitz*, a name rarely used at the time but now current to describe women troubadours. Though only twenty-seven or twenty-eight poems by some fifteen or twenty women have been identified, they are more personal and less unambiguous about their authors' experiences and feelings than those by their male counterparts. It has recently been said of the *trobairitz* that 'regardless of their intrinsic merit, which is considerable, they are worthy of study as a social and cultural phenomenon in an age which seems to show erratic oscillations between female emancipation and repression'.[57]

Once again, various factors contributed to the decline of the troubadours and the 'courtly' style, as it has come to be known. Although there were some four hundred troubadours still writing in Languedoc throughout the thirteenth century, the quality of their work slowly declined as their inspiration faltered and the courts which sustained them disappeared. Their work became ever more cliché-ridden and hackneyed and had nothing new to offer at a time when the northern poets, the *trouvères*, were finding a new vigour. The legal position of women had changed too; Acts of 1316 and 1322 brought to the Midi the Salic law which was in force in the north, and which, by enforcing primogeniture, prevented women, at least of the nobility, from inheriting family property and wealth.

With the decline of the troubadours and the eventual suppression of the Cathars, the Church was triumphant. Love for the 'lady' as expressed in the secular lyric was, as Marina Warner points out, subtly superseded by the growing cult of the Virgin Mary, 'who became an establishment prop, acceptable because . . . she could be used to affirm the legitimacy of the status quo'.[58]

One of the last poems in the *langue d'oc*, the *Breviari d'Amor*, was by a misogynist, Matfre Ermengaud, who died in 1288 at Béziers. He was attracted more by Franciscan spirituality than any love, let alone lust, for a real woman. The great wave of mysticism which swept the thirteenth century and which had led St Bernard of Clairvaux, whom we last met preaching against the Cathars, to write his learned commentaries on the *Song of Songs*, had finally borne fruit. But it was the poetry of the troubadours that inspired Dante's *dolce stil nuovo*.

The Montagne de la Clape is an isolated little hillock that rises out of the plain and the huge lagoons that run south from Narbonne to Perpignan and beyond. Although only 214 metres at its highest, it nevertheless effectively shields Narbonne from the sea. It is a little world of its own, with small ponds and deep ravines, amidst what used to be heavily wooded slopes until they were denuded by forest fires. The trees that have survived are mostly Aleppo and umbrella pines, and the *garrigue* is aglow with shrubs and flowers. Broom, cistus, the mastic tree (*pistachia lentiscus*) and juniper abound amongst the rosemary, myrtles and asphodels. Many varieties of orchid, a wild tulip and the odd camellia flower in April and May and a unique centaurea, *coryum bosa*, grows there.

The honey is particularly delicious. In the last weeks of April the bees have fed on the thyme and rosemary, and in May, when the *garrigue* has begun to dry out, the hives, with the young queens, are moved up to the hills for the summer. The new honey, collected in mid-June, then tastes of chestnut, acacia, lime and heather. The hives are brought back down to the plain in October. I had never imagined that bees were treated like sheep and moved to pastures new.

The whole area is alive with wild animals; foxes, hares, rabbits, badgers, squirrels and even boar; and there are eight thousand different insects, amongst them three grasshoppers only found there. A good road runs right round the Montagne, and it is altogether an attractive place in which to walk or picnic.

Some of the rather better local wines come from the vineyards that nestle in the valleys and flourish on the limestone slopes where they soak up sunshine and salt spray alike. The red wines are strong and rich in tannin, though quite how we are to interpret the information in one of the publicity leaflets that they are 'as solid as rugby goalposts', is unclear, except as further evidence of the Languedocian passion for rugby.

Beyond La Clape to the north is Narbonne Plage, a rather dull resort, and just to the south, Gruissan, on the northern edge of the Etang de Bages et Sigean. Gruissan is one of the few resorts, with a wonderful sandy beach and a yacht harbour created round an old fishing village, made the more picturesque by the ruins of the old château above it. The new architecture pleasantly combines apartment blocks with small villas, each with a tiny stone-walled garden, exuding the heady scent of rosemary and lavender, and swept by fresh sea breezes.

Near Sigean is the 'Réserve Africaine', a safari park which, apart from the birds whose natural habitat it is, contains bears, white rhinos, lions, giraffes, leopards, kangaroos, elephants and alligators.

The abbey of Fontfroide is now in private hands. It always seems ironic to me that communal buildings founded by and for people who wished to escape the world and family responsibilities should be turned into family homes. It was acquired by the ancestors of its present owners in 1908, and although in 1910 they had the good taste to employ Odilon Redon to decorate the library (which you are not shown), and they have spent untold sums on its restoration and furnishing, it is somehow very disappointing. The modern glass in the church is feeble and the pieces of furniture scattered about, while good in themselves, look out of place, as if they have been put there to be photographed for one of the fashionable interior decoration magazines.

The church itself was started at the end of the twelfth century, added to in the thirteenth century and a tribune (rather like that at Maguelone) put up somewhat later. It is impressive in its Cistercian austerity, with no figures on the capitals and no embellishments. The usual monastic offices, the chapter house, the dormitory and so on are still intact and well restored, but the abbey as a whole feels neither warm nor holy in the way that, say, that at St Guilhem-le-Désert does. One has to concede that the cloister is pretty, with an abundance of flowers and an effervescence of dark foliage winding up the yellow stone of the ogival arcades with their circular *oculi* above. Perhaps it is unfair to say it looks a bit as if an hotelier has taken the restoration work in hand.

The abbey enjoyed decades of prosperity in the twelfth and the thirteenth centuries, especially under the regime of two of its better-known abbots, Pierre de Castelnau, whom we have already met, and Jacques Fournier, whom we shall keep meeting again. There were 150–200 monks living here until about

1476, whereafter the abbey slowly declined until it was finally abandoned in 1791.

The monks owned a fortified barn at Fontcalvy, set in the rolling vinous countryside some 20 kilometres away. They used it as a storehouse for salt, which was produced from the lakes round the Aude delta and was the source of much of their revenue. As befits its Cistercian origin, it is a building of the utmost severity, with a square ground plan, crenellated towers at each corner and a tower above the entrance door. The size of some of the stone blocks incorporated in the walls suggests that they may have been hewn originally for the Via Domitia. It was only by a stroke of luck that the Germans were prevented in 1943 from dismantling the barn to use the stones for defensive bunkers on the coast.

The abbey to be found at Lagrasse is very different from that of Fontfroide in that it is not isolated in the countryside. Lagrasse itself lies in the very heart of the Corbières and is its capital. Surrounded by hills, it nestles in a hollow of the valley of the Orbieu, whose waters, like those of the Ariège, were reputed to contain gold dust. They certainly contributed to the wealth of Lagrasse which made its living from tanneries and the cloth trade. A number of fine bourgeois houses dating from the fourteenth to the seventeenth centuries are still extant, as are a few of the early fortifications and the magnificent single-span Pont Vieux. From here one gets a splendid view of the abbey, which was founded in 799 by a friend of St Benoît d'Aniane with the delightful name of Nimphridius.

The proliferation of classical forenames was very common in seventh- and eighth-century Gaul, when Orestes, Patroclus, Plato, Cato and Virgil were common. Names such as Martial, Félix, Hector, Auguste, Achille and Ulysse were given to children and by the nineteenth century denoted their parents' radical or socialist political views, or just their anti-clerical sentiments. Conservative Catholics continued to give their children more orthodox Christian names, though it is pleasing to find Marius-Jean-Antonin Mercié, a sculptor whom we shall encounter in Perpignan, whose parents obviously wanted the best of both worlds.

It is worth making a special journey to see the Benedictine abbey at Lagrasse, although for once its constituent parts are more interesting than the whole. It consists of a number of buildings of different dates. Only three of the original six apses remain from the eleventh-century church tucked in by the side of a stolid keep, out of which an unfinished hexagonal belfry starts to emerge like an underpowered rocket. It was put up in the sixteenth century and seems anachronistic even for that date.

The church itself was rebuilt at the turn of the thirteenth century, still in a simple and restrained Romanesque style. Between 1279 and 1309 a flurry of activity took place during the abbacy of Auger de Gogenx, who was also responsible for the chapel which, like the Ste Chapelle in Paris and that at the Palais des Rois de Majorque in Perpignan, is a two-storeyed construction. Here, in the upper chapel, all thoughts of austerity have been forgotten. As it was reserved for the Abbé's personal use, he allowed himself the luxury of having the walls covered with frescoes (only those on the west wall are still there), and the floor laid with black, yellow and green tiles, with highly decorative figures and beasts, real and mythical.

The monks' dormitory, a huge room, is above what was doubtless the cellar next door to the kitchens. It is magnificent and of a most interesting construction. Shallow pointed stone arches rise directly from floor level to span the entire width and to support a huge timber-framed ceiling. The arches are buttressed on the fortified exterior walls. Some of the other conventual buildings were renewed in the eighteenth century, as was the cloister, which is sober, classical and understated.

Bernard de Monfaucon, who became a Benedictine at Notre Dame de la Daurade in Toulouse, went on to study theology and philosophy at Lagrasse. Perhaps it was during the eight years he spent there that he acquired that love for ancient monuments, to the recording of which he was to devote the rest of his life. It is from his *Monuments de la Monarchie française* that we know of many works subsequently destroyed.

St Hilaire is built on a small spur above the River Lauger. A monastic foundation also existed here from the ninth century but the church was built between 1237 and 1260 and never completed. All that is to be seen is a short nave and a rectangular crossing which ends in a semicircular apse, and it is actually rather dull. The point of the visit, apart from the well-preserved cloister built 1323–40, is to see the splendid so-called tomb of St Hilaire decorated by the Maître de Cabestany.

The legend goes that St Hilaire was buried in it, but much ink has been spilled in trying to establish where it came from and what its purpose was. Alexandre de Mège, whom we shall find in Toulouse, went so far as to fake documents proving that it was of Toulousain origin, but in general it is thought on account of its measurements to have been a reliquary for the high altar of a church dedicated to St Sernin (or Saturnin). It is a most beautiful piece of work in white Pyrenean marble. The carvings tell the story of the arrest, martyrdom and entombment of St Sernin, the patron saint of Toulouse to whom the great church there is dedicated. The right-hand panel shows St Sernin, with St Papoul and Honest, Bishop of Pamplona by his side; in the central panel, in scenes alive with onlookers sculpted in telling detail, St Sernin is being tied to the bull which dragged him to his death; and in that of the left, he is being put in a tomb by the Stes Puelles, two women who rescued his body and were martyred for their pains. (There is a hamlet some few kilometres north of Castelnaudary called Le Mas des Stes Puelles.) To round the story off, two angels waft St Sernin's soul, in the form of a tiny nude figure, to heaven.

At St Polycarpe there are vestiges of another Benedictine abbey, also founded in the ninth century. The church, of eleventh-century origin, was added to in the fourteenth century. Though virtually in ruins, the semicircular apse with its lombard arcading is still visible. To see the two Carolingian altar tables and some fragments of twelfth-century wall-paintings inside, apply to the neighbouring house for the key.

Limoux lies at the centre of the Razès and the Kerkorb, the *pays* that run from the Ariège to Bas Languedoc, between the county of Foix and Carcassonne, and is perhaps best known for its sparkling Blanquette de Limoux, made by the *méthode champenoise*. This light, dry wine goes well with another of the town's specialities – the *fogasset al pebre*, a small twisted biscuit liberally sprinkled with pepper. The town is also proud of its *civet d'escargots*, yet another version of a snail stew.

Limoux is a busy and attractive town, and has a small museum which is something of a curiosity. Called the Musée Petiet, the house was given to the town by Auguste and Léopold Petiet whose studio it was. Not only were both brothers painters, but Léopold's daughter Marie was too, and her pictures are now enjoying a well-deserved if modest vogue. Marie, left motherless at birth, was brought up by the two men and taken to Paris to develop her talent. Although she exhibited at the Salons of 1878 and 1879, she really remained a gifted amateur. While too many of her works are both ill-constructed and sentimental, some, especially those of the girls and women of the neighbourhood, have freshness and charm as well as being of historical interest. After her father's death, Marie married Etienne Dujardin-Beaumetz, also a painter, who had a successful political career, becoming under-secretary at the Ministry of Fine Arts from 1905 to 1912. Marie died when she was only thirty-nine. The other paintings in the collection are mostly works by late nineteenth-century local artists, but include one by Chagall.

There are other monuments in Limoux worth a short visit; the parish church of St Martin, reconstructed between the thirteenth and the fifteenth century and heavily restored in the nineteenth; the Augustinian convent; the church of the Cordeliers; and a number of attractive but not grand bourgeois houses.

Alet-les-Bains, on the banks of the Aude, is a marvellously homogenous ensemble of pinkish stone houses with pink terracotta tiles surrounded by an undulating and shrubby landscape, with its two church towers standing out like marker beacons. The town exudes calm and is attractive with its quiet streets, six of which radiate out from a deserted small *place*. Many of the houses are still half-timbered, seemingly unchanged from the Middle Ages, and the beams of one are carved with mystical symbols that have never been explained.

It is however for the remains of the Benedictine abbey that Alet should be visited. The key which gives access to the precincts has to be collected from the baker's shop opposite the gate, so it is important to get the timing right, for you will not be able to get in between noon and 2 p.m. when practically everything is closed for a two-hour lunch-break, almost universally observed in these southern parts.

There seems to have been some form of monastic foundation at Alet from the early years of the ninth century which became progressively more influential, especially after its acquisition in 1059 of one more fragment of the True Cross. This attracted hordes of pilgrims who helped to augment the abbey's income, at least until the abbatial election in 1197 which

scandalized all Christendom. Bertrand de Saissac, regent of Foix, forced the monks, at a council over which the exhumed corpse of their previous abbot was set to preside, to cancel the election of their appointed candidate in favour of his nominee, the monk Boso: who within a year had ruined the abbey by selling off all its property to pay his debts to his patrons.[59]

Obviously the abbey recovered sufficient funds to continue building and what we see today are the remains of the main part of the church and the monastic buildings completed in 1223. The choir dates from 1318 when John XXII made Alet into a bishopric and the abbey enjoyed a new spell of prosperity.

Virtually the whole ensemble was burned down during the Wars of Religion and despite some modest restoration in 1594, no further repairs were undertaken and it was left to crumble away. The parlous condition of the abbey attracted Mérimée's attention in 1834, but it was not until much later that it was classed as an historical monument by Etienne Dujardin-Beaumetz, Marie Petiet's husband. It was certainly worth preserving for as a ruin goes it is very splendid, with wild flowers and tufts of grass sprouting romantically above the heavily decorated exterior of the choir, with a complicated corbel table and leafy capitals, and walls and arches soaring in silhouette to the sky above.

The parish church of St André, started between 1318 and 1333 is also worth a brief visit. The west door and the chapels were added in the fifteenth century and inside there is a fourteenth-century frescoed chapel. Further alterations were made by Nicolas Pavilion who became bishop in 1662 and who was amongst the founders of the Cabale des Dévôts, a secret society at St Sulpice in Paris, later to be banned by Louis XIV. Some have seen a Templar cross in the layout of the choir and attribute this to him.

The waters of Alet have been drunk since Gallo-Roman times and are still in vogue for gastric disorders. They cured Pantagruel of 'une maladie des plus particulières' and Nostradamus of some equally unspecified complaint.

The Corbières not only produces an enormous amount of wine, of which it is on the whole unjustifiably proud, but it also contains a number of fortresses, some but not all of which had Cathar connections. The theatre of war during the nine years between the triumph of the crusading army at Béziers and the death of Simon de Montfort, who had become its leader, was largely concentrated in and around the Corbières.

Simon de Montfort was an Anglo-Norman baron, Earl of Leicester through his mother. (He should not be confused with his third son, also called Simon and also Earl of Leicester, who led the baronial revolt against Henry III in England.) He was a brilliant choice as commander, experienced as he was from having taken part in the Fourth Crusade. His contemporaries held widely differing views about him. Sympathizers such as Pierre des Vaux-de-Cernay praised him for 'his aimiability, his gentleness, his modesty, his chastity, his prudence, his eagerness for action and his tirelessness in carrying it through' and his opponents, for whom the anonymous author of the *Chanson* spoke, vilified him by protesting that 'he earned his fame by butchering more women and children than men'.

Simon was above all a genius at organization and knew what he wanted, which is more than could be said of the southern lords who were hopelessly disunited. They also faced a seemingly insoluble dilemma: having protected the Cathars they now found themselves alienating a newly militant Church, but if they were to join in their persecution they would lose the support of many of their subjects, not least those in the towns.

For five years Simon pressed on with his conquests, burning Cathars and besieging towns and châteaux. His annexation of Raymond-Roger Trencavel's viscounties of Albi and Carcassonne and part of the Lauragais and Razès brought Pedro II of Aragon, who had an interest in conquering them for himself, into the war against him. Simon decisively defeated the southern forces in 1213 at the battle of Muret where Pedro was killed. Simon kept going and two years later, the French king's son Louis arrived in the Midi to help him besiege and capture Toulouse.

At the Lateran Council of 1215, Count Raymond VI of Toulouse was stripped of his possessions in the west, but not the east, of Languedoc, and these were given to Simon by right of conquest. He was then invested with the title of count of Toulouse by Philip Augustus. By now convinced of his invincibility, Simon set off to see if he could also conquer Nîmes, Beaucaire, the valley of the Rhône, and Provence. However he was defeated at Beaucaire by Raymond and his son, and in 1217, learning that Toulouse had revolted, hurriedly turned west again to recapture it. He failed to do so and was killed in June the following year by a stone fired from the ramparts by a woman.

By 1220 many of the southern lords were back in possession of their property and the Cathars were still at large. Simon's son Amauri was not the man his father was, and with his agreement the new pope, Honorius III gave his father's lands to the new king, Louis VIII, who was to die in 1226 leaving a young son, Louis IX, in the care of his widow, Blanche of Castille.

Six years later the royal forces had reduced Raymond VII and his vassals to submission, for the Regent was now committed to the acquisition of these territories for the crown. The Count of Toulouse was made to undergo the humiliation of public penance, like his father, only this time on the parvis of Notre Dame in Paris. By the Treaty of Paris of 1229 he had to undertake to suppress the Cathars and to give his daughter Jeanne in marriage to the king's brother, Alphonse de Poitiers. If the couple were to have no heirs, the county of Toulouse would go to France. The wars though did not end here; they were to rumble on for another twenty years until Raymond VII died and Alphonse de Poitiers became titular count. When in 1271 Alphonse and Jeanne died within a few days of each other childless, Languedoc was French at last.

It was inevitable that sooner or later the monarchy would have attempted to acquire this last semi-independent fief, though whether or not the process was hastened by the presence of the Cathars or whether they simply furnished an excuse, is subject to argument. Whether some of these châteaux were indeed Cathar strongholds is also open to question. Many of them were in fact built after their fall; moreover 'they are not affirmations of some vague religious quest nor are they sun temples, but mountain fortresses guarding passes and roads'.[60] Nevertheless, nothing can spoil the enjoyment one gets from scrambling up to see the ruins of these huge eagle's nests, perched atop bluffs where the wind always blows with almost demonic force. Not all are easy of access: the ascent (and descent) along steep and narrow rocky paths with loose stones requires determination, a steady head and stout shoes, but the view from all of them is superb with long vistas across wild, inhospitable and uninhabited countryside.

The ruins of the château of Arques, in the *pays* of Razès, are post-Cathar and the four-storey keep, started in 1284, despite being damaged during the Wars of Religion, still stands. The fourteenth-century church in the village has a fine stone statue of St Anne holding the Virgin holding the Infant Jesus, and was the birthplace of Déodat Roche, a recent scholar who founded the Cahiers d'Études Cathares. The small museum, dedicated to him, holds annual exhibitions of arts and crafts.

Simon de Montfort and his soldiers were at the château of Termes in November 1210, and the seigneur held out for four months before capitulating. Pierre des-Vaux-de-Cernay had obviously been there:

> Termes was an incredibly strong fortress; it seemed humanly impregnable. It was built on a summit of a high mountain, atop a huge crag, surrounded by deep and inaccessible ravines down which water poured in torrents . . . these ravines were bounded by cliffs so high and precipitous that whoever wished to reach the castle had first to creep along the bed of the ravine and then to scramble (so it seemed) heavenward.[61]

The château was one of those dismantled by Richelieu in the seventeenth century, and now there are only ruins of the double row of fortified walls and the twelfth-century keep. But what ruins!

It is a pleasant drive along the banks of the Aude from Couiza to Quillan which has a quiet sleepy air, despite being a minor industrial centre manufacturing footwear and furniture-making materials. The château, a perfect stone square with small watch-towers on each corner, which houses the town's water-supply is, for once, a real *château d'eau*. The church, of little special interest, was rebuilt in 1677.

Turning eastwards from Quillan in its hollow, a spectacular road leads through the Défilé du Pierre-Lys and past St Martin-Lys, whose *curé* Félix Armand persuaded his parishioners in 1814 to hack a carriageway out of the rock along what is now the D117. The château de Puylaurens is two kilometres to the south, its huge crenellated silhouette visible from the road. It takes about a quarter of an hour to walk up to the château, of which most of the exterior walls are still standing and which give some idea of the sophisticated system of defence. It was taken in 1250 by Louis IX and fortified as a frontier post against the Aragonese, who nevertheless managed to capture it from time to time. The Duc de Joyeuse (whose own château was at Couiza and is now an hotel) restored it in 1594 in his capacity as governor of Languedoc, but by the middle of the seventeenth century it had served its purpose. It was finally abandoned in 1804.

A few kilometres further along the D117, just off the road to the south, is Notre Dame de Laval, an attractive fifteenth-century church built on the site of a tenth-century sanctuary which became the centre of a Marian cult. It contains a much-venerated retable of the Virgin and Child, flanked by eight sculpted stone panels and one beneath with a crowd of rather crudely painted figures. Although known to have been executed in 1428 it is not attributed, and from its naive style is reckoned to be of purely local workmanship.

The D117 continues along through the vineyards of St Félix-de-Fénouillet and Maury. A turning to the north brings one to a tiny steep road leading up to the foot of the château of Quéribus. The climb to the ruins takes about half an hour. At 728 metres above sea-level, the château dominates the plain of Roussillon, and served as a refuge in the years after the French king had become involved in the campaign against the heretics. Benoît de Termes, the Cathar bishop of Razès, sheltered here for some time after 1230, and after Montségur had been taken in 1244, it was the last and only remaining Cathar stronghold until 1254 when Louis IX ordered its reduction. The royal troops took the château without a fight and many of the Cathars fled to Spain. Only the keep now remains.

To get to the château of Peyrepertuse, the grandest of them all, you go through the tiny picturesque village of Cucugnan principally renowned for its appearance in one of Daudet's stories – 'Le curé de Cucugnan'. Again, it takes a good half-hour to climb up to a height of 800 metres to the château, described as 'a celestial small Carcassonne' which, according to Julian Barnes, 'spectacularly fills in a mountain crest like a clever bit of bridgework by God the dentist'. It is really a walled town rather than just a fortress and is huge. The ramparts are 300 metres long and 60 metres wide and enclose two châteaux, one at the eastern end, properly called Peyrepertuse, and the other at the western, St Georges. By the early thirteenth century the châteaux belonged to the kingdom of Aragon, and were sold in 1239 to Louis IX. He improved the fortifications and built the 'San Jordi' keep, reached by a perilous stairway hewn out of the rock. The view makes its strategic importance immediately apparent. It commanded the frontier between France and Spain until it was made redundant by the Treaty of the Pyrenees in 1659, and only a token garrison was retained there until it was finally abandoned in the early years of the Revolution.

Retracing your steps through Cucugnan will take you past the ruins of the château of Padern, a good deal less spectacular than the others (as it was rebuilt in the seventeenth century) and on to that of Aguilar. Here it takes only ten minutes to reach the château, which also belonged to the Termes family, and was taken in 1210 by Simon de Montfort. It was recovered briefly by the family but in 1246 went to the crown and became a French garrison fort until the Treaty of the Pyrenees.

Between Aguilar and the small village of Tautavel, the limestone hills are riddled with caves. Serious excavation started at that of Caune de l'Arago and the site has produced evidence of an advanced form of Middle Pleistocene man. A jawbone was found in 1969 and two years later more pieces of skull, claimed to be those of 'the oldest human face in Europe', were discovered. These bones are thought to have belonged to a man of about twenty, with a receding forehead, prominent brow ridges and a jutting upper jaw. There is a small museum of prehistory, and the ruins of a thirteenth-century château.

126

The route from Quillan to Tautavel runs through the Fenouillèdes, a *pays* lying at the southernmost edge of the Corbières and extending into the valley drained by the River Agly in Roussillon. It is a superb and little-known region combining mountain and valley, limestone hills covered with holm oaks and lush Mediterranean valleys with olives and vines, vibrant with the rich colours of the ochre earth baked hard in summer and cinder-like in autumn.

Its geographical features have determined its history. A frontier zone from time immemorial, its inhabitants have had not only to contend with the savagery of nature but with innumerable invaders fighting for its possession until it finally became and stayed French. Though it has lost its autonomy, even today the posters by the roadside announce with pride that it is 'the gateway to Roussillon'.

5

Roussillon – Sea and Spa

Roussillon – Salses – Rivesaltes – Perpignan –
Cabestany – Elne – Côte Vermeille – Albères –
Vallespir – Aspres – Cerdagne

ROUSSILLON, like Languedoc, is a former province and though today it has been transformed into the *département* of the Pyrénées-Orientales, it too is very conscious of its past as French Catalonia. Though considerably smaller than Languedoc it is as varied. The plain of Roussillon proper, lying between the Rivers Têt and Tech, is wholly Mediterranean and wonderfully fertile, with vines and market gardens vying with each other. The valley of the Têt, the *pays* of the Conflent, is ablaze from February to May with mimosa and apricot and peach blossom, whereas the Vallespir, nourished by the waters of the Tech, is more mountainous and wooded. The littoral, dotted with fishing ports and summer resorts, has its own particularities – sandy in its northern stretches and rocky to the south along the Côte Vermeille. From the coast the Albères, the foothills of the Pyrenees, run along the Spanish border and shade into the Aspres, where solitary hermitages nestle amongst its verdant hills. Further to the west the Pyrenees rise to majestic heights and enclose the two high plateaux of the Cerdagne and the Capcir where there is marvellous summer walking and winter skiing. The local food reflects these differences, for it is wonderfully varied, with fish from the Mediterranean at one end and sun-dried hams and *charcuterie* made in the Pyrenean uplands at the other.

Despite consisting of these differentiated *pays*, Roussillon has always had and still retains its own sense of unity, a fact recognized when the county was integrated with France by the Treaty of the Pyrenees in 1659 and given its own administrative institutions. Today there is a modest separatist movement for an independent Catalan region which would incorporate Spanish Catalonia; red and yellow striped flags fly from many buildings, and Perpignan, for instance, labels its streets in both French and Catalan. At first sight, the Pyrenees appear to be a 'natural' frontier and an obvious territorial divide between France and Spain, at least in physical terms. Certainly Richard Ford thought so in the mid-nineteenth century: 'However tyrants and tricksters may assert in the gilded galleries of Versailles that "Il n'y a pas de Pyrénées", this barrier of snow and hurricane does and will persist for ever'.[62]

But whether natural or not, in political terms it was not always so, and as a border area Roussillon was for many centuries fought over and passed like a parcel from one owner to another.

Although Cardinal Richelieu is supposed to have said that it was his aim 'to restore to France the boundaries that nature allotted it . . . and to make Gaul coincide with France', at the time of the Treaty of the Pyrenees the theory of natural frontiers was rudimentary. The frontier line then drawn created a boundary where in fact there was none, and divided the Catalan people. However, with the odd exception, that line has remained unaltered since 1659, though General Franco told Hitler that he rather fancied having Perpignan.

The origins of Perpignan date back to the seventh century BC when Ruscino was the site of an Ibero-Ligurian *oppidum*. The Romans took it over when they colonized the plain, and excavations at Château Roussillon, as it is now known, are bringing to light foundations of buildings such as the forum.

By the fifth century AD Roussillon was incorporated in the Visigothic kingdom of Septimania, and in the seventh, occupied briefly by the Moors. After the Franks had expelled the Moors they created the March of Spain with the lands to the north of the Pyrenees, which consisted of Roussillon and the Cerdagne. By the early tenth century, the counts of both had established themselves as hereditary rulers, though still owing allegiance to the kings of France. To the south of the Pyrenees in Spanish Catalonia, the counts of Barcelona were attempting to impose their hegemony just as their neighbours, the counts of Toulouse, were in Languedoc. In 1172 the Count of Roussillon left his lands to Alfonso II, Count of Barcelona and by now king of Aragon, and the Count of Cerdagne followed suit in 1177. Thus it was that both Roussillon and the Cerdagne became part of Catalonia and in due course Spanish rather than French. Apart from brief, bloody and complicated intervals, they were to remain so for the next five hundred years.

Alfonso II, desirous of extending his power in territory belonging to the Count of Toulouse, married his son Pedro to Marie de Montpellier, but his ambitions there came to nought when Pedro was killed in 1213 at the battle of Muret. Thenceforward while Languedoc turned slowly and reluctantly towards France, Roussillon remained in the Spanish camp. The situation was formally recognized by the Treaty of Corbeil in 1258 when Louis IX renounced his claims to Catalonia, including Roussillon and the Cerdagne, and the King of Aragon his claims north of the Pyrenees except for those two counties.

Four years later, Jaime I split his realm in two, giving Spanish Catalonia, Valencia and Aragon to his older son Pedro, and the Balearic Islands, Roussillon and the Cerdagne, and Montpellier to his younger son, Jaime. This division only took effect on his death fourteen years later, and it was then that the younger Jaime founded the Kingdom of Majorca which he ruled from 1276 to 1311. Despite family rivalry, this independent kingdom flourished under his successors until Pedro II acceded to the throne of Aragon. He conquered the Balearics and then in 1344 invaded Roussillon, taking Perpignan and the Cerdagne and thus bringing to an end the autonomy of this short-lived kingdom. The deposed King Jaime II retreated to

Montpellier, which he owned, and promptly sold it to the French crown in 1349.

The fifteenth century was marked by troubles for Roussillon which was occupied by the French more or less continuously from 1462 to 1493. Juan II of Aragon died before he could recover Roussillon, but he had succeeded in uniting Aragon and Castille by the marriage of his son Ferdinand to Isabella. Charles VIII of France, now too preoccupied with his claim to the Angevin inheritance in Italy, and feeling he could not afford trouble in the western Mediterranean, returned Roussillon to Ferdinand by the Treaty of Barcelona in 1493. But as time went by, relations between France and Spain deteriorated, and the Catalans became progressively unhappier at being governed from Madrid. In 1640 they revolted and offered themselves to Louis XIII. The long years of Franco-Spanish conflict were not ended until the Treaty of the Pyrenees in 1659, and thenceforward Roussillon was to be part of France.

The great ruined châteaux of Termes, Puylaurens, Quéribus, Peyrepertuse and Aguilar, known as the 'five sons of Carcassonne' which stood guardian in the Fenouillèdes against attacks from the south-west had become, as we have seen, redundant. While invaders coming from Spain did cross the high passes of the Pyrenees, a more obvious and easier route was along the coast, the route taken by Hannibal in 218 BC.

For strategic reasons therefore there had always been some form of defensive works at Salses, which controls the narrow passage between the eastern slopes of the Corbières and the lagoons on the edge of the Mediterranean. No army could pass unobserved on the landward side or advance along the spit of littoral on the seaward side without being exposed to attacks by armed boats. There is known to have been a fortress at Salses since the twelfth century when it belonged to the King of Aragon, but the greater part of what we see today was built between 1497 and 1504. It is a mammoth construction of glowing yellow stone and pink brick, covering an area of three hectares, crouching sunken within a dry moat and marooned in the middle of a chequerboard of meticulously even rows of vines, stark against the dun-coloured earth. It was erected in an astonishingly short six and a half years, by three thousand workmen under the direction of one of the King of Spain's engineers, variously called Francisco Ramirez, Ramiro Lopez, Francisco Rodriguez or even Ramiro Ramirez. It owes its novel appearance to the need to provide a defensive system that would withstand the new techniques of artillery fire and gunpowder.

From the outside it has an air of solid impregnability. The surrounding walls are 6–10 metres deep and 20 metres wide, though their very thickness hindered the defenders' fire-power. The four corner towers and bastions in brick were rounded, not only to give better visibility and to discourage scaling, but also, since brick is more flexible than stone, so that bullets would ricochet.

The greater part of the fort is built round an enormous cobbled inner courtyard, in summer a magnificent setting for musical and dramatic performances. Apart from the walls, moats, drawbridges, watch towers, loopholes and so on, a number of other and original devices were incorporated to hinder invaders. A narrow underground corridor, which runs right round the courtyard, gave the defenders access to any part of the building without being observed by the enemy. It was equipped with water traps into which the unsuspecting fell, apparently exclaiming 'ha ha' (pronounced 'ah ah' in French) as they went to their watery deaths. In addition, some of the lintels in this corridor were set at different heights so that those who had not drowned would brain themselves, as the guides delight in telling you. (The Oxford Reference Dictionary defines a 'ha ha' as 'a ditch with a wall on the inner side forming a boundary to a park or garden without interrupting the view', and says that it comes from the French, 'perhaps from a cry of surprise at discovering the obstacle'.)

The governor and officers lived in a five-storeyed keep in relative comfort, and a chapel ensured that the men's spiritual needs at least were taken care of. Stabling for between a hundred and fifty and three hundred horses was also provided – lovely cool stone basements reached by narrow ramps. The horse-dung was traded with the peasants for fresh fruit and vegetables, but in other respects the garrison was self-sufficient, with its own oil and flour mills, bakeries and kitchens. An unusual refinement, unknown even at the château of Versailles some two centuries later, was the installation of a hundred and fifty urinals and sixty lavatories, which were drained through charcoal filters out into the lagoons.

The fort successfully withstood a French siege in 1503 but thereafter, despite occasional forays, its defences were hardly put to the test, for there was a long period of peace between France and Spain until France declared war in 1635. Salses held out during three sieges between 1637 and 1639, but was finally taken by the French in that year. Retaken briefly by the Spanish after the fall of Perpignan in 1642, Salses was then evacuated with full honours of war and was never again occupied by the Spanish. Louis XIV, however, was taking no chances and in 1691 Vauban reduced the height of the keep and removed some of the more decorative elements while strengthening the bastions. It then became a prison, and shortly afterwards housed some of the criminals involved in the 'affair of the poisons', (see page 158).

The Reverend S. Baring-Gould has a charming story about the last French governor who was

a nephew of Voltaire, named La Houlière, who . . . made wine . . . He sent a cask of the latter to his illustrious uncle, and entreated him to obtain a market for his wines in Russia. To which Voltaire replied, 'I am sorry not to be able to be of use to you in this matter, but the Empress at this moment is too much occupied with the Turks who drink no wine, and with the Germans who drink too much, to be able to turn her attention to your generous liquor'.[63]

It is sad to learn that La Houlière committed suicide in 1793 but obviously Salses had a sinister reputation, for no Perpignonnais would cross the border there until the eighteenth century without making a will. The fort became an ammunition store in the nineteenth century and has now been restored with great taste. It stands as a unique, fascinating and beautiful example of Spanish military architecture in France.

A fine example of ecclesiastical architecture, and a foretaste of what is to come in Roussillon, is to be seen in the church of Ste Marie in the small village of Espira de l'Agly. It is fortified and dates from the end of the twelfth century with black and white marble decorations on the walls, a squat tower and a splendid doorway surrounded by columns with elaborate capitals. The single nave unusually ends in twin apses, not apparent from the exterior since the chevet is square. Parts of the former cloister are now in Philadelphia.

The landscape hereabouts was, according to Arthur Young, an uninterrupted flat waste and by far the ugliest country he had seen in France. Even if there is an element of truth in what he says, the ambrosial nectar produced around Rivesaltes more than makes up for it. We had the good luck to choose the one café that stocked the best Rivesaltes, made by the Frères Cazes, whose *chai* is nearby and from whom you can buy it. It should be drunk ice-cold either as an aperitif or, since it is a Vin Doux Naturel, with cheese (especially Roquefort), pudding or fruit. It is similar to the dessert wine of Frontignan of which Jefferson opined that 'it would be far more appreciated, more seen at the best tables, if only it were not so cheap'. The wines of Roussillon in general are sturdy and strong enough to have been added in the eighteenth century to the thinner wines of the Orléanais to make fake Bordeaux and fake Madeira. Certainly in September there is no escaping the vinous smells which hang in the air at Rivesaltes and mingle with those of the sardines in barrels on the pavements, where old women sit and gossip in the heat.

The church of St André dates from 1675 to 1755 and is worth a visit, as is the little Romanesque chapel of St André in the cemetery. Jacques Joseph Césaire Joffre, the commander-in-chief of the French armies of the north in 1914 and responsible for the success of the battle of the Marne, was born here and there is a small museum devoted to him. He also has the honour of having had a tomato named 'Maréchal Joffre' for him.

Getting in or out of Perpignan is child's play compared to Montpellier, but the problem is what to do with the car once you are in the city. We had chosen a hotel that was central, but after twenty minutes of failing to find our way we finally resorted to driving the wrong way down several one-way streets on the advice of a friendly policeman.

From the moment we arrived at the Athéna Hotel we never looked back. We had an immense room on the third floor, under the eaves, with a skylight in the ceiling and an *oeil-de-boeuf* window from which we could glimpse the minute swimming pool installed in the courtyard; a shower and a basin in the middle of the room; and three double beds (for two of us). No television, no telephone, and the loo (a bit too smelly) twenty yards away along a creaky corridor. I thought I must have misheard the price when I made the reservation on the telephone and could not believe the notice on the back of the door, but when we came to pay we were correctly charged the princely sum of 149 francs per night. Things have certainly changed for the better since Augustus Hare was there and all he could bring himself to say of the hotels was: 'de Perpignan – best but horrors; de la Paix; du Nord; de l'Europe – all filthy'.

If you are only *de passage* and not sleeping the night in Perpignan (or even if you are), it is a good idea to start sightseeing at the Palais des Rois de Majorque because you can park there and do the rest of the city quite easily on foot. Like the château of Versailles, it started life as a simple hunting-lodge until Jaime became king of Majorca and transformed it when he made Perpignan into his capital. The palace is totally hidden from view by a huge and forbidding brick bastion erected in the sixteenth century and later reinforced by Vauban. The entrance is through over-arched ramps and staircases which lead up to a large and impeccably-kept formal garden from which you can see the outer façade of the palace pierced by small twin-arched windows. The masonry is in the local architectural style with rounded river stones laid in regular herringbone courses.

Across the moat, now dry, the entrance is by way of a large square tower, the Tour de l'Hommage, and up a flight of steps which takes you to an open, balconied passage. From here for the first time you can see the whole of the palace itself, for it is entirely inward-looking. All the rooms and apartments, arranged round one central and other smaller courtyards, are on the first floor, and in the early years the King lived in those in the west wing, then known as the Palais Blanc, from its plaques of white marble.

The huge state room, the Salle de Majorque, takes up the whole length of the south wing, while that to the east, neatly divided by another central tower, houses the King's and Queen's private rooms, both small and cosy, for the palace was designed to provide elegant living-quarters as well as to be secure. The central tower contains two superimposed chapels surmounted by a fortified keep and a little belltower. The chapels are lofty, with Gothic vaulting and painted walls, little natural daylight filtering through the lancet windows.

Though now bereft of furnishings, the whole palace exudes a feeling of well-being and luxury, and it is not difficult to imagine it peopled by a glittering array of courtiers. Tournaments and horse races were held in the large central courtyard where plays and concerts are now held in the summer months. Covered galleries known as 'paradises' were built on the upper floors to provide shadey roof gardens from which the view could be enjoyed.

After the collapse of the Kingdom of Majorca the palace became the property of the kings of Aragon. The *corts*, or Catalan *parlements*, met from time to time in the Salle de Majorque.

From the palace, you can either go down into the city or on round the outer boulevards to the church of St Jacques. There is something to be said for the latter approach because from the rather unkempt gardens of the Miranda by its side, you have a fine view out across to the east towards Château Roussillon. The church was founded in 1245 but was largely reconstructed in the fourteenth century and the nave given new vaulting in the nineteenth. There are a number of fine retables inside including those of Notre Dame de l'Espérance (late fifteenth century); Notre Dame du Rosaire (1643); and the high altar (1769). Amongst the paintings and sculpture a statue of St James the Greater in pilgrim attire (1450) may be singled out.

The eighteenth-century chapel of La Sanche (the Holy Blood) is the headquarters of a fraternity of the same name founded by St Vincent Ferrer in the early fifteenth century. Its members, whose vocation was to comfort prisoners condemned to death and on their way to execution, dressed in black or red robes with a *caperutxa*, a pointed hood, garments still worn when, every year on Good Friday, the Confrérie carries sacred relics through the town. Preceded by the Christ aux Injuriés (or Christ aux Outrages), one of those terrifying crosses made up of the instruments of the Passion, which normally hangs just inside the porch, the procession wends its way to the cathedral and back.

The present cathedral of St Jean stands at the end of a small square surrounded by lemon trees in tubs. It seems a pity that there is not a café in which to sit quietly and admire its façade, made like that of the Palais des Rois de Majorque of river stones with pink brick courses between them. Although the first stone was laid in 1324, not much progress was made until 1431, and it was not completed until 1509. The porch was added in 1631 and the delicate wrought-iron cage above, which houses a bell of 1418, was designed in 1742 by Philippe Barthélemy who worked at the Perpignan mint.

The huge single nave is lined by lateral chapels crammed almost to the ceiling with retables which can only be appreciated by electric light. Switches are thoughtfully provided alongside the chapels. Some of the retables are in marble and some in gilded and painted wood; all are elaborate, and dusty. The best are those of 'la Mangrana' – the Virgin with a pomegranate –

137

(early sixteenth century); Stes Julie and Eulalie (1678–88) by Jean-Jacques Melair; St Peter (Flamboyant Gothic); and the Immaculate Conception (c. 1700) by Onuphre Lazare Tremullus. That of the freestanding high altar is in marble and was started in 1618 by a Burgundian, Claude Péret and eventually completed in wood some twelve years later by a Catalan, Onuphre Salla. A gilded statue of St John the Baptist stands in its central niche in front of a red and yellow curtain, the Catalan colours of blood and gold.

The effigy of King Sancho and that of Bishop Louis de Montfort (c. 1700) by Jean Caravaque, who was in charge of the sculpture of the king's galleys at Marseille, lie on their tombs in the north transept. A passage leads under the organ into the chapel of Notre Dame del Correch which has a sixteenth-century painted wooden entombment and a dark cupboard said to contain ecclesiastical treasure which is hard to see in the prevailing gloom.

For those whose first passion is not Baroque altarpieces and who prefer something simpler, there is a beautiful and striking white marble font in the first chapel to the left of the main door. The marble tub has been worked as if it was made of some soft pleated fabric with a rope girdle around it and two small faces on each side. While it has until recently been considered to be pre-Romanesque, it is now thought to date from the twelfth century.

Beyond the south transept outside the cathedral is the chapel of the Dévôt Christ built 1535–43 to house a partially-gilded wooden crucifixion. Probably of Rhenish workmanship and at least as early as 1307, it arrived at Perpignan in the early sixteenth century. Christ's agony is made manifest in his pain-wracked face and body simultaneously schematic and realistic. It is strange how the Germans and the Spanish seem to have a similar ability to portray suffering.

On the far side and to the left of the cathedral is the earlier church of St Jean-le-Vieux. Consecrated in 1025, it was turned into a generating station in the 1890s by Edmond Bartissol (known as the Portuguese Rothschild) when he undertook to supply Perpignan with electricity, and the inside is now a wreck. Though Electricité de France still appear to own part of it, it is at last being restored, but at present you can only see the exterior. The white marble Romanesque portal has a majestic seated Christ, with knees like shiny footballs, by the same artist (Ramon de Bianya or Ramon de Via) who portrayed Guilhem Gaucelme at Arles-sur-Tech (see page 152).

A short walk takes you to the centre of the city, animated in a way that Narbonne is not, perhaps because a third of the population of the *département* of the Pyrénées-Orientales lives and works there, and most of them seem to congregate in the nearby place de la Loge, with its bronze statue of *Venus with a Necklace* by Maillol. You can spend many a happy moment with a drink or a meal in one of the cafés facing the Loge de Mer, with its sixteenth-century wrought-iron ship symbolizing Perpignan's maritime trade. The stone building of 1397 was put up to house the Maritime Exchange which had been created in 1388. It is in the Catalan Gothic style, though only the eastern part is original; the rest was altered in 1540 when the arcades on the ground floor and the windows on the first were added. The white marble at the base dates from the 1840s. In 1907 Baring-Gould noted that 'the lower storey was given up to be a café'; it now serves fast food.

Next to the Loge de Mer is the Hôtel de Ville, begun in 1315 to house the municipal government with its façade in river stones. The three bronze arms jutting from it represent the three categories of citizens who had the right to vote and were eligible according to their income bracket. Getting the key from the bureaucrats who inhabit the building (it is still the Mairie) to see the painted ceiling in the Salle des Mariages presents quite a problem, but Aristide Maillol's statue of *La Méditerranée*, exemplifying his statement that he wanted his figures 'to symbolize woman with her promise of motherhood', goes a long way to calm one's irritation.

The Maison Julia is in a little side-street nearby and it is worth trying to get into the courtyard to see its arcaded galleries.

Le Castillet is a sombre redbrick fortified gateway with two round towers built in 1368. It became a prison from the end of the seventeenth century until the Revolution and is now the Musée Catalan des Arts et Traditions Populaires and known as La Casa Pairal. It has a moderately interesting collection of regional furniture and folk art, and rather eccentric opening hours.

Beyond Le Castillet you are out of the medieval town and into a rather more spacious area, though Perpignan was not relaid out in any grand eighteenth-century scheme of urbanization. It is interesting to see how attitudes to size and space change over the years. We would describe the streets of Perpignan as narrow but Thomas Platter, there in 1599, found them

> wide and beautiful . . . The windows of the houses are mostly of marble and are arched and so wide that four or five persons might stand in them together. They have no glass and are never closed, because of the warmth of the climate. The town is divided by a stream not more than four paces wide, on the banks of which are orange trees full of ripe fruit; I counted more than fifty of these trees.[64]

Today in summer subtropical flowers are bedded out in the formal gardens which line either side of the River Basse, Platter's stream and a tributary of the Têt. The Basse runs round the city with its barbered lawns of an improbable green making it look like a tamed canal. Perhaps it was this that made Ibrahim Pasha's son, Mehemet Ali, observe in 1846 that he thought himself by the side of the Nile. Or perhaps it was the palm trees in some of the squares, like the place Arago, named for the astronomer François Arago whose statue by Marius-Jean-Antonin Mercié stands at its centre. (He was also responsible for a statue of Cabanel at Montpellier.)

There are more cafés and restaurants here, one of which was charmingly offering sorbets called 'le Black and White' and 'l'After Eight' and, more authentically, two of Perpignan's specialities, the cakes known as 'Bras de Vénus', a sort of scented swiss roll, and 'Pètes de nonnes'.

The Second Empire brick Préfecture faces the River Basse and the neo-Classical Palais de Justice is just beyond the place Arago. The Palais de la Députation was the seat of Roussillon's *parlement* in the seventeenth century and of the law courts until the Revolution. Like the Loge de Mer, it is a Catalan Gothic building and was put up in 1447. It is back in the old town in the place Jean-Jaurès.

A certain exoticism, whether Egyptian or just Catalan, is certainly evident in the centre of the city, even in the poverty-stricken quarter inhabited by North African immigrants from the Mahgreb between place Rigaud and place Cassanyes. Until about ten years ago, the Musée des Beaux-Arts was located up here but it has now moved into a more salubrious street in the pedestrianized centre amid sophisticated shops, where the red marble paving stones of the narrow streets glisten with a kind of frantic sheen in the rain.

The Musée Hyacinthe Rigaud is in the Hôtel Lazerme, a dignified eighteenth-century building, and contains some really lovely paintings. There are a number of early Catalan primitives, excessively rich and at the same time austere, of which the most striking is the *Retable of the Trinity*. It was painted in 1489 by the Maître de Canapost for the centenary of the Loge de Mer, though its predella is a somewhat imaginary representation of both the site and the building.

The outstanding works in the museum are of course the portraits by Hyacinthe Rigaud. He was born in Perpignan in 1659 and worked in Montpellier before going on to Paris where he won the Prix de Rome. Charles Lebrun dissuaded him from going to Italy, rightly perceiving that his vocation was as a portraitist. Indeed both his formal and intimate portraits are of the highest quality and never degenerate into mere cliché. In his self-portrait with a turban, painted when he was thirty-nine, he depicts himself as a humorous and slightly cynical fellow. He is as much at his ease with the full panoply of power and the sumptuous trappings of Church and State in his famous portrait of Cardinal Bouillon, which Voltaire thought 'a masterpiece equal to Rubens's best work'.

In addition to canvasses by the usual masters such as Brueghel, Greuze and Géricault, modern paintings are also exhibited, including several by Raoul Dufy who, like Jean Cocteau and Jean Marais, spent part of the Second World War in Perpignan. There is also a good collection of ceramics.

Not far away is the old Palais des Corts which housed various medieval law courts and dates from about 1310. It was given a new façade in the seventeenth century but the inner courtyard still has its arcaded gallery of 1424–7.

Perpignan, like most of the cities in the Midi, owed much of its wealth to its cloth trade, a fact reflected in its bourgeois hôtels of which the rue du Théâtre has some splendid if rather crumbling examples. Anne of Austria lodged in the nearby Maison de la Main de Fer (so named for the shipowner who built it in 1509) when she accompanied her son, Louis XIV, in April 1660 on his way to St Jean-de-Luz to marry Maria Theresa of Spain. This union was to set the seal on the Treaty of the Pyrenees. Mademoiselle de Montpensier, also a member of the party, disliked what she described as 'Spanish austerity, out-of-date clothes, boring fêtes, mediocrity, and the oddness of the dances'. If it is true that the only amusement that could be offered to the King was a fight between a bear and a dog in the courtyard of the Maison de la Main de Fer, it sounds as if she was right.

The Bibliothèque Municipale has recently moved out of the Hôtel Pams in the rue Emile Zola, and the wonderfully ornate *fin-de-siècle* creation by the Danish architect Petersen is to be renovated and opened as a cultural centre. Petersen also built the splendid ochre-yellow hôtel opposite for the Bardou family, with its initialized cast-iron balconies. The Bardous' claim to fame and fortune came from manufacturing cigarette papers as Baring-Gould noted.

On leaving S. Girons – about which I say nothing, as concerning it nothing can be said – the factory of La Monlasse is passed where cigarette papers are manufactured in large quantities. The man who started making them was named Jean Bardon [sic], and he put his initials on the little books of cigarette papers, with a lozenge between, thus J ◇ B. This was read as Job, and such papers acquired the name and became famous as Job's cigarette papers.[65]

They are still made, but the typography has been changed. Manufacturing cigarette papers was one of the city's most successful money-spinners from the middle of the nineteenth century, as was the production of bentwood whips. They were made at Sorède from the *micocoulier* by a man called Masson whose name, like those of Hoover and Singer, became a generic term for whips and actually appeared in the Littré dictionary of 1877 as such.

Salvador Dali, in one of his customary moments of excess, referred to Perpignan as 'the centre of the world' when he arrived at the railway station in 1965 having travelled all the way from Spain via Céret in a farm cart. I have failed to find his painting of this jape (it is not in Düsseldorf as one guidebook claims), and the ceiling in the booking hall of the railway station is not by him either (as another claims), but was painted in 1987 by Escoriguel-Kery and called *Point Zéro*.

There is a lavish new Palais de Congrès in the Bir Hakim gardens where there are a number of modern statues, a monument to Casals, the usual war memorial . . . and a red British telephone box.

Cabestany, between Perpignan and Elne, is worth a short visit to see the sculpted tympanum in the church of Notre Dame des Anges. The town is pleasant and sleepy, with runnels of water trickling along the gutters of the main street. The church has been considerably altered since the early twelfth century; it was enlarged in 1300 and a new nave and apse were added in 1934. It was during the course of these later works that the tympanum, then above the south porch, was discovered. For the time being it is on display inside the church where devoted ladies sweeping up and making great bouquets of flowers for the altar seem delighted that anyone should bother to come all the way to see *their* tympanum.

It was the examination of this work that enabled art historians to establish the Maître de Cabestany as a specific, if anonymous, individual working during the second half of the twelfth century. He appears to have been itinerant, for works by his hand, or those of his pupils, are to be found not only in Roussillon and Languedoc, but also as far afield as Navarre and Tuscany (in Sant'Antimo at Montalcino near Siena and San Giovanni at Sugana near Florence).

The tympanum at Cabestany tells a three-part story of the Virgin in the somewhat heavy but powerfully graphic style that has come to be associated with the Maître. On the left, Mary is emerging from the tomb to be greeted by her son; on the right, she is being borne aloft by four angels, one of whom looks exactly like ET; and in the centre, she sits in glory on Christ's left hand with St Thomas on his right. Thomas, according to the Golden Legend, arrived at Mary's bedside too late to receive her blessing before she died. However on his way to Jerusalem he encountered the angelic procession conveying her body to heaven. Mary gave him her girdle, clearly depicted in the sculpture, so that he would have evidence of her bodily assumption.

No one has satisfactorily explained the abnormal size of the hands in the Maître's work, nor his other hallmark, an inverted double scroll. Works by him are to be found at Rieux-Minervois, Le Boulou, St Papoul and St Hilaire. Cabestany also has a statue of St Gaudérique, whose boots seem an appropriate accessory for the patron saint of the *vignerons* who pray to him for rain.

The road to Elne plays box and cox with a series of small canals, lined with bulrushes amidst a flat landscape punctuated by cypresses and pines, and market gardens where rows of vegetables and fruit trees are sheltered by bamboo screens. Elne is now a centre for this produce, nicely symbolized by Maillol's statue of *Pomona*, the original of which is in the Mairie and a copy of which adorns his Monument aux Morts. The bust of a little-known local Fauve painter, Etienne Terrus, is also by him. Originally called Illiberis, Elne has been occupied since the eighth century BC and was the site of Hannibal's camp in 218 BC. The Romans changed its name in honour of the Empress Helena, Constantine's mother. It became a bishopric as early as 571 under the Visigoths and remained one until 1602 when the see was transferred to Perpignan.

The church of Ste Eulalie, consecrated in 1069, stands high and proud above the Mediterranean, with its two towers of unequal height making it a landmark from afar. The crenellated façade is simple and is pierced by one of those fine portals surrounded by marble of which there are so many in Roussillon. The capitals on the last two cruciform pillars in the nave are particularly attractive and the baldaquin was copied from that in the church of Val de Grâce in Paris.

The cloister is remarkable not just because it is the only one in the province that is virtually intact. The south gallery dates from the twelfth century and the other three some hundred or so years later, but they present an harmonious ensemble. The columns supporting the arches are of the wonderful greyish-white blue-veined marble that comes from Céret, and the historiated capitals are expressively carved with stylized floral motifs, animals and some rather archaic figures. There is a tiny museum giving the history of Elne in a room off the cloister.

The littoral is not a *pays* as such, and while the beach is sandy in its northern stretches from Canet Plage, it turns to rock at Argelès all the way down to the Spanish border. This southern stretch is known as the Côte Vermeille, a name it acquired at the turn of the century and appropriate enough to describe the silver-gilt or vermilion hues (*vermeil* can mean either) thrown off by the schist. Augustus Hare does not mention it and thought the fishing villages were only worth a few lines each.

While the coastline is spectacular, I am bound to say that I think the resorts are over-rated. Collioure may have been delightful fifty or perhaps even twenty years ago before it was turned into a sort of poor man's St Tropez and spoiled, like St Trop itself, by mobs of tourists and scruffy eating places. Its site is magnificent, built as it is in a semicircle round two natural bays with vine-clad hills rising behind and the sea stretching away in front. One can see exactly why it became the haunt of the Fauves.

Matisse took André Derain there for a holiday in the summer of 1905 and

> it became [for them] what Gardanne, in the heart of Provence, was for Cézanne and what Céret . . . was soon to be for Braque and Picasso. It was one of those rare places where privileged painters ripen their vision and create a style. If Céret was, as André Salmon put it, 'the Mecca of Cubism', Collioure was the birthplace of Fauvism, for it was there that the transition was made from the Neo-Impressionism of St Tropez to the new and brilliant manner that created a sensation at the 1905 Salon d'Automne.[66]

Derain was particularly struck by the quality of the light as he wrote to Maurice de Vlaminck in 1905:

> it's a golden-yellow light which has the effect of extinguishing shadows – maddening to work on. Everything I've done so far looks stupid to me. I'm taking advantage of a rainy day to write, because normally there is this brilliant sunlight which drives me to distraction by the sheer difficulty of recreating it . . . Otherwise it's a pretty place, sea in front, mountains behind.[67]

Subsequently both Derain and Matisse, through the good offices of Etienne Terrus, made the acquaintance of Maillol who 'opened their eyes to the almost Hellenic beauty of an Arcadian region where the gods of fable seemed to linger on in an eternal *Golden Age*'[68] (the title of one of Derain's paintings). Rather more prosaically, Maillol took them to see a collection of Gauguin's Tahitian paintings which Daniel Monfreid had at his house in Corneilla-de-Conflent. Both Matisse and Derain were much influenced by the way in which Gauguin dealt with flat tracts of pure colour and his handling of light and they, as well as Braque, Othon Friesz, Dufy, Marquet, Juan Gris and later Picasso and Foujita all found the strength and brilliance of the colours of the landscape magical, as indeed they are.

While Collioure may have changed since the Fauves were there, it is still an active fishing port, as it has been since medieval days, and specializes in anchovies, sardines and tuna fish. The anchovies, called *aladroc* in Catalan, have an exceptional flavour and are preserved in both tins and jars, as well as being used in a wide variety of dishes. Of the most interesting and easily manageable at home are a *feuilletée aux anchois*, small parcels of flaky pastry with anchovy fillets and olives; *pommes aux anchois*, a rather more unusual combination of fried apples, anchovies and parsley; and *anchoiade*, a delicious spread.

Amongst other fishy specialities of this coast are *bourride*, fish cooked in a *court-bouillon* with herbs and served with *aïoli*; and *bouillinade*, a thick mixture of fish, potatoes and garlic, flavoured with saffron. Saffron is a common ingredient in the cooking both there and in Languedoc. Since it takes 85,000 flowers of the autumn-flowering *crocus sativus* to make one pound of the dried styles, it is no wonder that it is so expensive.

Although important in military terms for both the Romans and the kings of Aragon, Collioure was also a thriving commercial port, exporting cloth from Perpignan until the nineteenth century, when it was superseded by Port Vendres. The royal château, which dominates both small bays and is built round a square keep, was adapted by the kings of Majorca from a former Templar castle, and transformed by the Emperor Charles V and Philip II of Spain into a powerful citadel. Vauban made some further alterations, and at the same time razed the church in what was then the upper town. Now Collioure consists mostly of the lower town where the late seventeenth-century church of St Vincent stands like a beacon on the westward arm of the sea wall. It is filled with superlative Baroque altarpieces, three of which are by Joseph Sunyer. He was born in Perpignan or Prades and worked at the end of the seventeenth century. It took him four years to complete the retable dedicated to Notre Dame de l'Ascension behind the high altar. The result is a perfect example of Catalan Baroque. There are a number of these altarpieces by him throughout Roussillon and all are highly coloured and gilded, and full of incident and movement. They carry the message of the Counter-Reformation with a restrained exuberance that manages to avoid the worst excesses of the Baroque. They are to be seen at Prats-de-Mollo, Vinça, Prades, Villefranche-de-Conflent and Font-Romeu.

Banyuls-sur-Mer, just beyond Port Vendres, is a small pleasure port, sufficiently sheltered from the winds for a number of exotic plants such as *caroubier* (carob tree) and eucalyptus to have been acclimatized there. They were originally planted by Charles Victor Naudin, who later successfully transplanted many of them to the gardens of the Côte d'Azur. There is also a marine laboratory run by the university of Paris.

Maillol was born here and though he lived in Paris, returned each autumn to work in his studio in his aunt's house. In the first decades of the twentieth century he turned from painting to sculpture and many of his drawings and statues are to be seen throughout the Midi, at Perpignan, Elne, Céret and in the museums in Montpellier and Bagnols-sur-Cèze. Here there is one of his Monuments aux Morts, and he himself is buried at the Mas Maillol.

The main road to Le Boulou turns inland at Collioure and runs along the foot of the Albères into the Vallespir where there are a number of small villages and remarkable churches. Those at St André-de-Sorède and St Génis-des-Fontaines are especially interesting because the lintels over their doorways are made from marble altarpieces thought to date from the early years of the eleventh century. With their charming and direct naïvety they are more like drawings in stone than sculpture and bear some resemblance to Carolingian goldsmiths' work. The lintel

1 The fair at Beaucaire; lithograph by Engelmann, 1827
(Musée Paul Dupuy, Toulouse)

2 The façade of the church at St Gilles-du-Gard *(FGTO)*

3 The Arènes at Nîmes *(Alain Patrice, Nîmes)*

4 Miniature of Molière as St John the Baptist
(Musée Vulliod-St-Germain, Pézenas/Lauros-Giraudon)

5 The *château d'eau* on the Peyrou, Montpellier *(FGTO)*

6 The foal in procession during the fête at Pézenas
(Marc Huygue, Pézenas)

7   The *oppidum* at Ensérune *(Yan/FGTO)*

8 Engraved stone showing bears and their trainers, in the
Horreum, Narbonne *(Richard Law)*

9 A satirical depiction of the Cathars in a medieval *Bible moralisé*
(Ms Bodl 270b, f. 123v) *(Bodleian Library, Oxford)*

10 The tympanum by the Maître de Cabestany, in the church at
Cabestany *(Jean Dieuzaide)*

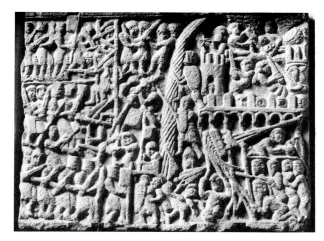

11 Stone depicting a siege, in St Nazaire, Carcassonne
(Charles Camberoque)

12 The ruined château of Montségur *(Mayotte Magnus)*

13 The fort at Salses *(Caisse Nationale des Monuments Historiques et des Sites)*

14 Predella of the Retable de la Trinité, showing the Loge de Mer, Perpignan *(Musée Hyacinthe Rigaud, Perpignan)*

15 The church of
St Michel-de-Cuxa
(FGTO)

16 Carcassonne *(Charles Camberoque)*

17 Ceiling of the church of the Jacobins, Toulouse *(Jean Dieuzaide)*

18 *Les Promeneurs,* with Jean Jaurès, by Henri Martin *(Jean Dieuzaide)*

19 The church of St Sernin, Toulouse *(Jean Dieuzaide)*

20 The Hôtel Assézat, Toulouse *(Jean Dieuzaide)*

21 Henri de Toulouse-Lautrec
by Edouard Vuillard
(Musée Toulouse-Lautrec, Albi)

22 Detail from *The Last Judgement*
in Albi cathedral *(Jean Dieuzaide)*

23 Albi cathedral with the Palais de la Berbie to the right
(Jean Dieuzaide)

24 Houses on the river at Castres *(Ville de Castres)*

25 The bleak uplands of the Cévennes *(Mayotte Magnus)*

at St Génis is one of the earliest to show human figures and depicts Christ upheld by two angels and six apostles. That of St André, also showing Christ, is rather clumsier, and though the carving is deeper, it is clearly still experimental.

Apart from the coast road, the only other road into Spain, until the new *autoroute* was built, followed the line of the Via Domitia going from Le Boulou to Le Perthus. Le Boulou has always been a busy town situated as it is at the foot of the pass of Le Perthus and used from time immemorial by the muleteers. When the railway was built it acquired a new lease of life as a junction for freight because of the difference between the French and Spanish gauges. It is still used as a base for long-distance haulage lorries. But, above all, Le Boulou is a spa, much favoured by those with liver and gall-bladder complaints, and nowhere near as elegant now as it was in the days of the Belle Epoque, to judge from the postcards on sale.

The church of Ste Marie is of no special interest, except for the frieze above the portal which is by the Maître de Cabestany. The scenes it depicts are of the Nativity, the infant Jesus being bathed, the Adoration of the Magi, the Flight into Egypt and other such episodes of Christ's childhood, but unfortunately they cannot be read by the naked eye. By contrast, the frescoes in the church of La Mahut at St Martin-de-Fenollar are, happily, visible, and dazzling. (It is easy to miss the way to this tiny chapel because it lies off the D618, a small road between the *autoroute*, the N9 and the D115.)

The frescoes on the vault of the choir, mostly in shades of red and ochre, were painted in 1123 and show Christ and four evangelists, a Virgin at prayer, the twenty-four elders of the Apocalypse, all with fiercely expressive faces, the Annunciation and the Nativity, in which the Child is shown rather oddly lying on an altar rather than in a crib.

L'Ecluse is to be found in a deep ravine nine kilometres before reaching Le Perthus. Not only are there remains of two old forts there, but also the last traces of the Via Domitia on the French side. It takes a bit of scrambling to find it and though it is only a path hacked out of the rock, it is thrilling to see the stones trodden by Hercules, Hannibal, Pompey and Caesar. Le Perthus, quieter now than it was before the *autoroute* was built, is still a lively frontier town.

The easiest way to reach the towns and villages in the lovely Vallespir is by retracing your path along the N9. At Maureillas-las-Illas, which used to be a haunt for highwaymen, nine of whom could hide in the hollow of the great oak tree, the Chêne des Trabucayres, there is a small museum devoted to cork.

Then there is Céret, a most enchanting and animated town. Enormous plane trees shade the streets and the remains of its stone walls, and it is especially renowned for its cherries which ripen in the mild climate as early as April. We had the good fortune to be there when the Saturday market was in full swing, and it seemed quite different from other markets. It certainly had its share of Guatemalan artefacts and the usual cheap clothes stalls, but the fresh produce came exclusively from the countryside around. I was delighted to hear purveyor and purchaser of that ewes' milk cheese known generically as 'Pyrénées' speaking what I took to be Catalan; both turned out to be Dutch. Freshly-made *tielles* were on sale, small rounds of frilly edged pasty stuffed with tomatoes and small cuttlefish; ideal for a picnic, or just a snack.

The situation and temperate climate of Céret has made it, like Collioure, a favourite haunt of artists, and the Musée d'Art Moderne is a great delight with the best small collection of its kind. It is housed in a simple building, a former convent, and the rooms with their white walls, pale tiled floors and natural light filtered through gently billowing white curtains make a perfect setting for contemplating the paintings. Only a few works are shown in each room so that each has the breathing space it needs.

The collection includes work by Matisse, Marc Chagall, Juan Gris, who spent the years of the First World War there, Albert Marquet, Pinkus Krémègne, Claude Viallat, Maillol and ceramics by Joan Miró. Picasso's 'Les Coupelles de Céret' are also here. He made these wonderfully attractive bowls in 1955 after seeing the bullfights in Collioure. A. S. Byatt recounts that in 1953 she was amazed to find the crowd booing at a bullfight in Nîmes. The explanation she was given was that 'the object of their derisive loathing was Picasso, whose black beret I could just see across the bloody dust. "They think his art is infantile and he has ruined the lovely traditional pottery at Vallauris"'.[69] Although Braque spent three summers in Céret from 1911, the museum has only one of his lithographs. But it has thirty bronzes by Manuel Hugue, commonly called Manolo, who lived at Céret for fifteen years from 1900. His statue of Déodat de Séverac is there, and one of his Monuments aux Morts can be seen at Arles-sur-Tech. The Monument aux Morts at Céret is by Maillol.

Just to the north of the town is the fourteenth-century Pont du Diable, a single-spanned bridge arching 45 metres above the River Tech, along which a pretty road runs up through the valley lined with fruit trees and olives shielded by bamboo screens to Amélie-les-Bains. Formerly called Arles-les-Bains, its name was changed in 1840 in honour of Louis-Philippe's queen. Although in 1890 Augustus Hare found life 'indescribably dull here . . . the same limited society necessarily meeting all day long', the sulphurous springs continue to attract curistes. The spa was put on the map in 1840 by a Dr Poujade who advertised his establishment as having 'humanitarian objectives' and explained that the exceptional mildness of the climate had led him to 'thermoclimacteric inventions'. But the beau monde did not come to sample the waters until fourteen years later when General Castellane installed a military hospital for invalid soldiers. The new thermal establishments built in 1902 'incorporating the very latest thing in modern hygiene' might have cheered Augustus Hare, though even today he would probably not find the company much more to his taste.

The next town along the river road is Arles-sur-Tech, built round Ste Marie, the earliest Benedictine abbey in Catalonia. The abbey church, consecrated in 1046, is basically a twelfth-century building and has the peculiarity of being orientated towards the west. Its main interest lies in the façade, with a lintel inscribed with alpha and omega and a rather mysterious double A; a tympanum showing Christ in glory with the four evangelists represented by their symbols in a style akin to that of Carolingian ivorywork; and a very pretty round-arched window above with a carved stone decorative surround. The interior has a lofty nave and two aisles, undecorated, a chapel dedicated to Sts Abdon and Sennen, and two silver reliquaries. The elegant cloister dates from 1262 to 1303.

By the side of the church, on a small platform, is to be found the Holy Tomb, with a rather battered effigy on the wall above of Guilhem Gaucelme, a local seigneur who died in 1304. The tomb has miraculous properties in that, although covered and completely freestanding, water collects in it. Every few years, on 30 July the lid is removed and the tomb is seen to be full. Despite scientific investigation, no explanation has ever been offered. A certain Arnulph, wishing to rid the countryside of dragons and suchlike, went to Rome to find some relics that would drive them away. Two Persian martyrs, Sts Abdon and Sennen, appeared to him in a dream and led him to their bodies, which in a cavalier fashion he removed. He packed them in a barrel of water and set off for home, accomplishing various miracles on the way. When he reached Arles-sur-Tech, according to Augustus Hare

> Arnulph drew forth his relics, and as for the water, emptied it into a vacant sarcophagus, where a leper washed and was instantly cured . . . The monks took possession of so valuable a source of income and the water is still sold by the clergy at 1 fr. the bottle, though only to those who ask for it in Catalan.[70]

The church of St Sauveur dates from the seventeenth century, there is a good 'Marianne' by the Mairie, and the monks' oil mill down by the river is now a factory for making traditional Catalan fabrics.

Beyond Arles-sur-Tech a minor road leads to St Laurent-de-Cerdans, famed for its espadrilles; there is a small museum devoted to them on the way to Coustouges, a pretty village with a fine church. Another leads to Serralongue, where there is another Romanesque church. The main road continues along the valley to Prats-de-Mollo and thence into Spain. At Prats-de-Mollo Vauban's ramparts and the church of Stes Juste and Ruffine (1649–81), with a stunning Sunyer retable (1693) are to be seen. Prats, like Arles-sur-Tech, still holds an annual bear festival at carnival time, though these days a man does duty for the bear, and allows himself to be hunted and captured to the delight of both children and adults.

It has been forbidden by law to hunt bears since 1962 and they are now an endangered species and a bone of contention between the ecologists and the local shepherds. They have vanished from the Vosges, the Jura and the Alps but there are believed to be about fifteen hereabouts and in the Ariège. They were already rare in Baring-Gould's day:

> Bears are no longer hunted on the French side of the Pyrenees, and those who seek for them must cross over the Spanish frontier, where a good many are still to be found in the forests. But . . . the demand for them has ceased, not only to be led about, but to show in barbers' yards as evidence that genuine bear's grease is sold on the premises.[71]

Macassar oil had by then replaced bear's grease for grooming men's hair, but old-fashioned London barbers' shops continue to display engravings of bears and their tamers.

The brown bear (*Ursus arctos*) is still very much part of the local folklore, and though welcomed by neither the shepherds nor the transhumant beekeepers whose honey they stole, they were viewed with a certain amount of affection, as those engravings in the Horreum at Narbonne show. They were also a source of income. The cubs were caught when they were very small and taken in to the farmhouses where at first they were treated like small dogs. Later their nails were cut and their teeth filed, and they were kept muzzled and chained. They were taught to perform at a school for bears in Ercé in the Couserans which still existed up to 1940, and then went out on the road with their keepers, many of whom came from Ustou in the Ariège, to amuse the crowds and earn an honest, if to our minds distasteful, penny. But performing bears, like bears themselves, are rare today.

There is no way across Mount Canigou rising 2,784 metres out of its massif, but from Amélie there is a beautiful if winding road across through the Aspres, a semicircle of hills covered with oaks and conifers, along which a number of churches and hermitages are to be seen.

The chapel of La Trinité, up at the Col de Fourtou which marks the separation of the valleys of the Tech and the Têt, is particularly beautiful, with strikingly decorative door-straps; the early parts date from the eleventh and the later from the thirteenth century. Inside there is a moving crucifix with a fully-clad Christ, and on the high altar a retable with a representation of the Trinity. God the Father sits in the centre with Christ on his right and, most unusually, the Spirit on his left is shown by a figure which may be female.

The church at Boule d'Amont has similar door-straps and a number of retables, touching in their simple piety. The priory of Serrabone, well restored some fifty years ago, is altogether more substantial and is reached by a series of hairpin bends as it is built in an isolated position on the side of a ravine. Its rather forbidding exterior gives no hint of the richness to be found within. Though the eleventh-century nave is simple, a tribune was added some hundred years later. Clad with decorative panels and supported by columns and capitals in pink marble from the quarries of Villefranche-de-Conflent, it makes an oasis of luminosity within the dark schist walls. The capitals here and in the adjoining gallery are profusely decorated with floral motifs and fabulous animals which constitute a sort of riotous bestiary amongst which lions figure large.

*

The D618 north from Serrabone wends through the gorges of the Boulès to join the N116. To the east lie Ille-sur-Têt, a lively little market town with a number of churches and a centre for sacred art which always has interesting and unusual exhibitions; Toulouges, where the church has a fine portal, and which was made famous by the synod of 1027 when the Truce of God, whereby warfare would be restricted to certain days of the year, was first proclaimed; Thuir, a charming village with pink brick houses, and a notable lead statue of the Virgin, and renowned for making Byrrh and suchlike aperitifs; and Monastir-del-Camp, where there is another priory whose eleventh-century church also has a good portal and a small early fourteenth-century cloister.

The road to the west goes through Vinça, with a seventeenth-century church in which there is a fine Sunyer retable (1710), and on to Prades. Prades is known primarily for being the town where in 1939 Pablo Casals, unwilling any longer to live in Franco's Spain, made his home. He started a Bach Festival there in 1950, and summer music festivals which attract big crowds are still held. A little museum is devoted to him. The seventeenth-century church of St Pierre has a wonderful Sunyer retable (1697–9) telling the story of St Peter's life.

Thomas Merton, the Cistercian monk, mystic and poet, was born in Prades during his parents' short stay there, as he relates in his autobiography:

Father wanted to get some place where he could settle in France, and raise a family, and paint, and live on practically nothing; because we had practically nothing to live on, and gaze out over the valley of the Canigou and at the monastery on the slopes of the mountain. . . . St. Martin and St. Michael the Archangel, the great patron of monks, had churches in those mountains. Saint Martin-du-Canigou; Saint Michel-de-Cuxa. Is it any wonder that I should have a friendly feeling about those places?

One of them, stone by stone, followed me across the Atlantic a score of years later, and got itself set up within convenient reach of me when I most needed to see what a cloister looked like, and what kind of place a man might live in, to live according to his rational nature and not like a stray dog. Saint Michel-de-Cuxa is all fixed up in a special and considerably tidy little museum in an uptown park in New York, overlooking the Hudson River, in such a way that you don't recall what kind of a city you are in. It is called The Cloisters. Synthetic as it is, it still preserves enough of its own reality to be a reproach to everything else around except the trees and the Palisades.[72]

The abbey complex of St Michel-de-Cuxa appears from the outside like a neat series of low-lying barns with modern red roof tiles contained within a barbered grassy precinct. Only its four-storey belltower indicates that there is a church there and even then the exterior walls and decorated portal give no hint of what is to be seen inside. No pink marble tribunes here, but cliffs of solid masonry where huge horseshoe and round arches are the only openings except for some small high windows that filter in the light. The church, one of the very rare examples of pre-Romanesque architecture in France, was consecrated in 975. Some scholars think that it shows Mozarabic influence from Cordoba, others that it was in a more local Visigothic tradition.

A further period of building took place under the Abbot Oliba in the first half of the eleventh century. He extended the chevet and built a circular chapel west of the church on a lower level, of which the crypt has a single massive pillar holding up the annular vaulting.

The cloister, or such of it as is *in situ*, dates from the mid-twelfth century, and the columns have richly ornamented pink marble capitals, though many of them have been restored. Most though were acquired in 1907 by the American sculptor George Grey Bernard, bought by the Metropolitan Museum of Art in 1925 and reassembled in 1936 at The Cloisters in New York where they gave Merton so much comfort. Benedictine monks now live at St Michel.

There is a charming photograph of Rudyard Kipling at Vernet-les-Bains in 1911 with friends and sundry French officers. In his morning coat, striped trousers and bowler hat, Kipling looks just like the butler, except that he has his hands in his pockets. Perhaps it was of here that he wrote in 1933 with the nostalgia of hindsight:

> There is a certain little meadow by the sea, under Mount Canigou, which Spring fills with narcissi when she first sets foot in Europe . . . From the tourists' point of view March is not a good season. Winds blow, there may be snow-drifts on the lower passes that a month later would be clear. Yet, for those who love the land and its people, March is the month above all; for then France, who never stops working, begins her spring cleanings, loppings, and prunings.[73]

Vernet-les-Bains as a spa is nothing like so fashionable now, but it is the starting-point for an excursion to the church of St Martin-du-Canigou. This is perched on a vertiginous cliff at a height of 1,094 metres and dominates a great ravine. The only way up to it is by foot (the return walk takes about two hours) or by jeep (which, with a driver, can be hired at Vernet). Founded by Abbot Oliba and funded by his brother Guifred, Count of Cerdagne, it was started in 1007, consecrated a first time two years later and then again in 1026.

The church is two-storeyed, with lombard arcading round the apses and the great square tower. The lower part, built in the tenth century and referred to now as the crypt, is dedicated to Notre Dame sous Terre and has a banded barrel-vault ceiling, while the upper, dedicated to St Martin, also has a barrel-vault ceiling, but without the bands.

Apart from its stark beauty, it is of great architectural interest because it was one of the first churches in France to have a fully vaulted nave and aisles, albeit of modest dimensions, supported by simple but massive monolithic pillars. The capitals are carved in low relief with sketchy floral motifs.

Much of the abbey was destroyed by an earthquake in 1433 but it was rebuilt some years later. It was totally abandoned during the Revolution, restored in 1902–32 and enlarged in 1952–72; the cloister is now being restored.

The abbey owns the relics of St Gaudérique, stolen by its monks from another church, and to whom there is a statue. The tombs to the north of the church are those Guifred cut out of the rock for himself, one of his wives and his brother.

There is another tiny Romanesque church at Corneilla-de-Conflent, with an eleventh-century belltower, a decorated twelfth-century portal and amongst several statues of the Virgin, one of exceptional simplicity and beauty.

Villefranche-de-Conflent, by contrast, offers architecture of military rather than ecclesiastical interest, though the church of St Jacques has a fine pink marble façade with two portals and, inside, a Sunyer retable (1715) and some seventeenth-century tombstones with macabre grinning death's heads. The town, founded in 1092, was surrounded by ramparts in the thirteenth and fourteenth centuries as befitted a frontier town controlling the valley of the Têt. These were later strengthened by Vauban. It was a French garrison from 1659 to 1925 and the fort served as a prison.

Sabine Baring-Gould thought Villefranche 'a dreary little place', which is rather unfair considering that it is built almost entirely from pink marble from the local quarries. Perhaps like Augustus Hare, he did not care for the company; but he tries to cheer his readers up by telling them that this was where 'La Chappelain' and 'La Guesdon' died in 1717 and 1724 respectively. These women, unlike their accomplices who were confined at Salses, were imprisoned here for their part in the 'affair of the poisons' which centred round the infamous Marquise de Brinvilliers. Nancy Mitford recounts the story in *The Sun King*:

> In 1676 the Marquise de Brinvilliers, a gentle mousey little person much given to good works, was brought to justice . . . She had poisoned and killed her father . . . then she had done the same thing for her two brothers and had tried to polish off her husband. Luckily for him, her lover and accomplice had no wish to marry

somebody as evil as he was himself, so every time the Marquis was given a dose by his wife, the lover gave him an antidote; the result was that he survived, with a greatly impaired digestion . . . She confessed everything, repented and made a good end after suffering appalling tortures – probably no worse, however, than those she had inflicted. The whole of high society attended her trial and the execution; she was beheaded and then burnt 'so that,' said Mme de Sévigné, 'we are all breathing her now'.[74]

From Villefranche-de-Conflent to Latour-de-Carol the road, and a railway serviced by 'le petit train jaune' as it is always affectionately referred to (its rolling-stock is indeed painted a vivid yellow), winds its way to and fro through the Cerdagne. The narrow-gauge railway was laid in 1910 and the rolling-stock dates from then too. The little puffer creeps over viaducts and in and out of tunnels several times a day and is a recommended option for those who feel the exigencies of driving allow them too little time to devote to the landscape.

The Cerdagne, claiming to be the sunniest region in France, is a saucer-shaped plain well over 1,000 metres above sea-level and ringed by mountains, with Pic Carlit (2,921 metres) to the north and Puigmal (2,902 metres) to the south, which remain snowcapped until late summer. The plain itself, criss-crossed by mountain streams like the Eyne and the Sègre, the products of the melting snows, presents an open, smiling landscape, intensively grazed and cultivated; oxen were still to be seen ploughing as late as 1983.

The works of nature rather than of man are the great attraction of this sun-soaked enclave. This is especially so in early summer when the fields and mountainsides are a mass of wild flowers; some very common, like alpine roses, marsh marigolds or anemones; others so rare, like the bird's nest orchid (*Neottia nidus avis*) and lady's slipper (*Cypripedium calceolus*), that enthusiasts come from afar for a sight of them. By August and September it is too hot, and the brilliant mountain flowers are already over. It is ideal country for walks and one that is particularly to be recommended is that from Saillagouse, a village which faces north towards Font-Romeu from the steep side of Puigmal, to Llo, a mountain village tumbled like a waterfall down the mountainside, with a church with an especially fine portal.

The road winds through meadows where the great height and the clarity of the air lend a unique intensity to the colours of the flowers, and the larks in the early morning can reasonably be called deafening. The clang of cowbells can be heard on all sides in summer when the herds are driven up the hillsides and can be seen picking their way very surefootedly for such heavy animals. Groups of farmers employ cowherds in summer on a co-operative basis. Each man will watch out for several hundred head spread out over some eighty square kilometres, the tools of his trade a pair of binoculars and a jeep and, in emergencies, a helicopter.

For the dedicated sightseer and lover of small early Romanesque churches there *are* works of man to be seen in the Cerdagne, though getting round to them involves some rather roundabout driving.

Mont-Louis, for example, at the foot of the Col de la Perche where the River Têt rises, was created by Vauban in 1679 for Louis XIV and named for the King, to keep guard over the new frontier. It was never called upon to defend itself and is perfectly intact. The entrance is through the classical Porte de France and one can stroll round the ramparts admiring the view. The citadel, built in 1681, is privately owned.

A short detour off the main road takes one to Planès to see an eleventh-century church with an unusual plan, in that it is trefoil, with three semicircular apses surmounted by a central dome.

Back on the main road and down a small turning on the north just before Font-Romeu is a charming hermitage. The little group of seventeenth- and eighteenth-century buildings nestles greyly on the green hillside. There, in a small chapel which contains one of Sunyer's most lavish retables, is to be found in its central niche the much-venerated Vierge de l'Invention. A beautiful twelfth-century figure. Her fête is celebrated annually on 8 September when she is carried in procession to Odeillo and remains there until Whitsun. Behind the chapel is 'le Camaril', a tiny room decorated by Sunyer and wholly Spanish in feeling.

Font-Romeu was put on the map a good deal more recently. Its pure air and sunny climate attracted asthmatics seeking a cure, once it was accessible by train and a decent hotel was built. It was developed into a centre for skiing in the 1920s and has grown into a popular and well-equipped resort.

From here still going west, one road leads to Angoustrine (an eleventh to twelfth-century church) and Ur (a church with a trefoil apse and more iron door-straps). Another, lined with the granite from which these Cerdagne churches are built, goes to Odeillo, where one is startled to see huge glinting mirrors capturing the sun's rays above the experimental solar energy plant, and through or round Llivia to Bourg-Madame on the Spanish frontier. Llivia in fact is Spanish territory. By a quirk of verbal inexactitude when the frontier line was drawn by the Treaty of the Pyrenees (it was signed there), France took the whole of Roussillon and the Cerdagne, and it was agreed that thirty-three *villages* along the frontier should go to France; Llivia was considered to be a *town*.

Bourg-Madame was originally called Guingettes d'Hix (*guingette* being a suburban place of refreshment or a cottage in the country), but was renamed in 1815 after the downfall of Napoleon, when the Duc d'Angoulême entered France by this route. Its inhabitants asked him if they might alter the name of their village to that of his wife, known as Madame Royale, to commemorate the event. Nearby at Hix there is a particularly fine Romanesque church which contains good statues and a fine retable.

From Bourg-Madame, the road goes on into Andorra and Spain, or back to the west of the Canigou across the Col de Puymorens into the old county of Foix, now the *département* of the Ariège.

Although in summer there are a fair number of tourists and, in winter, skiiers, these eastern Pyrenees seem like a haven of peace and quiet. However, even a hundred years ago an enthusiast like Henry Beraldi recorded the Pyrenees' majestic peaks

vulgarized, besmirched, behotelled, serving aperitifs and *biftecs*, where terror and exaltation once reigned. The mountains of the 1890s, he lamented, placed a café next to every natural marvel, matched pints of beer with torrents, cascades and lemonades, glorious vistas and aperitifs. Worse, the new generation, heedless of past glories, *liked* the new comforts, decent roads, mountain railways, hostelries. There, commented Beraldi, was the havoc that vulgarity and utilitarianism had wrought: '*A nous les Pyrénées*, let's make a profit from them'.[75]

6

Caves, Carcassonne and Canal du Midi

Ariège – Niaux – Foix – Le Mas d'Azil – Pamiers –
Montségur – Mirepoix – Fanjeaux – Carcassonne –
Canal du Midi

THE River Ariège rises in Spain just to the west of the Col de
Puymorens in the central Pyrenees and runs through Haut
Languedoc almost all the way to Toulouse. It has given its name
to a *département* of great natural beauty with ever-changing
scenery and criss-crossed by lots of little valleys. Like Roussillon, it is made up of a number of *pays*. The Haute Ariège is wild
and mountainous, and shades off into the Couserans to the
west, which is almost in Gascony. The Lèze and Arize, named
for the two rivers, is a small but enchanting enclave of tree-lined
slopes contrasting with the rich agricultural plains and low hills
round Pamiers in the Basse Ariège. The *pays* of Olmes over
to the east is by contrast rocky and has a pre-Mediterranean
climate and flora.

Ax-les-Thermes is, as its name implies, a spa and specializes
in the treatment of rheumatic and respiratory diseases. It boasts
no less than eighty sulphurous springs whose curative powers
were first sampled by soldiers after Louis IX had founded in
1260 an establishment for those of his troops who returned from
the Crusade with leprosy.

The spa buildings are of some architectural interest in themselves, especially the Breilh, a charming neo-Baroque affair

erected in the nineteenth century with marble columns and a portico and rebuilt in 1969.

Tarascon-sur-Ariège, at the junction of five rivers, was in the past important both strategically and commercially, but little remains of the medieval town where Gaston de Foix had a hunting-lodge, or of its château which was demolished by Richelieu in 1632, because it was virtually destroyed by a disastrous fire in 1702. But it makes an agreeable place from which to visit the *grotte* at Niaux.

This cave, sometimes called 'the Versailles of prehistory', whatever that may mean, has been more seriously described as

the sole cave-system which rivals Lascaux for the technical quality of its paintings and their state of preservation, for the sweep of its designs and the inspiration which gives them life. Elsewhere one can find excellent pieces, even ample processions of figures but nowhere, except in the Altamira ceiling, such artistic power.[76]

Niaux is one of twenty-three known painted caves in the Pyrenees, and indubitably the best. Two kilometres of galleries have been excavated, and at least three-quarters of them contain prehistoric paintings. Their 'discovery' in 1906 excited intense interest in the archaeological world, though their existence had obviously been known about in previous centuries to judge by the graffiti, the earliest of which is dated 1612. During the nineteenth century nearby Ussat-les-Bains was popular for its treatment of neurological and psychosomatic diseases – Louis Bonaparte and Lamartine were among the more distinguished visitors – and plenty of visiting patients went to see Niaux. They seem however not to have taken much notice of the wall-paintings, or if they did, not to have realized what they were. Perhaps they were distracted by the pieces of stalactite and stalagmite that were sold to them as souvenirs, like so much Brighton rock.

There are paintings, drawings and engravings of bison, deer, ibex and horses, all of which are depicted with a wonderful economy of line that nevertheless catches the essence of the animals and their movements. There is one mysterious silhouette which some have seen as anthropomorphic and, in addition to the more usual arrows and harpoons, a number of other marks, either on their own or in groups. Their arrangement and significance remain unexplained though it is thought that they might be part of a directional signposting system. These signs, like the paintings of the animals, are in both black and red. The pigments were mixed with animal fat and applied with a stick. There are also charcoal drawings made directly with the end of a burnt twig, and engravings of auroch, bison, perhaps a rhinoceros, and a salmon-like fish.

The cave seems never to have been lived in and it is from the style of these splendid works of art, almost certainly created for magico-religious purposes, that archaeologists have dated them to the end of the Palaeolithic era.

Over-exposure to light and human breath has led to the complete closure of Lascaux. At Niaux, to avoid that necessity, only two hundred visitors a day are allowed in, so you need to make careful plans if you want to see the cave. Elaborate atmospheric controls are in force, so one must hope that the cave will still be open for many years to come and that the owners will not have to resort to showing the public a photographic reproduction on the lines of Lascaux II.

Sabine Baring-Gould, a hard man to please, was not enamoured of Foix. He thought it 'a very dull place, its sole feature being the castle, like a very plain man with a very prominent nose'. Dull, Foix is not, as we found in late September when the autumn sunlight played on the red and yellow banners flying from all the public buildings and strung out across the streets, without any apparent reason for them being there.

Foix occupies a fine site, neatly tucked between the Ariège and Arget rivers and in a commanding position. In the early Middle Ages the *pays* of Foix was originally part of the duchy of

Aquitaine until it passed to the counts of Carcassonne, one of whose sons founded his own dynasty at Foix. At the time of the Albigensian Crusade, while the ruling count Raymond-Roger was not himself a Cathar, his wife was, and his sister Esclarmonde, who owned the château of Montségur, was a Parfaite. Simon de Montfort failed to take the château after two attempts, but in 1229 the new count, Roger-Bernard III, was obliged to swear homage to the French crown. This did not suit his son, not a scion of a family known as the 'Capetians of the Pyrenees' for nothing. He attempted to establish his own autonomy, until a campaign led by Philippe III in person in 1272 forced him to capitulate.

Roger-Bernard III became co-prince of Andorra in 1278 and inherited the viscounty of Béarn and its capital, Pau, on his father-in-law's death in 1290. The château, which had originally been built in the twelfth century for purely defensive reasons, had no living-quarters, so Roger-Bernard III promptly moved to Pau well beyond the writ of the king of France.

Foix saw little more of the family, though Gaston III (1331–91) lived in the town for a while. Gaston was an exceedingly colourful character – a 'Renaissance man' before his time – renowned for his military skill and his intellectual brilliance, and arrogant enough to add Phoebus (which he spelled Fébus) to his name. Amongst his other claims to fame are that he had his brother and his son killed, believing that they were poisoning him. He wrote a detailed and valuable treatise on hunting, in which he has a lot to say about bears.

During the fourteenth century the counts of Foix-Béarn were united to the kingdom of Navarre, and in 1485 its queen, Jeanne, married Jean d'Albret. Their great-grandson was Henri IV and when, in 1589, he acceded to the throne of France, Foix became crown property. It seems that it was this royal connection that prevented Richelieu from dismantling the château; on the other hand he may well have thought that it posed no threat.

Once its rulers had left Foix, only a small garrison remained in the château, to which there was no access other than on foot. A carriageway was not built until 1835–40 and then only to link it to the fortifications in the town below. It was used as a prison until 1864 and remained empty until 1950 when it was turned into a museum.

By comparison with the other châteaux we have seen, that of Foix, despite its impressive appearance from a distance, is tiny. There are two square towers and a guardroom dating from the eleventh century to which crenellations were added in the fourteenth when the round tower was built. The keep was put up in the early fifteenth century. Originally the round tower had a conical roof but this was not replaced after the roof timbers caught fire during a firework display in the middle of the nineteenth century, after, one supposes, the prisoners had departed.

The museum was rearranged in 1987 and though not ideal for displaying works of art, contains a number of prehistoric tools and beautiful bone carvings from local sites. There is also a room arranged as a kitchen–living-room (*oustal*), displaying the kind of domestic and agricultural objects that a family of prosperous nineteenth-century peasants would have owned. The knitted silk and cotton stockings with embroidered patterns are particularly interesting. Other prehistoric and medieval objects and some armour are displayed in the rooms in the round tower.

In the town, the abbey church of St Volusien, with a huge stone belfry, has a single nave in the meridional Gothic manner. The supports to the stone arches are in brick and there is a curious band of low relief doing duty for capitals painted in shades of terracotta, red and dark green, all highlighted in gold. There is a Renaissance polychromatic Entombment and handsome late seventeenth-century choir stalls, which were originally made for the church of St Sernin at Toulouse.

Foix was an important centre for the wool trade and still makes textiles in traditional Catalan style. For centuries too it was a mining town and indeed, the last ironworks only closed in 1931. During the nineteenth century it also attracted gold-diggers, for the Ariège contains modest amounts of gold, but today it is largely populated by bureaucrats.

Some 25 kilometres to the west of Foix in the escarpment of the Planturel is the cave of Le Mas d'Azil. Oddly, the River Arize and a stretch of the D119 goes right through it. The cave consists of a tunnel nearly half a kilometre long with winding galleries and chambers. Unlike that at Niaux, Le Mas d'Azil was inhabited and has no wall decorations. Both human and animal bones (including those of bears) dating from the end of the Palaeolithic period have been found there, together with a number of painted stones for which no one has yet found a satisfactory explanation. There is a small museum on the site.

If Baring-Gould was lukewarm about Foix, Arthur Young was downright rude about Pamiers

> which is situated in a beautiful vale, upon a fine river. The place itself is ugly, stinking, and ill built; with an inn! Adieu, Mons. Gascit; if fate sends me to such another house as thine – be it an expiation for my sins![77]

I am sorry to say that we too found Pamiers pretty scruffy, and that I came away riddled with flea-bites, but it would be a pity not to stop if you are in the vicinity.

The most striking architectural feature about the city is the number of towers that still remain. The cathedral of St Antonin (for Pamiers became a bishopric in 1295) has an octagonal tower, though only the rather dilapidated twelfth-century portal is of much interest. Notre Dame du Camp, whose south wall is barely six feet away from the houses on the opposite side of the street, has a fourteenth-century brick façade, with a monumental doorway put in in 1870 and flanked by two towers. There is the belltower of the Cordeliers and that of the Monnaie (1419). The square tower by the Carmelites was originally Raymond-Bernard III's keep. Parts of the conventual buildings with seventeenth-century woodwork and an eighteenth-century chapel embellished with Pyrenean marble may be seen. From the Promenade du Castella by the ruins of the old château there is an agreeable view across the plain which gives the impression of being planted with maize as far as the eye can see. In fact enormous quantities of white haricot beans, known as *cocos*, are grown there and these are highly prized for making *cassoulet*. *Azinat* or *potée de choux ariégeoise* is the town's gastronomic speciality. It is basically a form of cabbage soup and is to be found in various forms throughout the Ariège.

Gabriel Fauré was born in Pamiers. He spent the first four years of his life with a foster nurse in Verniolle and then joined his parents at Foix where his father was a teacher. His studies at the Ecole Niedermeyer in Paris, to which the journey then took three days, were paid for in part by a grant from the Bishop of Pamiers. It was with the help of Saint-Saëns that Fauré was commissioned to write a lyric opera for the Arènes at Béziers. *Prométhée* was scored for three wind bands, a hundred strings, twelve harps, choirs and solo voices so that the sound would carry, and the performances given in August 1900 were a huge success.

It has been said that Wagner took the château of Montségur as his model for Montsalvat in *Parsifal*, but there is no evidence for this assertion. However the fate of the Cathars there has certainly been the subject of a large number of books, both fact and fiction. Zoé Oldenbourg's novel *Montségur* is the most famous and certainly the most balanced, though that by the Duc de Lévis-Mirepoix, also called *Montségur*, expresses charitable sentiments not always evident in other authors.

> For centuries the din of battle has been hushed; grass and peace together clothe your fields, O Montségur! and now from north to south French people, united and reconciled, have only to pass before you and gaze in wonder upon the mighty shell of your departed glories.[78]

Although in fact the château of Quéribus was the Cathars' last stronghold to fall in 1255, and Cathar communities thrived until the early fourteenth century, the final drama took place at Montségur.

In the years after 1229 there was relative peace and the Cathars who had taken refuge there in 1232 must have thought themselves safe. But two events were to prove them wrong. The Treaty of Paris had called for the Count of Toulouse's territories to be organized into two royal *sénéchaussées*, that of Beaucaire and that of Carcassonne, and Raymond was left with only the Toulousain and the Albigeois north of the Tarn. Raymond and the Trencavels rose against the French in 1240 in the hope of regaining their power. But Raymond was forced to surrender and moreover to agree to rid his lands of the heretics. The Cathars' fate was finally sealed when in 1242 a group of about fifty of them from Montségur murdered two members of the Inquisition (founded in 1233 by Gregory IX) and their entourage at Avignonet-Lauragais, sixty kilometres away as the crow flies.

Neither the Crown nor the Church could tolerate this and, in reprisal, a Catholic force reputed to number ten thousand men – and which included the Count of Toulouse – was sent in 1243 to capture and destroy the château. When it became obvious that it could not be taken by assault, it was encircled and the siege was continued throughout the ensuing winter months.

At the end of February 1244 Pierre de Mirepoix, Montségur's military commander, offered to abandon the château in return for the lives of the occupants. A fortnight's truce was arranged, but apart from four Cathars who were thought to have escaped with the 'treasure', no one fled, and on the morning of 16 March, 207 (or 250) of the Parfaits, men and women, refusing to abjure their faith, marched out to be burned alive at a gigantic stake in a field still known as the Prats dels Cramats. The remaining Believers were taken off to be dealt with by the Inquisition.

The ruins are certainly spectacular, perched on a steep hill no easier to climb today than it would have been for a besieging army. It takes about half an hour to get to the top and the path is in some places perilous. The ruins consist of a pentagonal surrounding wall pierced by two doors only, part of the keep wall and a number of foundations. Many of these were in fact built by Guy de Lévis (to whom the château was given in 1244) and his descendants. There is a small museum in the village below.

There have been innumerable attempts to link the Cathars with the Templars, and the Cathar 'treasure' with the Holy Grail itself. The Nazis sought to find connections between them, both before and during the war when a group of SS men appear to have camped there seeking some mysterious revelation. Steven Runciman deals with the problem with his usual learned commonsense:

> Modern Occultists show a marked determination to claim the Cathars as their medieval brothers. There is a tendency amongst them to mix up the Cathar church with the Grail legends, while a society has been recently formed called *Les Amis de Montségur* [Runciman was writing in 1960], which elevates that castle into the Mecca of Occultism and the home of the Grail itself. The Cathars certainly gave Montségur, as their one physical place of refuge, high-sounding titles – as for example Mount Tabor – but such names should never be taken literally. The castle had no spiritual significance to them. Its destruction was a great material blow to them, but they were perfectly prepared to seek other refuges elsewhere. As for the Holy Grail, though Grail legends undoubtedly flourished in the Middle Ages, they can have had little connection with Cathar mythology . . . But Catharism had nothing to do with Magic, Black or White. The idea that the treasure smuggled out of Montségur on the eve of its fall was the Grail itself is picturesque but untrue. The treasure may have included sacred books, but was chiefly material treasure, money, a worldly commodity but one very necessary to a church.[79]

There we should leave neo-Catharism but not the Cathars themselves. Although most of them fled to Spain or to Lombardy, small groups persisted in Languedoc until the early fourteenth century. The tiny and now deserted village of Montaillou, just south of the D613 between Ax-les-Thermes and Quillan, was the last place where they were active after they had all but disappeared elsewhere in the Midi. In the early fourteenth century, when Catharism enjoyed a brief revival, the Inquisition tried many of its inhabitants. It was from the registers of Jacques Fournier's courts, which sat at both Carcassonne and Pamiers, that Emmanuel Le Roy Ladurie was able to analyse the lives and habits not only of the community at Montaillou but of Catharism in general in his fascinating book, *Montaillou*.

From Montségur the road to Carcassonne goes through the active little town of Lavelanet with its Musée du Textile et du Peigne à corne, which contains a reconstruction of a spinning-mill and where the machinery for making horn items is still in action. The combs and shoe-horns are all made locally and are a very good buy. Here it is worth making a detour, if you have time, through Bélesta and on past the small late fifteenth-century chapel of Notre Dame du Val d'Amour, in a quiet leafy spot in the wide cultivated valley of the Hers.

Puivert is so sleepy that it seems almost dead, but its invisible inhabitants have thoughtfully put up signposts to indicate where such things as the grocery store are to be found, perhaps for the benefit of campers. The few houses are reached across a slimy empty riverbed by a bridge which still has two thunder-boxes perched precariously on it. Above the village, perched on a low plateau, is the ruined château. Although it is walled and has towers and a keep, it seems to have been built less for defensive purposes than to house a small seigneur's court. Simon de Montfort captured it in 1210 but the ruins that we see today are later in date. It is the keep that is of interest for it has three magnificent rooms in it, one above the other. One has lofty Gothic vaulting and another is decorated with small carvings, probably fourteenth-century, showing musicians and their instruments.

Mirepoix, which advertises itself as the 'Gateway to the Pyrenees', is a charming and more attractive town that makes a good centre for excursions or for walking, as there are a number of villages in the district with pleasing if not spectacular churches and châteaux.

The town, at that time on the right bank of the River Hers, received its charter from the Count of Foix in 1207, but two years later its luckless citizens found themselves in the hands of Simon de Montfort. He subsequently gave it to Guy de Lévis as a reward for services rendered and Lévis' position was confirmed in 1229.

Some fifty years later a catastrophe overtook the Mirapiciens when floodwaters destroyed the entire town, but spared the château. A new town in the form of a *bastide* on the better-protected left bank of the river was built in 1289 by Guy de Lévis' son. This in turn took a hammering from the Black Prince during his famous *chevauchée* of 1355. Edward III's son, known to us though not to his contemporaries as the Black Prince, 'set out', in Stendhal's words, 'to pillage Languedoc, profiting with true English phlegm from the mutual rivalries of the English generals'. However, notwithstanding, he found him to be 'so modest, so generous and so great that he seems the embodiment of the virtues of an earlier age'.[80] An English historian saw his exploits through less rosy spectacles: 'He spent the autumn in congenial fashion, firing the ancient cities of Narbonne and Carcassonne, and ravaging the Mediterranean provinces'.[81]

The bands of *routiers* who followed him caused yet more destruction, so that Mirepoix had to be rebuilt once more at the end of the fourteenth century. But its basic shape has remained the same though the Porte d'Aval is the only extant gateway of the original ramparts. Mirepoix is a typical *bastide* with its grid-iron pattern of streets and a central *place*. Houses, many of them half-timbered, surround the principal square, with covered arcaded galleries (*cornières*), some still supported by stout timber beams. The house known as the Maison des Consuls is the most elaborate and has odd little faces carved on its joists.

There is a huge and fine nineteenth-century cast-iron canopy above the market-place by the side of which is the church of St Maurice. The early church, dedicated in 1298, was considered to be too small and insignificant when John XXII elevated Mirepoix to a bishopric in 1317. Work on a new one was initiated by Jacques Fournier when he was bishop. Competent, conscientious and incorruptible, Fournier, whom we have just met as Inquisitor at Montaillou, was born at Saverdun in the 1280s. He became bishop of Pamiers in 1317, of Mirepoix in 1326, cardinal in 1327, and as Benedict XII, pope in 1334, when he loyally employed Pierre Poisson, a Mirapicien, to start work on his new palace at Avignon.

Real progress was not made on St Maurice until 1327–48 when the polygonal chevet and chapels were added with their individual roofs like a pleated fan. Work on the building continued spasmodically until 1497 when the portal was enlarged and the belltower received its spire. It was consecrated in 1507. Major works of restoration took place in 1858 to 1865 and the ceiling was vaulted, with flying buttresses put up to support it, in 1867.

Perhaps because it took so long to build, the interior proportions are unsatisfactory, for the nave is too short and the ceiling too low for its huge width. In fact the nave is the widest in France. At 22 metres, it beats Albi by two and a half metres. But whereas the nave at Albi is 111 metres long and 32 metres high, that of St Maurice is only 48 metres long and 24 metres high. St Maurice is lovely just the same, with a row of rose windows high up along the side walls letting light in onto the altar.

Though Mirepoix cannot itself claim to have invented the sauce (of diced onions, carrots and celery) which bears its name, it may justly be proud that it originated with one of Guy de Lévis' descendants. The Duc de Lévis-Mirepoix was Louis XV's ambassador to Vienna in 1737 and governor of Languedoc from 1755, and he, on behalf of one supposes one of his cooks, has achieved lasting fame for this culinary achievement rather than for any diplomatic or administrative skills.

*

Fanjeaux takes its name from Fanum Jovis in the days when there was a Roman temple dedicated to Jupiter on the site, and it has always kept its religious aura. Today it has become a sort of shrine to St Dominic. It is perched up on one of those hillocks that rise from the plain in this southern part of the Lauragais, and catches the wind. No wonder that Dominic had a vision there as he stood on the eminence called Le Seignadou at the very top of the hill looking out at the plain below and across to the Montagne Noire. It is pleasing but misconceived to wonder if he shared the troubadour Peire Vidal's view that the château of Fanjeaux 'seemed like paradise'.

St Dominic's house at Fanjeaux, the saddlery of the château which no longer exists and now a centre for Catholic studies, has been rather clumsily done up, but the Dominican nuns in mufti who show you round are full of a quiet devotion to their founder and you may even find a novice at prayer in the tiny chapel. There is a fourteenth-century meridional Gothic church attached to the Dominican convent.

Dominic de Guzman was born at Calaruega in Catalonia and became head of a community at Osma until 1203, when he accompanied his bishop on a preaching mission to Languedoc. He was appalled by the heresy he found, just as St Bernard had been fifty years before in Toulouse. He chose Fanjeaux as a base because it was where Guilabert de Castres, the famous Cathar bishop, was to be found, and he spent nine years there. A celebrated *colloque* took place in 1207 between the Catholics and the Cathars, though whether at Fanjeaux or at nearby Montréal is a matter of dispute. But wherever it was, it was the scene of the 'miracle du feu'. The Catholic case had been prepared by Dominic (he was not actually present) and after fifteen days of argument, it was decided to submit the texts used by both parties to a test. Those of the Cathars burned to a cinder; those of Dominic rose from the flames three times, leaving only a scorch mark on a beam, and flew away intact. The sacred beam was preserved and is now to be seen in the chapel of St Dominic in the parish church, another meridional Gothic building, with a decorated eighteenth-century choir. (A painting of this miraculous event by the Dominican Fra Angelico hangs in the Louvre in Paris.)

By 1214 Dominic's plans for founding his own order were under way. Although a man of great humility, courage and heroic sanctity, he was also a superb organiser – and by 1215 he had the support of the Bishop of Toulouse, where his first house was opened. He obtained formal sanction from the Pope a year later for the Order of Preachers. It was the Pope and not he who was responsible for setting up the Inquisition in 1233, but the papacy saw fit to have Dominic canonized the following year.

Dominic's first converts were two Parfaites, and he opened an institution for them at Prouille, at the foot of the hill, in 1206. Dominican nuns still live there in their nineteenth-century convent.

The collegiate church of St Vincent at Montréal is in the austere meridional Gothic style and has an elegant porch and an organ by Cavaillé-Coll.

While there is much still to be discovered in Languedoc even for the seasoned traveller, there can be few today who, like Stendhal, come upon Carcassonne unawares, though many may sympathize with his attitude to sightseeing.

> I always make a point of visiting towns before reading them up in a guide book or calling on my contacts there. It is to this habit that I owe my extreme surprise at the first site of Old Carcassonne when, walking by chance through a gate of the New, I beheld it on its solitary hillock across the Aude.[82]

Carcassonne indeed consists of two separate towns, the upper one, the Cité and the lower, the Ville Basse or Bourg, joined, until the nineteenth century, by only one bridge across the River Aude. The Cité looks very different now from what it did in Stendhal's day for it is the largest, most impressive walled city in Europe. Its silhouette, resembling nothing so much as one of the illuminations from the *Très Riches Heures du Duc de Berry*, has only to be glimpsed from the motorway to convince even those reluctant to brave a town so thronged with tourists. Go out of season if you can, but at all costs, go; you will not be disappointed.

The site of the Cité was occupied from pre-Roman times, and the *castellum* and a first fortified wall were erected by the Romans. It was later occupied by the Visigoths and, for a short period, the Moors. One of the most entertaining explanations given for the city's name is that it derived from Dame Carcas, the wife of the Saracen Balaak. When Charlemagne and his Frankish paladins failed after a number of years to take the city (pure fabrication as they were never there), the garrison consisted only of Carcas.

> But she ran from one tower to another with astonishing agility, letting fly an arrow from one point, hurling a javelin from another so that it seemed a numerous army manned the walls. There remained the hope of reducing the place by famine, but Carcas read the besiegers' minds. She threw down into the fosse a pig* gorged with maize; and the French [Franks] concluding that the garrison had an abundance of provisions, prepared to lift the siege. They would in fact have given up their attempt on the town had not a miracle supervened. One of the towers . . . bowed down before Charlemagne, as though in homage to the Emperor of the West.[83]

This is how Mérimée tells the story, but the sting lies in his footnote; '* the pig seems an error of detail in a Saracen town; but local colour had not yet been invented'.

Carcassonne then became the capital of three successive and interrelated families of feudal counts of whom the Trencavels were the last. Bernard Aton Trencavel, inheriting from both his father and his mother, found himself overlord in 1074 not only of Carcassonne and the Razès, but of Agde, Béziers, Albi and Nîmes as well. For most of the twelfth century the Trencavels sought to free themselves from the suzereinty of the counts of Toulouse but failed to do so. Carcassonne capitulated to the Albigensian Crusaders after only a fortnight and Simon de Montfort incarcerated the 24-year-old count, Raymond-Roger

Trencavel, in one of its towers, where he died a year later. Simon de Montfort's son ceded Carcassonne to the crown in 1226 whereafter a second encircling wall was built. In the revolt of 1240 Raymond-Roger's son, another Roger, failing to recover his property, fled to Barcelona. Louis IX, newly-king, ordered the destruction of all the dwellings which had grown up around the fortifications and exiled the inhabitants for seven years. Then, in January 1248, he relented and allowed them to build a new *bastide* on the far side of the River Aude. This lower town – the Bourg or Ville Basse – soon came to rival the Cité, and by the mid-fourteenth century Froissart described it as 'a prosperous and flourishing conurbation of 7,000 houses'. Geoffrey Le Baker talks of 'a finely built wealthy town that was larger than London *intra muros*'. In 1348 the population was swelled by sixty burghers from Calais, resettled there after they had been exiled for not being willing to swear fealty to their English overlords.

Balducci Pegelotti, a contemporary Italian merchant, talks of Carcassonne cloth being sold at Naples, Messina, Famagusta, and even Constantinople. On the whole this cloth was coarse stuff sold to the lower classes for winter wear, but the quality steadily improved and later qualified for the 'woolmark'. It was, however, a false dawn, and although by the end of the century Francesco Datini (Iris Origo's 'Merchant of Prato') recorded that over half of a shipment of four thousand lengths came from Toulouse and Carcassonne, trade foundered. Both the Ville Basse and the Cité, which no longer had any military function, became ever more impoverished and Carcassonne lost its last vestiges of strategic importance with the Treaty of the Pyrenees. The cloth trade did however recover at the end of the seventeenth century and survived through most of the eighteenth, when the best wool came from Spain, since its quality was better than that produced in Languedoc. There was a brisk export trade via Montpellier and Marseille to the Near East, and the finest cloths were called 'mahoux', because only Moslems descended from the Prophet Mohammed were entitled to wear them. These cloths were by now renowned not only for their quality but also for the permanence of their dyes, mostly imported, via Cadiz, from South America. A sheet of samples to be seen at the Archives in Carcassonne lists the shades available: scarlet, crimson, canary, pistachio, lemon, dragon's blood, nine different blues, as many greens, and such copywriters' fantasies as 'bottle bottom', 'hay flower', 'Spanish tobacco', 'gunpowder', and 'wine soup'.

Carcassonne remained moderate during the Revolution, though it produced its fair share of heroes in the Chénier brothers and Fabre d'Eglantine. Although neither André-Marie nor his younger brother Marie-Joseph Chénier were born in Carcassonne, Carcassonne claims them as its own. They spent much of their youth there (in a house in the rue de Verdun in the Ville Basse) and certainly felt themselves to be Audois. André, a poet who, though dedicated to the idea of liberty was opposed to the excesses of the Terror, went to the guillotine on 7 Thermidor (25 July) 1794, three days before Robespierre fell. He is better known today from Umberto Giordano's opera *André Chénier*, still performed quite regularly, than for his poetic works.

Marie-Joseph Chénier was a hack writer whose play *Charles IX* had been the most popular theatrical event in 1789. He went on to produce stirring words for Robespierre's set pieces on occasions such as the Apotheosis of Voltaire, the Festival of Unity and Indivisibility, and the Festival of the Supreme Being, though he was equally adept in a different political climate when he drafted the text inviting Talleyrand to return to France.

Fabre d'Eglantine, born in Carcassonne as plain Philippe Fabre, the son of a clothworker, was educated at Limoux and Toulouse, where he won the prize, an eglantine – a golden briar rose – for his sonnet to the Virgin. He was also a leading member of the committee (on which Marie-Joseph Chénier also sat) which was responsible for reorganizing the calendar. His poetic bent can surely be seen in the choice of such names as 'Fructidor', 'Thermidor' and the like for the new thirty-day months, and the inspired invention of 'sans-culottides' for the five odd days left over at the end of the year. This was surely a dig at the Midi which had been known in Roman times as *Gallia braccata* (breeched). The house in which Fabre d'Eglantine was born is in the rue Pinel in the Ville Basse.

The Revolutionary wars, the Napoleonic wars and the supremacy of the British in the Mediterranean put an end to the short spurt of prosperity from the revivified cloth trade, and the Ville Basse now followed the Cité into economic decline. Carcassonne enjoyed a temporary respite during the wine boom of the late nineteenth century and now derives a handsome income from its flourishing tourist trade which Eugène Viollet-le-Duc did so much to create.

At the beginning of the nineteenth century, the Cité was a dilapidated rabbit warren, crumbling and insalubrious, with narrow streets and the château in ruins. Stendhal grumbled about the silence and emptiness, though in fact two thousand people lived there. He bewailed 'the absence of everything which betokens civilization; even many of the windows had oiled paper instead of glass', until at last it dawned on him that he was in 'a fifteenth-century town'. The church has some decent stained-glass windows, a rarity in Languedoc. It also houses a tombstone reputed to be that of Simon de Montfort, and a carved stone depicting a siege, perhaps that of Toulouse at which he was killed.

Viollet-le-Duc's restoration work was not without its frustrations:

> I've really only the church of St Nazaire to make up for so many vexations [he wrote]; so I cling to its columns, its stained glass and its sculptures with a passion born of despair. I spend the livelong day amid a pack of old women who come to confess their sins but have no scruples about passing on to me their fleas.[84]

One feels quite sorry for him though one cannot but sympathize with the inhabitants of the Cité who objected not only to having their property compulsorily purchased before being evicted, but also to being dictated to by the central government, Monu-

ments Historiques or not. The whole subject of the restoration
of ancient buildings excited fierce argument then as now. One
apologist for Mérimée claims that his intervention was justified
because

> for centuries, Gothic architecture had been disdained as barbaric
> by both architects and public, brought up in a narrowly classical
> tradition, and little had been done to protect medieval buildings
> against the ravages of time.[85]

Taine in 1865 complained bitterly that the restorations at
Carcassonne were all in 'very poor form, this latter-day town of
the translated south, converted by the north to peace, civilization and prosperity'[86]; and a twentieth-century critic blames
both Mérimée and Viollet-le-Duc: 'they are inseparable
and carry the crushing responsibility for the false witness
unwittingly borne by the most venerable monuments of French
art'.[87]

Work however proceeded at Carcassonne, costing the
government enormous sums of money, though no one was quite
sure what was to become of this huge white elephant (it was not
actually completed until 1930). Luckily it rapidly became a
curiosity and once it was accessible by railway, tourists flocked
to see it, the English and honeymoon couples in the lead. The
Cité was illuminated for the first time on 14 July 1896 and a
tourist information bureau, only the third of its kind in France,
was set up in 1902. It has never looked back, though people like
Henry James were still doubtful about the whole procedure:

> The process of converting the place from an irresponsible old town
> into a conscious 'specimen' has of course been attended with
> eliminations; the population, as a general thing, has been restored
> away. I should lose no time in saying that restoration is the great
> mark of the Cité. M. Viollet-le-Duc has worked his will upon it, put
> it into perfect order, revived the fortifications in every detail. The
> image of a more crumbling Carcassonne rises in the mind, and
> there is no doubt that forty years ago, the place was more affecting.
> On the other hand, as we see it to-day, it is a wonderful evocation;

and if there is a great deal of new in the old, there is plenty of old in the new.[88]

It did not take long for forgotten legends to be resurrected and 'authenticated' by local historians: the Cité was founded by Anchises, the son of Aeneas, or better still, by the Hebrews, led by one of Esther's eunuchs. Souvenir shops, with brand-new 'Gothic' signs hanging above them, soon cashed in. They offered a variety of goods, including fanciful cakes and biscuits, sweets and liqueurs, and Dame Carcas's pig, worked in pink sugar. Alas, none of the last were on sale when we enquired, though I am sorry to say we were offered sandals 'as worn by the feudal counts'.

The Cité is enclosed within two rows of concentric defensive walls, of which the outer measures 1,672 and the inner 1,287 metres. Between them are the *lices* (tiltyards). Both sets of walls are punctuated at intervals by fifty-two mostly conical towers, nearly all of which are roofed in blue slate instead of terracotta tiles because when Viollet-le-Duc came to restore them he supposed that the men of the north would have used their habitual style and materials.

One can walk around these walls and it is for them, for the great gateways and towers and for the Château-Comtal, built by Bernard Aton Trencavel in about 1125, that one admires the Cité. One cannot but agree with Viollet-le-Duc's own verdict (and he should know). 'I do not think', he said 'that there exists anywhere in France such a complete and formidable ensemble of defence works'.

There was intense rivalry between the inhabitants of the Cité and the Ville Basse on the western bank of the Aude. There are fewer tourists in the Ville Basse, a *bastide* constructed by St Louis about 1260 and fired by the Black Prince some hundred years later. But it too was reconstructed and vestiges of the bastions and ramparts remain along with what are now the outer boulevards. It is a pleasant place in which to stroll or take a meal, and I had the best *cassoulet* I have ever eaten at Le Languedoc there.

There are two churches of interest; the cathedral of St Michel and, to the north, that of St Vincent, both of which are in the meridional Gothic style. St Michel, restored by Viollet-le-Duc, has some good fourteenth-century stained glass in the windows of the choir; and the nave of St Vincent is the second widest in France, at twenty metres, two metres fewer than that at Mirepoix. There are a number of bourgeois houses, much less grand than those in Montpellier or Pézenas, particularly in the rues Bringer, de Verdun and Aimé Ramon, where the Maison du Sénéchal' (also restored by Viollet-le-Duc) and the birthplace of the painter Gamelin are to be found.

The place Carnot, at the centre of the *bastide*, is small but agreeable enough and very jolly on market days with its vegetable, fruit and flower stalls, and its pretty eighteenth-century Fontaine de Neptune in red marble from Caunes-Minervois. Nearby is the Halle au Grain, no longer either a corn market or the site of the pillory, with a fine eighteenth-century wooden ceiling. The Portail des Jacobins is the only remaining gateway and also dates from the eighteenth century as do the former bishop's palace, occupied by the Préfecture, and the Hôtel de Rolland, now the Mairie.

The Musée des Beaux-Arts was virtually empty when we visited it and the curator was further depressed by the fact that all his colour postcards had been stolen. I was sad not to be able to buy one of a really lovely still-life by Chardin shining out amongst the otherwise mostly indifferent works. There were some tolerably good portraits, by Rigaud, Pierre Subleyras and Jacques Gamelin; plenty of late nineteenth-century genre paintings which are slowly coming back into fashion and are worth taking at least semi-seriously; and a modest collection of twentieth-century art.

When the Canal du Midi was being planned, the municipality was unwilling to contribute to its costs to enable it to run just below the walls of the Cité. It therefore went some two kilometres to the north, too far away to be of much commercial use to the Carcassonnais. They eventually had to build their own canal to join it, but it was not operational until 1810.

The Canal du Midi runs from Toulouse through the Lauragais, the Minervois and the Corbières to the Etang du Thau and Sète. It lies in a magnificent wide valley framed to the west by the Pyrenees and to the east by the Montagne Noire. Travelling on or alongside it well illustrates the difference between Haut Languedoc with its fields of wheat and maize, where Ernest Renan noted on a journey from Sète in 1852 that 'the countryside grows green again', and Bas Languedoc, covered with vineyards, orchards and market gardens.

Whether you drive to and fro across the Canal, float along by boat, or bicycle or walk along its banks, you are offered an ever-changing landscape of great beauty, from the gentle greens and yellows in the spring through to the sun-baked crispness and golden aridity that comes with the stifling autumn heat. There is plenty to see *en route*. There are many graceful bridges and aqueducts with elegant sculptural decorations, and most of the tunnels and locks are much as they were when they were built. Some of the buildings, painted green or pink and with lovely red roof tiles, erected to service the bargees and their passengers, still grace its banks.

The idea of some artificial waterway that would link the Atlantic, by way of the Garonne which was navigable from Bordeaux to Toulouse, to the Mediterranean had occurred to Augustus, and eight centuries later to Charlemagne. It would do away with the long sea-journey along the Aquitanian coast, all the way round the Iberian peninsula and through the Straits of Gibraltar. But the first practicable scheme though for a canal seems to have been suggested by Nicolas Bachelier in 1539, and it aroused François I's interest; Thomas Platter heard talk of it in 1599 when he was in Narbonne. Forty years later the idea was brought up again, but another twenty were to pass before a more serious and practical design appeared. This came from Bernard d'Arribat, a Biterrois who, in 1618, submitted to the Estates of Languedoc a scheme for a canal from Toulouse to Narbonne. It was rejected under pressure from groups such as the hauliers who complained that it would be dangerous, it would take work away from the muleteers, it would – literally – stir up mud and result in stagnant and insalubrious waters. But the most crucial opposition came from the landowners in Languedoc who feared that the price of their land would go down, as would the price they could charge for their wheat and maize when faced with competition from the cereal growers of Aquitaine, who would now be able to sell their products to the eastern part of the province.

Neither this nor another scheme of 1644 came to anything, partly because none of their progenitors had solved the major technical problem: how water was to be fed into a canal at the watershed at the Seuil de Naurouze, about half-way between Toulouse and the Mediterranean. At a height of 194 metres, it was the highest point that would have to be circumvented.

However, by 1662 when Pierre-Paul Riquet came up with a viable proposition, political, military and economic conditions had changed. Colbert was in power, and a waterway which would bring prosperity to a huge area of France, not wealthy despite its natural fertility, had an obvious appeal. Colbert even contemplated the possibility that French warships might use it to bypass Gibraltar; of course they never did.

As a young man Riquet must have heard discussions between Arribat and his father, a none-too-scrupulous Biterrois lawyer and financier, and he certainly became obsessed with the idea of a canal from an early age. Although he was not particularly well educated (he even boasted to Colbert that he knew neither Latin nor Greek, and was barely proficient even in French), he was a good mathematician and clearly a master of organization. He began his professional life in the salt farm and quickly rose to become Fermier-Général for Languedoc, the Cerdagne and Roussillon, thereby not only acquiring a good working knowledge of the land but amassing, by somewhat dubious means, a huge fortune.

In 1651 Riquet had acquired the fief of Bonrepos near Verfeil, where he rebuilt the dilapidated château and employed Antonio Verrio, who went on to work for Charles II at Windsor.

Here, on his 210 hectares, Riquet experimented, with the help of Pierre Petit and Pierre Campmas, on miniature versions of the canal, of which alas no trace remains. Riquet's first stroke of genius was to solve the problem of supplying the canal with water at the Seuil de Naurouze. He saw that if he could increase the flow of water rising at the Fontaine de la Grave and separate it into two streams, one running east and the other west, he could create a reservoir which would contain enough water to feed locks on either side of the watershed. If at the same time he could collect the waters of a number of small rivers running off the Montagne Noire, he would have enough to supply the canal with all that was needed.

Through the good offices of the Archbishop of Toulouse, he was introduced to Colbert, to whom he submitted an extremely detailed plan, including estimates of costs and a note of the money he was prepared to put up himself. Complex negotiations followed, resulting in approval four years later in 1666. This time the Estates of Languedoc voted in favour of it. The scales may well have been tipped by the agreement of the twenty-two participating bishops who reckoned that if they supported a scheme that had Colbert's blessing, he might help them in their persecution of the Protestants.

The first stone of the Bassin de St Ferréol was laid in 1667 and water from this reservoir, which was the largest in the world at the time, with an area of 67 hectares and a capacity of 6.3 million cubic metres, ran into a channel which supplied the canal. There are lovely drives and good walks all round this reservoir (which has subsequently been enlarged) and the little town of Revel nearby. The stretch from the Seuil de Naurouze to Toulouse was completed by the spring of 1668 and watered two years later, while that from the Seuil to the Etang du Thau and Sète was finished in 1681 just after Riquet's death – the whole measuring 240 kilometres. When it was joined in 1856 by the Canal latéral de la Garonne, which went from Toulouse to just west of La Réole, it brought the whole waterway to its present length of 450 kilometres.

Riquet achieved this feat in fourteen years by sheer administrative ability. He split the area into zones, putting each under the command of an officer with five brigadiers and fifty workers. Women were employed as well as men, on the basis that three of them counted as two men. In 1669 some 600 women worked amongst 7,200 men, and their main job was to carry the earth away. In all, as many as 12,000 labourers struggled on the canal, and Riquet had no difficulty in attracting them as he offered above-average wages. He was ahead of his time persuading his employees to work on Sundays and holidays and paying them if they were off sick. He also provided all the tools, and lodgings.

If the physical achievement puts today's construction industry to shame, Riquet was no different from contemporary financial forecasters. The actual cost far outran the estimate. The original estimate was for 5,262,935 livres, of which the construction would account for 3,700,000; the rest going towards acquiring the land and so on; all to be financed by the Treasury, the Estates of Languedoc and Riquet himself. How much it actually cost is difficult to calculate but it was in the region of fifteen to seventeen million livres.

Arthur Young, who was appalled by the poverty he saw in general in Languedoc, where many of the women were barefoot, thought that the creation of the canal was entirely praiseworthy and money well spent. The locks at Fonséranes were

the best sight I have seen in France. Here Lewis XIV thou art truly great! Here with a generous and benignant hand, thou dispensest ease and wealth to thy people! *Si sic omnia*, thy name would indeed have been revered. To effect this noble work of uniting the two seas, less money than was expended to besiege Turin, or to seize Strasbourg like a robber. Such an employment of the revenues of a great kingdom is the only laudable way of a monarch's acquiring immortality; all other means make their names survive with only those of the incendiaries, robbers, and violators of mankind.[89]

Although on Riquet's death he was in debt to the tune of two million livres, his work lived on to transform the economy of Languedoc, and the fortunes of his heirs. From 1724 onwards they had a monopoly on the barges, the waterborne postal service, the leasing of warehouses and mills and, above all, the seven tollhouses, of which the only one still to be seen is by the round lock just to the north of Agde.

Vauban, who was involved in the last decades of the seventeenth century in supervising the Canal and its works, thought that 'it was undeniably the finest and noblest work of its kind ever undertaken' and said that he would have 'prized more highly the glory of having been the begetter than anything else of mark he had done or might yet do'. His own contribution was equally remarkable; he oversaw the building of forty-nine aqueducts, was responsible for the vaulting of the 122-metre-long underground tunnel at Les Cammazès and for the raising of the height of the reservoir wall at St Ferréol.

Although two-thirds of the freight carried along the canal consisted of grain, other less mundane articles found their way on to the barges. In 1722 thirty crates containing paintings by Raphael, Titian, Tintoretto, Veronese, Correggio, Guido Reni and Rubens, which had been acquired in Rome for the Regent, travelled by sea from Civita Vecchia to Agde and thence by the Canal and the Garonne to Bordeaux, and on up to Nantes, Orléans and Paris. As we have seen, the statue of Louis XIV destined for the place du Peyrou at Montpellier arrived there by canal; in return, marble from Caunes-Minervois went north to be used for the pillars of the Trianons at Versailles. Many years later Charles Garnier found some unused in the stores at Chaillot and promptly incorporated them in the Paris Opéra.

By the 1840s the canal was carrying some 100 million tons of freight (one barge could carry 1,200 quintals – 12,000 kilograms – whereas it had taken 200 mules to carry 1000 quintals) and 30,000 passengers a year; fifty years later these figures had fallen catastrophically. The Canal had been taken over in 1858 by the Compagnie des Chemins de Fer du Midi who virtually abandoned it to stop it from competing with their new iron horses. The history of Riquet and his Canal is told in a fascinating open-air museum at Port Lauragais.

Canal boats can be hired now at Toulouse, Castelnaudary,

Carcassonne, Bram, Homps, Trèbes, Pérols, Capestang, Marseillan and Agde. A wide choice of companies offer floating hotels, cruises and day-trips, and hire out houseboats advertised as having 'le look britannique' or 'l'élégance française' throughout the summer from Easter to early November. There are few more enjoyable ways of seeing this countryside than on board one of them, undisturbed by the noise and pollution of the modern world. Nature is at her most graceful; poplar and planes in the northern stretch, cypresses and umbrella pines to the south line the banks of fields alive with wild flowers and birds.

Today, time is no object for holidaymakers and discomfort not a problem, but when the Canal was first opened, the journey for passengers from Toulouse to Sète took ninety hours. By 1845, although it could be done in thirty-five, Hans Christian Andersen did not find it to his liking:

> In the Languedoc Canal we had all to get into a large boat which had been constructed more for goods than for passengers . . . It was impossible to move; no railing surrounded this pile of boxes and people, which was drawn along by three or four horses attached by long ropes. Beneath in the cabins it was as crowded; people sat close to each other, like flies in a cup of sugar . . . I made myself a way through boxes, people, and umbrellas, and stood in a boiling-hot air; on either side the prospect was eternally the same: green grass, a green tree, flood-gates – green grass, a green tree, flood-gates – and then again the same; it was enough to drive one insane . . . the sun burnt infernally. People say the South of France is a portion of paradise; under the present circumstances, it seemed to me a portion of hell with all its heat.[90]

7

Cassoulet and the Land of Cockagne

Castelnaudary – St Papoul – Lauragais – Toulouse

CASTELNAUDARY is very much a canal town, well situated between Carcassonne and Toulouse, and has one of the largest and prettiest basins, ringed with low-lying red-tiled houses whose reflections shimmer and break as the swans and small boats make gentle ripples. This tranquillity belies the activity elsewhere, for Castelnaudary, as befits a county town, is full of bustle and commercial business. There are few monuments of note apart from a restored windmill and the church of St Michel, rebuilt in the fourteenth century, with a high belfry-porch and a double doorway, one Gothic and the other Renaissance. The nave is Gothic, there are good rose windows and another of those organs by Cavaillé-Coll.

If you see an old faded fascia-board advertising 'Alleluias et Glorias', do not suppose that you are amidst a group of revivalists or that the shop specializes in the elaborate funerary decorations so loved by the French. 'Alleluias' are little scented cakes, named in honour of a pope who was passing through, and are made to a recipe given to a local *pâtissier* in 1800 by one of Napoleon's veterans. Their ingredients should include *cédrat*, a relation of the grapefruit, not to be confused with *citre* (*cucurbita melanospermum*), a kind of marrow used only to make a jam and occasionally on sale in the markets.

Ford Madox Ford, amongst others, might well have cried 'Alleluia!' when in 1925 he made a special journey to the Hotel de la Reine Jeanne (alas no longer) to eat the *cassoulet* there, 'which had sat on the fire for the last three hundred years'. For Castelnaudary claims to have invented the dish that Prosper Montagné, a Carcassonnais, called *le dieu occitan*, and the taste of which Anatole France likened to that 'which one finds in the paintings of old Venetian masters, in the amber flesh tints of their women'.

Many years ago in our poverty-stricken days, we lived on *cassoulet* – or at least that was what we called it in a way that makes me now blush with shame for both our pretentiousness and our inaccuracy. It was merely a dish of baked beans with as much bacon or sausage as we could afford, and perhaps, if we had guests, a piece of pork. It bore absolutely no resemblance whatsoever in quality, ingredients, cost, time of preparation or taste to real *cassoulet*, or even to the American version, which Ford Madox Ford claimed had spread 'from Montpellier, France to Montpelier, Vermont, and so to Massachusetts, where, simplified, it became Boston baked beans and pork'.

Arguments over the origin and the ingredients of this dish have entertained gastronomes for years, and the battle lines between the Chauriens (as the inhabitants of Castelnaudary are called), the Carcassonnais and the Toulousains, each of whom claim it as their own, are still firmly drawn.

Henry Clos-Jouve, a Burgundian, and therefore, one would suppose, not *parti pris*, starts his recipe for the Castelnaudary version thus:

The base is a stew of strongly-flavoured beans, of Cazères or Pamiers, together with a rind of pork, soaked for eight to ten hours until they begin to germinate (at which point they can become poisonous until cooked). It is of the utmost importance that the cooking vessel should be of glazed earthenware, since this permits the liquid to be entirely absorbed without being delayed by the precipitation of mineral salts, as can happen when a metal pan is used. The traditional seasonings are garlic, an onion pierced with a single clove, a sliced carrot (for its sugar), a sprig of thyme, a bay leaf and a small spray of parsley. Simmer gently without stirring so that the beans remain unbroken.[91]

All the pundits are at one about the quality of the white haricot beans, but exactly what the other ingredients should consist of has resulted in rivers of ink. Curnonsky, the 'Prince Elu des Gastronomes', says one specific cut of pork and a particular sausage is vital, whilst Prosper Montagné has a different cut of pork and a different kind of sausage, and is adamant that lamb and either duck or goose be included. It is difficult to find the correct ingredients in this country.

The final touch is its crust, and how that should be dealt with gives rise to yet further dispute. The breadcrumbs sprinkled over the top become crisp and brown as the *cassoulet* cooks slowly in the oven. They should then be broken with a spoon and gently stirred in, so that the full flavour permeates the whole dish, but whether it should be done once, or twice, or even seven times – that is the question.

Curnonsky, an Angevin, tells a charming story about his friend and rival Montagné who went out on a normal working day to collect his shoes from the cobbler in Castelnaudary only to find the door locked, and a notice saying 'Maison fermée pour cause de cassoulet'. It is true that it is a substantial dish and Dr Edouard de Pomiane (whom Elizabeth David thinks was really the inventor of *cuisine nouvelle*), includes *cassoulet* in his *Vingt Plats qui donnent la Goutte* (*Twenty Dishes which give you the Gout*). This entertaining little book was distributed free to all French doctors by the Laboratoires Zizine, a pharmaceutical company selling medicine to cure, amongst other ailments, gout. Two of the other dishes included are *soupe aux oignons* and *bouillabaisse*; all good Midi fare.

Apart from the restaurants, many of which in a rather lily-livered way simply advertise the dish as 'languedocien', perhaps to avoid sectarian dispute, most of the *traiteurs* sell *cassoulet* ready-prepared in the *cassoles* which have given it its name. They are round, shallow, terracotta bowls with gently sloping sides, and glazed on the inside only. Originally made at Issel, near Castelnaudary, they can be bought in a wide variety of sizes in all the local *quincailleries*, and very pretty and useful they are too.

An enjoyable excursion from Castelnaudary is to the church of the oddly named St Papoul, a disciple of St Sernin and, like him, a martyr. A Benedictine abbey was founded on the site in the ninth century and it grew in fame and importance partly because of the miracles which took place at the tomb of St Béranger, a Toulousain noble who died in 1093 in the odour of sanctity. The only twelfth-century remains of the church are the main apse and two smaller ones, for the nave was rebuilt in 1317 when John XXII, as part of his campaign to restore orthodoxy, made St Papoul the seat of a bishopric and the church a cathedral.

Four of the corbels on the chevet (one needs binoculars to see them in detail) are attributed to the Maître de Cabestany; two decorated with foliage, one showing Daniel with seven lions being fed by Habbakuk whose beard he is pulling and the other, five people being eaten by lions. The fine square belltower with a spire is of uncertain date, as it, like the rest of the church, has been endlessly rebuilt or restored.

The entrance to the cloister, and the church, is through a seventeenth-century gateway. All four galleries are intact, with rounded arcades resting on twin pillars, many of which are made of octagonal red bricks and were plastered in the past. Those that are bare make the oddest impression but that may simply be because they are so unusual. The cloister was completed in 1347 and by the late fifteenth century was being used for stables. There are some charming decorated capitals, of which one shows a man holding a roundish object in his hand; some have seen it as St Papoul with his head in his hands, but I like to think of it as the precursor of a rugby football.

There are some good capitals inside the church too, which has only recently been restored, as have some of the Baroque decorations installed by François de Gramont de Lanta, bishop for forty years in 1677–1716, and by his successors. Viollet-le-Duc found the interior in very poor taste, clad as it was with panelling and stucco, for he and his contemporaries were really only interested in medieval, and more specifically 'Gothic', buildings. Interest in 'Gothic' architecture was more than a revival, and in some senses, the Middle Ages were reinvented in the middle decades of the nineteenth century.

If the Canal du Midi was built to join Haut and Bas Languedoc, the drawing of the regional boundary between Languedoc-Roussillon and Midi-Pyrénées some fifteen kilometres to the west of Castelnaudary is nothing other than an administrative label, for it in no way marks either a geographic or an historical division. It cuts right through the Lauragais – which became a county in 1477. The Lauragais is a smiling, rolling landscape with few trees or hedges, vast fields of wheat and maize, and grazing for cattle. It benefits from rain from the Atlantic, though it is swept by the desiccating *vent d'autan*. It has always been populous as it was on the well-trodden path from Bordeaux through Aquitaine to the Mediterranean from pre-Roman days, and the present roads, both the N113 and the Autoroute des Deux Mers, more or less follow the same route.

Long low farmhouses, each with immense barns, dot the countryside, and more Renaissance-style manor houses were built here than in any of the other *pays* we have visited, though few are grand enough to qualify as châteaux. Amongst the peaceful villages that make this such an attractive area to wander through at leisure is St Félix-Lauragais. Built on a small hill, it commands a splendid view across the plain ringed by the Pyrenees to the west and the Montagne Noire to the east. St Félix-Lauragais is a *bastide* and many of its small half-timbered houses are untouched from earlier days. It has a large central market-place which becomes the main stage for a splendid three-day fair at Easter and where, in 1990, two bears were amongst the entertainments on offer. The fair had a commercial rather than a religious origin for the Lauragais lived from the dye obtained from woad, and St Félix was a prosperous centre in the fourteenth century with a population of 5,000 (it is now 1,188).

It was the birthplace of Guillaume Nogaret, the lawyer who prosecuted the Templar leaders for Philippe IV, and of the composer Marie-Joseph-Alexandre Déodat de Séverac. The latter's father Gilbert was a prominent Toulousain painter (whose works hang in the Musée des Augustins and the Musée du Vieux-Toulouse). Déodat de Séverac was passionately attached to the Lauragais countryside, in which he found inspiration for a style at once impressionistic and descriptive. Amongst his piano pieces are two called 'En Languedoc' and 'Cerdana'. He died in Céret, and the centenary of his birth was celebrated in the arena there in 1972 with a performance of his opera *Héliogable* which had had its première in August 1910 in the arena at Béziers.

We spent the night at a charming hotel called the Auberge du Poids Public where we had an excellent dinner and a blissfully quiet bedroom. We paid the bill next morning and left in the pouring rain, and it was not until we were ten kilometres away that we discovered that there had been some mistake and that we had been grossly undercharged. Natural decency struggled with the inclement weather and the exigencies of our schedule, but we did turn back and found the proprietors juggling with their accounts and a whiff of divorce in the air. They were duly grateful (no perfidious Albions we) and gave us in thanks a *cassole* that I had admired the previous evening. It has a gratifyingly rough surface and a genuine rusticity, but although my *cassoulets* nowadays are a great improvement on my past efforts, I have to admit that I still cannot even approximate those served in the Toulousain.

By the Seuil de Naurouze, which played so vital a part in the realization of the Canal du Midi, an obelisk was erected in 1825–7 to the memory of Riquet. It is enclosed by a railing, more often locked than not, but for those frustrated by not getting up to see it and interested in hydraulic engineering, inspecting the feeder channels and locks in the immediate vicinity makes an instructive diversion.

A few kilometres to the north, Avignonet-Lauragais is a beautiful walled town built in glowing yellow stone with vestiges of two former châteaux and a modern statue of a crusader. The church of Notre Dame des Miracles was, sadly, shut but it has a wonderful tower, a four-square block of solid stone with blind arcading, a hexagonal upper storey and a small spire above. While we were admiring it, we noticed an agreeable young woman having trouble getting her car started, and in return for giving it a push, she decided that we deserved a history lesson. She was the mayor's wife, and I must say she did him, and us, proud. She told us that in 1242 the citizens of Avignonet-Lauragais had supplied the weapons used by the Cathars who came from Montségur to murder the Inquisitors and their party. Thereafter the church was closed, but when thirty years later the *curé* heard the bells ringing again of their own accord, he found the door open. He went inside, and was vouchsafed a vision of the Virgin. Today, if you can get inside, you will be vouchsafed a view of a 1631 painting of the murder.

The church at Villefranche-de-Lauragais was built in 1271 by Alphonse de Poitiers and Jeanne de Toulouse, just a year before they both died within so short a time of each other. It could hardly be further removed from that at Avignonet-Lauragais, being built of brick in the Toulousain style. The area from this northern stretch of the Lauragais right up into Quercy at Caussade beyond Montauban is one of the very few areas of France where there is no local stone, so brick is used instead. The church at Villefranche has a narrow belfry with two small towers at either side, and between them open triangular-topped apertures in which the bells hang. This distinctive style can be seen again in a rather more elaborate form at Notre Dame du Taur in Toulouse itself.

The N113, the railway and the River Hers all pass through Villefranche, and the *autoroute* and Canal du Midi run just to the south of the town. At Gardouch there is a charming lock and range of canal buildings, and it is pleasant to weave one's way to and fro across these major arteries by the little side-roads and come upon small, out-of-the-way villages.

Fourquevaux is one such, very spick and span, at the confluence of two valleys from which it gets its name (forked valleys). Because it is all in brick, for a moment one thinks one is no longer in the Midi, but the intensity of the heat and the quality of the light soon dispel that impression. There is a large château of feudal origins which at one time belonged to a family who were bankers to the Cathars. It was rebuilt in the fourteenth century by a Toulousain named Yzalguier, and enlarged in the sixteenth and eighteenth centuries, when the orangery was built.

Jean-Paul Laurens was born in this pretty village and his painting of the Lauragais which hangs in the Capitole at Toulouse marvellously captures the essence of this landscape.

The vineyards and fields of the Lauragais and the Albigeois provided fertile ground for woad, as the rich soil (known as *terrefort*), small danger of frost, ample spring rains and dry summers are all propitious for its growth. In the mid-fifteenth century the plant spread rapidly and its increased cultivation led to the boom which made Toulouse and much of its surrounding countryside rich for the better part of a century.

Woad, called *pastel* or *guède* in French, is *Isatis tinctoria*, a biennial or perennial plant of the mustard family found growing wild all over Europe. It has small yellow flowers atop a thin stem, and reaches its full height of 1 metre 40 centimetres some sixteen months after sowing. The leaves, after a smelly and laborious process, were used to make an indelible blue dye, much sought after in Europe until it was superseded by the indigo plant, imported more cheaply from India. Today woad is still used by hardy home-dyers who grow and process their own, but commercially it is now only used as a starter to ferment indigo.

The larger leaves were harvested in June, just as they started to turn yellow, and the remainder were picked at monthly intervals until November. The peasants crushed them to a pulp and rolled this into balls of approximately fifteen centimetres in diameter, which were then left to dry. These were known as *coques* or *coqagnes* and brought such wealth to the area that it came to be called the 'land of cockagne', a phrase now synonymous with a land of luxury and ease. The *coques* were taken to be milled and left to ferment for four months, a nauseating business requiring great stamina on the part of the millers as the mixture, which often included urine, had to be stirred constantly. Queen Elizabeth I found the stench so objectionable that she forbade the processing of woad within five miles of any royal estate.

The final product, a hardened blackish mastic, was taken by road by muleteers, mostly from Béarn, and by river by the boatmen of the Garonne, many of whom came from Moissac. In spite of the extra expense of the tolls – and there were thirty-two between Toulouse and Bordeaux – it cost as much to take these *coques* the 75 kilometres from Albi to Toulouse by mule as it did for the 250 kilometres by river from Toulouse to Bordeaux.

The muleteers and boatmen, like the peasants and millers, had to be paid in cash, as did the shipowners who transported the product from Bordeaux to the main markets in Antwerp and London. The whole process was a lengthy one, taking three years from start to finish, and it was financially risky, but the entrepreneurs stood to make a lot of money if the woad harvest was good. Some Toulousain merchants certainly made great fortunes and built themselves not only fine country houses, like that of St Michel-de-Lanes (south of Avignonet-Lauragais) but also exceedingly grand houses in Toulouse itself.

Tolosa was referred to by Cicero as 'a sentinel and a fortress', and Martial, in the first century, called it Tolosa Palladia, 'beloved of Pallas Athene, goddess of letters and the arts', though he did say that the cheese made there 'was shunned by gourmets in Rome and served as food only for the poor'. However fine a city in Roman times, the fact that it was built of brick, which is so much more perishable than stone, has meant that there are no visible remains today.

The Toulousain, like the rest of the Midi, was part of the Roman Narbonensis. Then for some two hundred years after the battle of Vouillé in 507, it constituted a March, cut off from the Mediterranean. In 789 Guilhem de Gellone (or Guillaume d'Orange or St Guilhem) was appointed to the county of Toulouse and his descendants subsequently acquired huge tracts of land including both the Toulousain and Septimania. The enormous semi-independent principality was later split up and the title, if not the territory, of the duke of Aquitaine passed to the counts of Poitou.

Thereafter these counts were to be a thorn in the flesh of the counts of Toulouse who, to salvage their pride at having lost the title to the Duchy of Aquitaine (and to confuse matters for us) called themselves marquises of Gothia. Guillaume IX, Count of Poitou, Duke of Aquitaine and the first troubadour, invaded and held Toulouse for several years in the late eleventh and early twelfth century. One can hardly blame Raymond of Toulouse (or St Gilles) for finding it easier to go on crusade than trying to keep his patrimony together. For his heirs, worse was to come on the northern frontier when Guillaume IX's granddaughter Eleanor, having divorced her first husband Louis VII of France, married Henry Plantagenet, who became king of England in 1154.

Toulouse itself was taken and lost by Simon de Montfort in the early years of the thirteenth century, and the next two hundred years were made miserable for its inhabitants, what with constant incursions by the English, the plague, bands of brigands and finally, in 1463, a disastrous fire. The Toulousains, as perhaps the only possible form of self-defence, withdrew into their shells and simply survived as best they could until woad came to their rescue and provided them with an economic miracle which lasted a century.

Even so, they still seemed to prefer 'honour to profit and art to business', and when the woad boom was over, they retreated into their former lethargy. By the late seventeenth century, as Basville recorded in 1698, 'the canal linking the two seas which debouches here might have seemed ready-made to bring Toulouse all the produce and plenty which the Atlantic and the Mediterannean can be made to yield. But in fact it carries hardly any traffic'. He also complained of the 'Spanish indolence' of the

Toulousains, and Stendhal found the vulgarity and uncouthness of the common people incredible when he was there in 1838, though he approved of the coffee he was given.

Toulouse has taken many years to emerge from being nothing but 'a large village', but today with a growing population, a thriving industry and a metro, it is very much alive and go-ahead. All the new development has taken place on the outskirts of the city, so its historic centre, virtually untouched since the destructive vandalism of the nineteenth century, can be seen on foot. One way to orientate oneself is to be aware that many of the streets parallel to the Garonne are labelled in yellow, while those at right or oblique angles are in white. The plaques were made in 1815 by the Faïencerie Fouque.

However, be warned. It gets *very* hot in high summer and Adolphe Joanne in his guidebook of 1879 thought it 'a monotonous and wearisome town, excessively hot in summer and excessively windy all year round'. He was right in terms of heat, for in high summer the *vent d'autan* blows up hot and humid from the south-west, and on 9 August 1923 the temperature reached 44°C, the highest ever recorded in France. The only advantage of being there in August is the absence of some seventy thousand university students.

Joanne was emphatically not right about Toulouse being monotonous, either in terms of colour or of boredom. It is justly called the 'rose-red' city, because so many of its buildings are made of those elegant small hand-made bricks, and there is a considerable number of absolutely first-class churches, hôtels and museums to be seen.

St Sernin (an abbreviation of Saturnin), to whom the largest Romanesque basilica in the Midi is dedicated, was martyred in the early days of Christianity, under Decius. He was attached to a bull and dragged round until he died (as we saw at St Hilaire), and his cult became so popular that thirty communes were named after him.

The original church was on the site where today Notre Dame de Taur stands (an interesting church in its own right with an amazing belfry), but a new one was started in 1080 to cope with the inordinate number of pilgrims who flocked to St Sernin's tomb, and its size and plan are those of a pilgrimage church. Building continued through to the fourteenth century, but the exterior presents an entirely homogeneous whole. The walls are in pink brick and yellow stone, with the stone used to outline the windows of both church and tower, and the effect is dazzling. One should walk round the outside slowly taking it all in, from the Porte Royale (at the end of the northern transept) clockwise to the eleventh-century chevet. Then pause to admire the splendid sight the church presents, dominated yet lifted by a five-storeyed belltower, and crowned by a spire soaring to a blue heaven.

Viollet-Le-Duc made substantial alterations between 1860 and 1879, in particular to the roofing, and now, because more repairs are necessary, the whole of Toulouse is up in arms about whether Viollet-le-Duc's work should be removed or restored. The argument has become politicized and for the time being no decision has been made.

The Porte des Comtes (which leads into the southern transept) is filled with sculptures, one of which shows St Sernin himself, and by its side is an enclosure containing antique tombs reused to hold the bodies of the eleventh-century counts. The Porte Miègeville is preceded by a freestanding Renaissance archway surmounted by one of Viollet-le-Duc's least successful inventions.

Continue round clockwise, pausing to admire the pink brick façade which contrasts so strikingly with the honey-coloured interior with its high barrel-arched nave. The ambulatory, with its radiating chapels, is lined by display cases which house some of the church's many relics and reliquaries. To make the 'circuit of the Holy Bodies' as it was known, was one of the attractions for the pilgrims who came to venerate St Sernin, whose body lies under the high altar. Though today we find the workmanship of greater interest than the contents, it was not so in the

seventeenth century when the latter aroused Locke's splendidly
Protestant scepticism:

> At the Church of St. Sernin they tell us they have the bodies entire
> of 6 of the Apostles and the head of a 7th. This is much, considering
> what need there is of such reliques in other places, but yet
> notwithstanding they promise you 7 of the 12 Apostles . . . we saw
> not these Apostles, but being told by a spiritual guide of the
> infalible church, we believed, which was enough for us.[92]

The crypt is two-storeyed with seven beautiful eleventh-
century bas-reliefs embedded in the outer walls of the upper
one. Inside both there are more reliquaries and other ecclesiastical treasures.

The church of the Jacobins could hardly be more different,
and is altogether more original, though no less beautiful. St
Dominic, as we know, founded the Order of Preachers in 1215
and the Black Friars started building their church in 1230,
though the main structure was not completed until about 1340.
The exterior is dour and fortress-like, its high brick walls
relieved only by narrow slits for windows and *oculi*. The façade
is sombre, with an unassuming entrance, two ogival windows
with two roses above, and a modest balcony linking three small
pointed towers. Only the hexagonal belfry, whose five storeys
echo the top two of that at St Sernin, affords the slightest
decorative embellishment.

In 1845 Mérimée had difficulty in seeing the interior, for the
church was still occupied by the artillery regiment to whom
Napoleon had given it. With a fine disregard for anything
except their own convenience and that of their horses, the
soldiers had put in a mezzanine floor, demolished many of the
side chapels, blocked up the windows, and raised the level of
the cloister to make equine access easier. Even so, Mérimée
wrote

> It is wonderful . . . the whole built in brick on a most original
> system: all this I have seen . . . plus five hundred horses munching

their oats, and as many gunners drawing pictures [on the walls] of an unmentionable kind. Despite both the horses and the men, the fabric of the church itself is wonderfully preserved.[93]

Getting the army out was a major problem but eventually it was achieved and the restoration work began, which included having to scrape off the brilliant red paint with which the bricks had been covered. Taine saw it at this time and has left an exact and splendid description which holds good today:

> It is divided into two naves by a row of very high round columns, like the trunks of palm-trees, spreading out into fillets above. On this slender support the whole roof rests. The last column ends in a cluster of twenty-three arches, supporting the apse. So high are they, and so straight, so white with their crown of black arches against the white walls, that these columns are like an enormous firework, or the continuous play of a fountain. Nothing finer can be imagined than their curves, nothing richer than their clusters . . . This epoch of the Middle Ages was perhaps the most triumphant and ecstatic. It was the zenith of the power of the Church.[94]

Restoration has been continuous since the mid-nineteenth century; new glass was recently commissioned for the windows and all the missing bits of the cloister have been found and bought back, or made anew. With its grey-white marble columns set off by the pink brick, it is a haven of peace and quiet, surely very close to the original. The refectory, which like the church was used for all sorts of other purposes, such as a concert hall, an assembly room for political meetings, a market for violets and a boy's school, has also been restored.

One of the stipulations of the Treaty of Paris in 1229 was that the defeated Count Raymond VII of Toulouse should found and endow a university in Toulouse, to be run by the Dominicans. Its most famous pupil was Thomas Aquinas, one of the foremost medieval theologians, who was largely responsible for making Aristotle's works acceptable in Christian Western Europe. The students at Toulouse university were permitted to read Aristotle though those in Paris were not. Although

Aquinas died in Italy in 1369, shortly after his canonization Pope Urban V sent his mortal remains to the Jacobins, where it was thought fitting that he should rest. His tomb is now beneath a marble altar in the centre of the church on the site of the earliest sanctuary.

The 'angelic doctor' would have been horrified at the depths to which his university had sunk some three hundred years later, if we are to believe the comment of an English visitor, Charles Bertie. The colleges, he said were 'not to be compared to ours in England, being pitiful holes and in them nothing remarkable . . . We viewed the schools of Divinity, Physic and Civil Law, which are very poor. A good barn would make a better show'.[95]

The third great church in Toulouse, St Etienne, must be one of the oddest of all the cathedrals in France. Its west front, seen from a charming triangular *place* lined with attractive houses, is wildly asymmetrical and makes it obvious that it was built in fits and starts with no attempt at unification. Its erratic appearance was in part due to lack of money, brought about by the dismemberment of the diocese of Toulouse by John XXII when he carved it up to make all those bishoprics we have seen, for example, at Pamiers and Mirepoix.

Its façade, with a huge rose window of about 1229, is in stone, though the rest of the building is in brick, including a huge heavy tower added in the fifteenth century. The present nave, on the site of an earlier church erected at the end of the eleventh century, was started in 1210 and is in the typical meridional Gothic style. The cross of Toulouse, now the city's device, is to be seen sculpted on the roof boss of the third bay of the nave and the walls are covered with sixteenth-century tapestries telling the story of St Etienne. Of the later church only five bays and a choir with five radiating chapels were built, tacked on as it were to the earlier structure. They are the work of Jean Deschamps who started in 1272, though the side chapels with stained glass date mostly from the fourteenth century. The 'royal' window depicts Charles VII and the future Louis XI, and Riquet is buried under one of the stone flags which were being relaid when we were last there by very jolly workmen grumbling that they were not the men their forefathers were.

After St Etienne became the seat of an archbishopric in 1611, some attempt was made to embellish it with woodwork in the choir, a new high altar and retable and a new organ. The beautiful wrought-iron grille round the choir dates from 1767. The chapter buildings, like so much else in Toulouse, were destroyed in the nineteenth century, but many of the stone sculptures, with those of the other convents which no longer exist, are to be seen in the Musée des Augustins.

'This place', said Arthur Young rather disparagingly of Toulouse, 'has always prided itself on its taste for literature and the fine arts. It has had a university since 1215; and it pretends that its famous academy of Jeux Floraux is as old as 1323'.[96] It is interesting that he uses a *faux-ami*, 'pretends' to mean 'to claim', but he was right to be dubious, for the origins of this academy of the 'Floral Games' are pretty suspect.

In November 1323, seven so-called troubadours, mindful of the glories of their predecessors, announced that a competition would be held to judge poems dedicated to the Virgin. The first prize was to be a *violette d'or*; subsequently prizes of a silver marigold or a silver eglantine were given for poems on other subjects. The choice of a violet as first prize was not fortuitous for it is a flower that grows profusely in the region.

A hundred and fifty years later, a benefactress by the name of Clémence Isaure is reputed to have produced funds to revive the poetry society which was by now moribund. Called at first the 'Compagnie de Gai Sçavoir', it later became the Académie des Jeux Floraux. Ford Madox Ford indulged in a little quiet fun when he reckoned that the after-effects of eating *cassoulet* could induce strange hallucinations, like seeing Clémence Isaure 'in her steeple-crowned hat and trailing, scarlet sleeves, bestowing upon a kneeling bard the first golden rose of her Floral Games . . .'[97]

The society changed name and fortune several times over the

centuries but it continued in existence and amongst its best-known laureates were Ronsard, Fabre d'Eglantine, Chateaubriand and Victor Hugo. To this day the flowers awarded to the prizewinners are blessed on 3 May at the altar of the Vierge Noire in the church of Notre Dame de la Daurade. This church was a Benedictine priory and was given a massively heavy pillared stone façade at the end of the eighteenth century. It is on the quayside, and has a splendid view across the Garonne to the domes of the Hôtel Dieu St Jacques and the Hôpital de la Grave on the far bank.

Toulouse, though dedicated to the arts, worshipped mammon for a century and with the wealth that accrued from the production of woad, its citizens erected a number of magnificent hôtels, many begun between 1500 and 1560. They were built not only by the twenty-odd newly-rich merchant families, but also by the cohorts of lawyers who did a roaring trade after Toulouse had become the seat of the Languedoc *parlement* in 1420 and who were not to be outdone by the *pasteliers*.

The Hôtel Assézat, the headquarters of the Académie des Jeux Floraux today, is perhaps the finest of them all. There is much uncertainty about the authorship of many of these hôtels but Anthony Blunt thought that Assézat can be attributed to Nicolas Bachelier, or if not, he says 'whoever the architect may be he must rank with Lescot and de l'Orme as one of the creators of the classical style in the middle of the century.'[98]

Pierre Assézat was a woad merchant but also a Protestant, and although his hôtel was started in 1555, he was exiled for ten years and died in 1581 before it was finished. It consists of two main buildings round a vast courtyard, each three storeys high, and a small pavilion. The bleached brick walls and pale stone decoration of the pillars, whose capitals work through the three orders as they rise, and the window-surrounds and marble insets all combine to give an effect of the utmost elegance and grandeur.

The Hôtel de Bernuy, now a *lycée*, was started rather earlier, in 1504, also by a woad merchant, the extent of whose wealth may be gauged from the fact that he went bail for François I after his capture at the battle of Pavia and later entertained him in his magnificent house. He too died before it was finished – he was killed by a bull during a fête – obviously one does not want to encounter a bull in Toulouse – but his son continued work on the hôtel from 1538 to 1555. This second stage displays a greater architectural delicacy than the first, despite some deliberate antiquing in the stone window and door-surrounds. It too is set round a courtyard and the style is a combination of Flamboyant Gothic and Italian Renaissance.

It is beyond the scope of this book to go into the details of the eighty-four hôtels to be seen (some of which date from the eighteenth century). Suffice it to point out the most spectacular. The Hôtel du Vieux Raisin or Béringuier-Maynier, built in two stages, 1515 and 1547, is rather clumsy and overpowering but impressive none the less; and the Hôtel de Bagis (or de Clari), known as the Hôtel de Pierre because of its stone façade, which is grossly over-egged but imposing, has an inner courtyard in brick with a gallery of great delicacy. The Hôtel de Pierre is to be found in the rue Dalbade, which has no fewer than ten more of these astonishing mansions. The Hôtel des Chevaliers de St Jean de Jérusalem stands out for having been started in the twelfth century, and for being severely classical; it was rebuilt in 1668–72 to the plans of Jean-Pierre Rivalz.

Notre Dame de la Dalbade, at the corner of this street, looks like a typical meridional Gothic church but was in fact put up at the beginning of the sixteenth century. The highly-coloured ceramic tympanum, based on Fra Angelico's *Coronation of the Virgin*, was inserted in 1874.

The emergence of the *capitouls* (town councillors) in Toulouse at the end of the twelfth century is a perfect example of the peaceful acquisition of legislative and judicial powers by the bourgeoisie. Partly because of differences in landholding and partly because so many of the southern towns had a flourishing commercial life, they moved towards self-government earlier than those in the north. The movement was strengthened because the lesser aristocracy frequently sided with the merchants against the local seigneur, and even more importantly, against the bishop. In the case of Toulouse, its counts were hardly ever in residence there. A municipality is first mentioned in 1152 when Alphonse Jourdain extended its commercial privileges, and by 1192 the *capitouls* were exercising full power; but it was a short-lived interlude, for their independence was ended after Simon de Montfort took the city and their powers were curtailed once Languedoc went to the French crown. Nevertheless they continued to deal with purely municipal affairs in their headquarters, always known as the Capitole.

Stendhal found the building 'the last word in ugliness but the rest of the city so mean that the site of this massive building fronting an open space that is nearly square, make a pleasing contrast'. Henry James too was less than ecstatic about it:

> The Place du Capitole, which is the heart and centre of Toulouse . . . bears a vague and inexpensive resemblance to the Piazza Castello at Turin. The shops are probably better than the Turinese, but the people are not so good. Stunted, shabby, rather vitiated looking, they have none of the personal richness of the sturdy Piedmontese . . . At Toulouse there was the strongest temptation to speak to people simply for the entertainment of hearing them reply with that curious, that fascinating accent of the Languedoc, which appears to abound in final consonants and leads the Toulousians to say *bien-g* and *maison-g* like an Englishman learning French. It is as if they talked with their teeth rather than with their tongue.[99]

Nowadays the place du Capitole, filled on market days with gaudy awnings covering the stalls, is not at all shabby, though the stallholders speak with many tongues.

Although the Capitole has been the seat of the municipality since the early twelfth century, most of the present building dates from the mid-eighteenth century when Guillaume Cammas, who was a painter and not an architect, was employed to turn it into a palace. The façade, which takes up the whole of one side of the *place*, is brick but punctuated by stone pilasters rising from a first-floor balcony to a crowning balustrade. The pediment in the centre is supported by stripey pink marble columns, to represent the *capitouls* (of which there were eight from 1438), and were brought to the city from Caunes-Minervois via the Canal du Midi.

In the centre of the pediment is a cartouche bearing the initials 'RF' (for République Française) which have been there since 1871; it initially depicted Louis XV, and then became successively the goddess of Liberty, Napoleon, Louis XVIII and then Liberté–Ordre Public. The crowning statues above have been less subject to political conformism. On the left, Clémence Isaure and Pallas Athene stand for Art and Science; in the centre, durable as ever, are Force and Justice; while to the right, Tragedy and Comedy commemorate Toulouse's long and proud connection with the performing arts. Molière was here in 1645 and 1649, and today the Orchestre National du Capitole de Toulouse is one of the best in France.

A statue of Henri IV, in what looks like a faded blue jogging suit but is in fact black, green and white marble, peers down from Nicolas Bachelier's ornate classical doorway in the inner courtyard on to the stone slab recording the execution of Henri de Montmorency on 30 October 1632 (see page 71). When news of the court's grief at Montmorency's sentence was relayed to Louis XIII, he is reported to have said while playing chess, 'I would not be king if I had the feelings of a private person'. He was to show a markedly similar reaction later to the execution of Cinq-Mars (see pages 109–10).

On the upper floor of the Capitole, reached by an imposing staircase reconstructed in 1912, there are a number of rooms pompously redecorated in the nineteenth century. Although many of the specially commissioned paintings are fairly feeble, there are some good ones amongst them. Those of Henri Martin were, for me at least, a real discovery. One lovely sunny view of promenaders strolling along the quayside of the Garonne includes Jean Jaurès lost in thought, in a boater and a beige overcoat with his hands clasped behind his back.

The paintings in the Salle Gervais are all allegories on the subject of love by Paul Gervais; the room was formerly used for marriages, though these are now celebrated in the Salle des Illustres where works by Benjamin Constant, Edouard-Bernard Debat-Ponsan and Laurens are not without merit and depict some of Toulouse's finest hours.

The 'donjon' or tower, on the far side of the Capitole, in ruins by the end of the eighteenth century, was transformed by Viollet-le-Duc to house the municipal archives and serve as a meeting-place for the town councillors. The tourist office is now to be found there, plate glass and all, topped by his Flemish-style belfry.

Toulouse remained staunchly Catholic during the Wars of Religion and its parlementarians deeply conservative, which was rather an anomaly as the surrounding towns and countryside were Protestant. Consequently the Huguenots were persecuted with more than usual savagery as Pantagruel soon discovered, having been sent

> to Toulouse, where he quickly became skilled both at the dance and the two-handed sword – as scholars of the said university make their wont. But he did not bide long among them, when he saw how they grilled their tutors like kippered herrings. 'God forbid that I should die in such a fashion', quoth he, 'since I am parched enough already, not to require further cooking.'[100]

In the aftermath of the Wars of Religion – and the city was racked with civil war for thirty-six years – Toulouse saw the establishment of a number of new religious foundations, of which only the Carmelite convent, now used for university offices, still exists. It is worth wandering in to see the courtyards with their unkempt rambling greenery, and the recently restored chapel. Louis XIII laid the first stone in 1622 but it was not completed for another twenty years and even then was left undecorated. Eventually the walls and ceilings were painted, first by Jean-Pierre Rivalz and then in 1747–51 by Jean-Baptiste Despax, and their Rococo exuberance, albeit on religious themes, affords one of the very few examples of eighteenth-century decoration in the region.

In the middle of the century, Toulouse found itself at the centre of a *cause célèbre*, made public by Voltaire. The son of Jean Calas, a linen merchant and one of the few Protestants left in the city, was found hanged in October 1761. Calas was alleged to have killed his son to prevent him from turning Catholic, though in fact he committed suicide in frustration at not being allowed to become a lawyer. Calas *père* was condemned to death, first by the *capitouls* and then by *parlement*, and he was broken on the wheel, strangled and burned. His case was taken up by Voltaire and one of his pupils, and they succeeded in getting Calas rehabilitated in 1765. The scandal caused at the time was in some measure responsible for the Protestants being given full rights as citizens, though this did not happen until 1787. An American historian thinks that this violent outbreak of religious intolerance, in an age dubbed 'Enlightened', may have been sparked off by the fear of a possible British invasion.

The abolition of the *parlements* by the National Assembly in 1790 contributed largely to the decline of Toulouse. By then pre-eminently a city of wealthy lawyers, with little commerce, its working class became poverty-stricken when legal business all but dried up, and rallied to the left-wing faction that called itself Jacobin. (The Dominican friars have always been called Jacobins because their first house in Paris was in the rue St Jacques; the revolutionary politicians took their name from another Jacobin house in the rue St Honoré.) The names of the Jacobin clubs in Toulouse remind one of nothing so much as the SDP. The first was called the Société de Club littéraire et patriotique de Cent; it then became the Club des Amis de la Constitution; then the Société de la République; and finally the Société républicaine des Sans-culottes de Toulouse.

It is generally believed that Toulouse played a vital part in the continued existence of the Republic when it refused to join the federalist movement and even considered seceding with the Bordelais and Provence as an independent 'Republic of the Midi'. Although only thirty-one people were put to death during the Terror, Toulouse, unlike most of the other large French towns, remained predominantly Jacobin in the final years of the Revolution and it was then that it went from being known as the 'rose' to the 'red' city.

At the time when the revolutionaries were expropriating church property, the convent of the Augustins was one of the first to fall victim. The refectory was sold and in 1793 turned into a store for cattle fodder, and in 1794 the Museum provisoire du Midi de la République was installed in the church, which had been built in the first half of the fourteenth century. A few years later a curious figure appeared on the scene. Alexandre de Mège took over the museum and arranged the collections as 'a pantheon to the glory of Languedoc and the monarchy'. Not only did he indulge his own taste to the exclusion of scholarship, but he had tombstones, sarcophagi, statues and documents fabricated to bear out his theories. His romantic fantasies even extended to turning the chapel of Notre Dame de la Pitié and the chapter house (both now restored to their pristine fourteenth-century glory) into a neo-Classical temple, a transformation which would never have occurred to Viollet-le-Duc.

In the meantime other buildings in Toulouse were left to collapse and it is no wonder that Montalembert called it 'the metropolis and as it were country of vandalism'. The general outcry about the parlous conditions of these early buildings started in the 1820s and he and Hugo were in the van. The level of ignorance at the time may be judged from the fact that most architects thought that Romanesque and Gothic styles were contemporaneous, rather like Ionic and Corinthian orders, and that people sometimes built in one way, sometimes the other, according to taste.

The church happily was spared any further acts of vandalism

but not the refectory, which the municipality had bought back and then had demolished in 1868 in the service of art. A new museum was constructed in its place in 1880–96 on the basis of a project by Viollet-le-Duc. It stands at the corner of the rue d'Alsace Lorraine and the rue de Metz, two thoroughfares cut through the city in 1864–8.

The Musée des Augustins, as the whole complex is now known, was completely restored between 1950 and 1980. The beautiful cloister is a sculpture gallery and contains many of the capitals from other churches in Toulouse, so much easier to see here than *in situ*; the church is used to display religious paintings and the museum building houses a fine collection of paintings and sculpture, many by local artists, including the native-born Jean de Troy.

Toulouse is rich in museums to suit every taste. That devoted to Vieux-Toulouse is in a small side-street in a wonderful crumbling building with just the right kind of creaky floorboards, peeling distemper and dim lighting to make the past seem like the present. It is full of lovely minor objects of which one of the most charming is Jules Léotard's model of his own gym. Léotard, who called himself a 'gymniasiaque' in his memoirs, was a Toulousain cyclist and is credited with having invented the flying trapeze on which he first appeared on 14 December 1859 at the Cirque d'Hiver in Paris.

The Musée Paul Dupuy, named for a local art-lover who left his collection to the city in 1944, is a small hôtel made of pink brick again, and reconstructed in the seventeenth century by a rich parlementarian. The interior has been recently restored and the collections are now displayed in small rooms with pretty pink and green furnishings – the very acme of modern decorators' taste. There is an exceptionally good collection of local artefacts ranging from silver, china, scientific instruments and clocks, all of which are going and keeping time. A pharmacy from the Jesuit church of 1632 has been reassembled in the basement where, in the vaulted cellars, there are religious statues and a variety of ironwork and arms. The museum also has an important collection of engravings and a library.

The Musée St Raymond, devoted to prehistory and classical antiquities, is housed in a building opposite St Sernin. It was originally a hospice for pilgrims, erected in 1080 by Raymond Gayrard when he was overseeing the building of the church. The house was rebuilt in the sixteenth century and restored by Viollet-le-Duc.

The Musée Georges Labit, by the Jardin des Plantes, specializes in oriental works of art, and there is a fine museum devoted to natural history.

For people with plenty of time, a visit to the Galerie municipale du Château d'Eau provides a good excuse to get out of the centre of the city and appreciate the beauties of its site on the Garonne. The museum, which has a large collection of photographs, is on the west bank just across the Pont Neuf, built with some difficulty between 1544 and 1632. The Garonne is liable to heavy flooding, and the medieval Chaussée du Bazacle just beyond it to the north was constructed to serve both as a barrage and as foundations for the city's water-mills, owned as early as 1190 by a group of citizens who were in effect shareholders. If you continue along the west bank, past the meridional Gothic church of St Nicolas and the Hôpital de la Grave, and return across the Pont de St Pierre, you could see the remains of the church of St Pierre des Cuisines, or the Canal de Brienne, built between 1766 and 1777 to join the Garonne to the Canal du Midi, and its junction with the Canal latéral de la Garonne – opened in 1891 – at the Bassin de l'Embouchure. There by the two bridges is a statue by the eighteenth-century sculptor François Lucas representing the Atlantic and the Mediterranean, and nearby is that of *Herakles* by the Montalbanais Antoine Bourdelle.

After years of stagnation, the First World War finally put Toulouse on its feet again; the city not only supplied a quarter of the boots and many of the uniforms for the army, but since it was well away from the front it was an obvious place for making ammunition. After 1914 it became the home of France's nascent aircraft industry, perhaps not unconnected with the fact that Clément Ader was born in nearby Muret. Ader is credited, at least in French reference books, with having made in 1890 the world's first powered flight, and 1990 was declared 'Clément Ader Year' by President Mitterand in celebration of this achievement. The firm of Latécoère made aeroplanes used during the war and then turned to civil aviation, inaugurating the first postal services to South America and Africa. Amongst its famous pilots was Antoine de Saint-Exupéry, known for his writings which include *Le Petit Prince*. Today Toulouse is the home of Aérospatiale, which builds Concorde and the Airbus.

Toulouse also benefitted from becoming the centre for the manufacture of synthetic nitric acid, used for making explosives, when France was awarded the German patent after the Treaty of Versailles. A less synthetic speciality of the city, whether rose or red, comes from the violet. The flower is depicted on postcards, still in an amazingly 'Victorian' idiom, which are on sale all over the city, as is the scent, made curiously enough from the leaves. The plant is grown under cold frames and flowers from October onwards. The violets are sent to market in the normal way, and then in April, when no more are produced, the whole plant is cut and the leaves are processed to produce the essence for the scent, which is made at Grasse. It is a complicated and delicate business, though sweeter-smelling than that of producing woad. It takes two thousand kilograms of leaves to make one kilogram of this concentrated essence; hence the very high price of 35,000 francs a kilogram which it commanded in 1989. A liqueur is also made from the flowers, but inevitably it looks like methylated spirits. I am afraid I have not been brave enough to taste it, though the crystallized violets are a different matter. They are to be found in the excellent *confiseries* which jostle amongst the few remaining half-timbered houses and the smart shops and boutiques of this flourishing metropolis.

Here too, as one would expect from the fourth largest town in France, the food is superlative. There are three restaurants which, by any standard, are amongst the best in France. At

Vanel the eponymous proprietor has had the good sense to bring with him the *crêpes de grand'mère* from Quercy; at Les Jardins de l'Opéra, Dominique Toulousy brings invention to old regional specialities; and at Darroze one is delighted to find, amongst so many *machos mousquetaires*, a woman in charge of the kitchen.

The Toulousains have always been both *gourmands* and *gourmets* from the days when they founded the first gastronomic association in France, in the early eighteenth century. The Confrérie de la Jubilation, with a constitution in pretty feeble Latin, enjoined its members to moderation as well as to good eating. The Confrérie has recently been revived as a dining club and its members, Les Quarante du Pilon d'Oie (The Forty Goose Drumsticks) keep the tradition going. Meals are eaten to the accompaniment of a violinist to remind the diners that gastronomy has its place amongst the arts. The officers are dignified by titles such as Grand Pilonier, Cuissardier, Croupionnier (Parson's Nose), Grand Frère Propagateur and Noble Gueule, and the club's coat-of-arms displays a flagon, a ham, a glass, a *pâte-en-croûte* and a violin, topped by a barrel of grapes, and surrounded by a string of sausages.

Toulouse sausages are certainly world-famous and where would Toulouse be without its geese? The Toulousains boast that their method of serving fresh *foie gras* spiked with truffles and baked in flaky pastry is the best in the world. I only hesitate to agree because I live for part of the year in Périgord, where the *foie gras* and the truffles are second to none. Alexandre Dumas has a good story about Tsar Paul I reprieving a Pole who had committed some political crime because he managed to supply him with *pâté de foie gras* direct from Toulouse to St Petersburg without it going rancid *en route*.

8

Dame de Pierre and
Dame de Brique

MONTAUBAN is unlike Toulouse or Albi in more than one respect: it is little visited by tourists, a fact underlined by the closure of three of its restaurants from mid-July to mid-August, and it hardly advertises itself at all. It certainly does not bother to call itself 'rose' or even 'the Geneva of France', though it had some claim to the latter in the sixteenth century. However, it cannot resist a mild joke at the expense of its more boastful gastronomic neighbours by selling *cassoulet Montalbanais*, which turns out to be sugared almonds in pink, cream and green.

'This town is sculpted in autumnal tints, this countryside flushed crimson with its vines, lit at night by potters' fires and in the day gilded by a burning sun and by the glow of its ripe fruits',[101] wrote Bourdelle in a prose style only too akin to his sculpture, but if you approach Montauban by way of the Pont Vieux you will see what he means. This fortified bridge was begun in 1311 and is still standing, though the fortifications have gone. Its seven pointed brick arches rest on stone piers surmounted by five large apertures to let the floodwater through, for the exceptional depth of the riverbed causes frequent and appalling floods. The last, in 1930, killed two hundred people and destroyed over two thousand houses.

To the south of the bridge on the tree-lined quay is a handsome red brick building, which was formerly the bishop's palace and is now the Musée Ingres. Beyond it lies the small city itself filled with small brick houses, some stuccoed, which while of no great distinction in themselves lend it an agreeable air. Its central *place*, the place Nationale, surrounded by more brick houses and a double row of arcades, is attractive without being elegant; there are charming squares with fountains such as that by the Palais de Justice, and the little side-streets which run out of it are lined with fifteenth- and sixteenth-century houses with simple but satisfying façades.

They seem very much in keeping with Montauban's general air of modesty, though it has cause enough for pride in its history. The inhabitants of Montauriol, a small village centred round the eleventh-century abbey of St Théodard, petitioned the Count of Toulouse in 1144 to be allowed to found a new town because of 'the rotten treatment they were getting from the abbot and monks of St Théodard'. The Count acceded to their request, glad to enhance his prestige at the expense of the Church and to earn their grateful support in a site of strategic importance. Indeed, it was unique in the Midi for a town to be founded at the behest of its future burghers and not by a seigneur, a bishop or a king. The new citizens called their town Mont Alba and their coat-of-arms still displays a willow atop a hill (*alba* being a willow in the *langue d'oc*), perhaps because the underside of the leaves blow white in the wind.

The Montalbanais sided with their overlord when the English invaded in 1159, 1186 and 1188 and stuck grimly to him in 1212 when the Abbot of St Théodard took Simon de Montfort's part. The town became relatively prosperous during the twelfth century, trading wheat, salt and wine for wool and luxury goods from England, Spain and Italy. The account books of Barthélemy Bonis, a fourteenth-century merchant of some standing, show a sale of two dozen pairs of English gloves which had become all the rage. He also had a substantial banking business, but shortly after the outbreak of the Hundred Years War, he smartly switched to arms-dealing.

When Edward III claimed the French throne in 1337 and Philippe VI confiscated the Duchy of Aquitaine, Montauban found itself in the front line, situated as it was in a key position on the borders of Gascony and Languedoc. It was constantly beset by English troops, though spared during the Black Prince's *chevauchée* of 1355, and in 1361 it was handed over to the English by the Treaty of Brétigny. The Black Prince visited Montauban in 1363 and started to build a palace, but by the time the English left eight years later, only one floor had been completed. It contained an enormous guardroom with a high vaulted ceiling, where one roof boss shows the English leopard, and another quarters the arms of both England and France. Now the basement of the Musée Ingres, it has been laid out with medieval arms and armour and houses an extremely rare example of a *banc de question*, the rack used for wresting the 'truth' from virtually all criminals.

By the mid-fifteenth century Montauban had begun to depend commercially on Toulouse, and a hundred years later was almost entirely Protestant, with some aspirations to independence. Its citizens concentrated on strengthening the fortifications with an almost obsessional fervour and between 1573 and 1584, seven meetings of the United Provinces of the Midi were held there. By the time of the Edict of Nantes, there were two temples (as Protestant churches were called), a college and an academy for training ministers on which Thomas Wentworth commented:

> Hear is an university for them of the religion . . . Hear be many Scotsmen and many of the professors are of that nation . . . Thear is one colledge; itt is properly but a scoole for thear be no fellows, only a colledge to read in and not so much as lodging for the professors.[102]

But after the death of Henri IV the Counter-Reformation gathered strength and when Henri, Duc de Rohan led a new revolt, it was put down by royal troops commanded by Louis

XIII. He failed to take the city by siege in 1621 but the dents made by the cannonballs are still to be seen on the tower of the church of St Jacques. This brick church of thirteenth-century origin was also badly damaged during the Hundred Years War and the apse was replaced in 1481 by the one we now see. The interior is typically meridional Gothic with a high single nave.

After La Rochelle had fallen in 1628 Montauban gave in without a struggle and inevitably its fortifications were dismantled by Richelieu. Many of the Huguenots fled as the Catholics returned, and a new era of prosperity began when the city was made the capital of a *généralité* (an area roughly equivalent to a province). New houses were built throughout the seventeenth century, many of them by the magistrates and lawyers who flooded in when the Cour des Aides (the court which handled disputes over indirect taxation) was moved there from Cahors in 1661. By now Montauban was firmly Catholic and the building of both a new bishop's palace and a new cathedral were set under way.

Pierre de Bertier, bishop from 1652 to 1674, employed Pierre Campmartin (who also restored the place Nationale) for the former, which rose on the foundations laid so long before by the Black Prince. Three wings in red brick surround an inner courtyard; their style is curiously anachronistic, reminiscent of the palaces built during the reign of Henri IV rather than in tune with contemporary trends.

The cathedral, by contrast, started in 1692 and designed by François d'Orbay, Jules Hardouin-Mansart and Robert de Cotte, is more typical of its time. Arthur Young found it 'modern, and pretty well built, but too heavy', and indeed its stone façade is rather overpowering. It looks less dilapidated now than it did since the badly weathered statues by Marc Arcis have been replaced by modern copies. The interior, where the original statues, including one of St Hugh, Bishop of Lincoln, with his mitre and a swan at his feet, are now to be seen, is warm and friendly, with a canopy over the high altar. Ingres's *Le Voeu de Louis XIII*, with its banana-fingered Virgin, hangs in the left transept.

The city, which produced a certain amount of cloth, was badly hit by the disappearance of its main market when France lost Canada. Its economic decline persisted throughout the eighteenth century and when the new *départements* were created during the Revolution, Montauban was demoted in administrative terms. It was not until 1808 that the municipality persuaded Napoleon to carve out a new *département*, the Tarn-et-Garonne, of which it became, and has remained, the *préfecture*. Despite a modest silk industry, specializing in stockings made from a technique learned from the Nîmois, and the manufacture of very fine sieves for the bakery trade, the combination of political indifference and latter-day religious conformity reduced the city to an apathy from which it is only just emerging.

The bishop's palace, known as the Palais Berbier, was turned into a museum in 1846. It has good archaeological and medieval sections and a fair collection of paintings dating from the sixteenth century to today, including some by the Montalbanais François Desnoyer. But it is best known for those by Ingres who was born in Montauban in 1780. He studied first in Toulouse and then in Paris, only returning for a few days in November 1826 to accompany his *Le Voeu de Louis XIII*, which had been commissioned for the cathedral and which had been hugely successful in the Paris Salon two years earlier.

He subsequently made up for his absence by giving the museum an enormous number of paintings and drawings, and by leaving others to it in his will. While there is no doubt that Ingres was a superlative draughtsman and portraitist, many of his larger pictures, such as the *Dream of Ossian*, are less immediately attractive. It is good though to see a selection of his possessions, including an elegant and practical trolley for his paints and his marl stick. There is also a painting of him in his studio in Rome in 1818 by J. Alaux, holding his violin, and the instrument itself. Playing the violin was Ingres' hobby and although he knew that he was an indifferent fiddler he preferred being complimented on his playing than on his painting. *Le violin d'Ingres* has since come to mean 'second-best'.

Thomas Merton's family found Montauban 'a good enough town but it was dull'.

> The only thing that interested Father was the Musée Ingres, filled with meticulous drawings by that painter . . . and that collection of cold and careful sketches was not enough to keep anyone at a high pitch of inspiration for much more than fifteen minutes. More characteristic of the town was a nightmarish bronze monument by Bourdelle, outside the museum, which seemed to represent a group of cliff-dwellers battling in a mass of molten chocolate.[103]

Antoine Bourdelle is the only other native of whom most of us have – just – heard. The Musée Ingres has forty of his sculptures and a large number of drawings and watercolours. Although he lived and worked in Paris, in a house now turned into a little-known museum devoted to him tucked away by the Tour Montparnasse, he was, unlike Ingres, a constant visitor to his home town. He felt himself very close to his peasant and artisan origins as the grandson, as he was fond of repeating, of a goatherd and a weaver. 'I have sculpted', he said, 'in the *langue d'oc*'.

Bourdelle worked for Rodin from 1893 onwards but developed his own characteristic style. From 1893 to 1909 he worked in what he called his 'dionysiac' manner, which laid more emphasis on structure than on modelling, and from 1910 to 1929, in an 'apollonian' manner, which was more linear. Rodin thought highly of him and sprang to his defence when the critics savaged his Monument aux Morts as being, for instance, 'a negroid monstrosity which sets at naught every law of anatomy' or a work 'which carries singularity to the limit'. Nowadays Bourdelle's work is better liked and his *Herakles* was exhibited in 1989 in the Yorkshire Sculpture Park at Bretton Hall, where he was billed, in Rodin's phrase, as 'the Pioneer of the Future'.

Visitors to Montauban can make their own minds up about his sculpture in general and his Monument aux Morts in particular. The latter is just outside the Musée Ingres in the *place* in front of the elegant old Cour des Aides, which now houses both the Musée du Terroir devoted to local history and another museum specializing in natural history and archaeology.

There is, as one would suppose, relatively little industrial archaeology to be seen in Languedoc, but a fascinating excursion can be made to the west of Montauban to see both a derelict brickworks and an unusual example of modern technology. The brickworks at the junction of the Canal de Montech which links Montauban to the Canal latéral de la Garonne still has its two stacks intact and some antiquated machinery rattling away operating a small sluice, but otherwise it is a ghost factory. The contrast between it and the experimental lock just to the north of Montech could not be more poignant. At what is known as the *pente d'eau*, there is a new mechanical lock where the boat is taken into the lock and the gates before and behind it are closed. The boat in its pool of water is propelled mechanically by wheeled hydraulic rams up (or down) an even gradient, about 450 metres long, until it reaches the new level, whereupon the gates are opened and the boat floats off.

St Antonin-Noble-Val, to the east of Montauban, lies between the Rivers Aveyron and Bonnette within a circle of wooded hills dominated by the Rochers d'Anglars, in a land that was, according to Thomas Merton, 'long wild with heresy, and the fake mysticism that tore men away from the Church and from the Sacraments, and sent them into hiding to fight their way to some suicidal nirvana.'[104]

St Antonin was evangelized by its eponymous saint, and grew into a prosperous village. It suffered some damage during the Albigensian Crusade but recovered in due course as the imposing town hall built in 1312 testifies. Viollet-le-Duc, called in to restore it, said that 'it is certainly one of France's most curious civic buildings . . . with sculptures of unusual delicacy and purity, the figures all of an excellent style and perfectly carved', and while the architect left the façade much as it was, he thoroughly enjoyed himself by adding a sort of Florentine campanile which now looks like a joke in execrable taste. Even so, the hotel next door recently changed its name to 'Viollet-le-Duc', apparently untroubled by any aesthetic doubts.

The town, which lived by processing leather, has many old tanneries on the riverside and a number of late medieval houses, some half-timbered, with arched shopfronts, nail-studded doors and mullioned windows. There are arcaded streets, one of the usual covered markets, and the elegant mid-eighteenth century presbytery is now used as the tourist information office.

Thomas Merton was only ten when he arrived at St Antonin-Noble-Val in 1905, and in retrospect it seemed to him that 'the church had been fitted into the landscape in such a way as to become the keystone of its intelligibility. Its presence imparted a particular significance to everything else that the eye beheld . . .'. It is certainly of little architectural significance, it must be said.

To the northwest of St Antonin lies the Rouergue which is more properly dealt with in a book on the Auvergne, while to the south the main road leads to Cordes. It runs for a short stretch along the still turbulent Aveyron which grows calmer as it leaves the gorges, and then on through the wooded valley of the Cérou, aflame in autumnal sunshine. Just outside the town there is a splendidly old-fashioned restaurant, the Hostellerie du Parc, where the dining-room still has its dark red walls and an ornate nineteenth-century mantelpiece. It was good to be offered so local a dish as *tripes à l'albigeoise*, tender and succulent, scented with saffron and capers.

Cordes-sur-Ciel is sometimes known as the 'Dame de Pierre' in contrast to Albi, the 'Dame de Brique' or, more quaintly still, as the 'Toledo of France'. In the Middle Ages Cordes, like St Antonin-Noble-Val, was famed for its weavers and its tanners –

its name may even be a derivation from Cordoba, the home of a special kind of decorated worked leather.

The town, founded as a *bastide* on the northern confines of Languedoc in 1222 by the young Raymond VII, Count of Toulouse, lies along its rocky eminence 291 metres above sea-level and dominating the valley of the Cérou below. Albert Camus found the view enchanting:

> A light haze drops from the night sky towards the mists of the valley, mingles with them for a moment, then flows on downwards while the exhalations of earth rise one after another to disperse under the bright stars. Anything seems possible at such a moment: it is an image of reconciliation. I tell myself that this hulk, encrusted with old and precious shells, has beached at the end of the world, on the border of another universe – that here, estranged lovers will finally embrace, love and creation achieve perfect equilibrium.[105]

Cordes was elaborately fortified with a series of ramparts (though not apparently with a defensive château), but of the first wall to be built only the Porte des Ormeaux remains, and from a later one, two more gateways, the Porte de la Jane (or de la Viguerie) and the Porte du Planol, have survived. A third wall, which necessitated partially demolishing the first, was erected at the end of the thirteenth and the beginning of the fourteenth century. These three walls protected the *bastide*, while a fourth enclosed the *faubourg* which had grown up at the foot of the hill. The stairway which leads to the Porte de l'Horloge is called Pater Noster because it has the same number of steps as there are words in the Lord's Prayer.

A fair number of medieval houses, such as the Maisons Gorsse, Carrié-Boyer, Fontpeyrouse, Prunet, Gaugiran and Ladevèze are still extant. Dating them is difficult but some are thought to have been built between 1295 and 1320, and others during a second wave of prosperity in 1330–40. The ground floors have mostly been restored and present fairly uniform façades with arcaded windows letting light into the artisans' workshops or sales counters, which are used for the same purposes today. The rings on the house walls have puzzled architectural historians, but it is generally thought they were used to display banners on feast days or for hanging newly-dyed textiles out to dry.

The sculptural decorations on the façades of the three largest and most elaborately decorated houses led Mérimée to call them, rather fancifully, the hôtels of the Grand Ecuyer (Groom), the Grand Fauconnier (Falconer) and the Grand Veneur (Hunter), though there is no evidence that they were indeed occupied by such high-ranking seigneurial officers. Be that as it may, they are striking in their Italianate style.

Although Cordes had been a Cathar stronghold, by the sixteenth century it had become staunchly Catholic and suffered some destruction at the hands of the Huguenots in both 1568 and 1574. Thereafter it fell on evil days apart from a brief revival at the end of the nineteenth century. Two of its inhabitants, exiled to Switzerland with the army of General Bourbaki (who had commanded the Imperial Guard in Paris in 1870), returned from St Gall, renowned then as now for its embroidery, with new machinery, and for fifty years more than three hundred looms were busy clacking away, turning out material for skirts and curtains.

The Musée Charles Portal has some exhibits relating to these textiles as well as to local archaeology and history. A most entertaining little museum in the Maison Prunet, the Musée de l'Art du Sucre, has recently opened to display the skills of confectioners who specialize in sugar, both raw and cooked. It sells, amongst other things, delicious chocolates called *pastel Cordais*, filled with a pale blue cream flavoured with curaçao and orange-flower water, and wrapped to resemble miniature *cocagnes*.

There are also a number of ecclesiastical buildings of which the only really interesting one is the parish church of St Michel. The belltower, on a square base and mounting to an octagon, dates from 1369 to 1374; the church, completed in 1287, was given a new nave in the fifteenth century after an earlier one had collapsed. There is a good rose window, and some amusing capitals in two of the chapels. The organ, which was bought second-hand from Notre Dame, Paris in 1842, had been played at the funeral of the Duc d'Orléans, the son of Louis-Philippe, and at the baptism of his grandson, the Comte de Paris. There is also an early medieval covered market-place, the roof of which was replaced in 1358, though the pillars were mostly refashioned in the nineteenth century.

Gaillac, twenty-four kilometres away, on the right bank of the Tarn, is the centre of one of the oldest vineyards in France, reputed to have been planted by the Emperor Augustus's legionaries. Henry VIII prized the wine and imported twenty barrels a year, but later the wine-growers suffered from competition and the restrictive practices of the Bordeaux merchants, and it was less highly prized. Despite recent efforts to improve its quality, the reds, whites and rosés are still of greater interest to the historian than to the wine-lover.

Gaillac is an animated, small, brick-built town and with its flourishing commercial life is very different from Cordes. Its cypresses and umbrella pines give it a much more pronounced southern, indeed Mediterranean air. The former abbey buildings are occupied by a wine co-operative; and its church of St Michel, in the meridional Gothic style and built of brick, has an interesting thirteenth-century Virgin known as the Vierge Médiatrice, where the Christ child points a finger up to draw attention to his interceding mother. The organ is by Dominic Cavaillé-Coll, a member of the family of organ-builders who lived here and of which four generations made some six hundred instruments between 1709 and 1889.

The church of St Pierre was restored in the eighteenth century; the Tour Pierre de Brens contains an ethnographic collection and a museum devoted to Compagnonnage which shows the work of journeymen masons and carpenters, and wine. On the southern edge of the town there is the charming seventeenth-century brick château de Foucaud, now a museum of fine arts. It is surrounded by an attractive park, attributed to Louis XIV's great landscape gardener, André Le Nôtre, with a small pavilion and an eighteenth-century orangery.

It is hard luck on Albi that it has given its name to the crusade against the Cathar heretics, for although it counted Cathars amongst its citizens, they were neither numerous nor influential in the twelfth century and in fact the city welcomed Simon de Montfort when he arrived there in 1209. It was Geoffroi d'Auxerre, the biographer of St Bernard of Clairvaux, who first blackened the reputation of the Albigeois when, in 1145, he said that 'the people of this city are contaminated by a greater degree of heretical depravity than in any of the surrounding region'. This was a view subsequently endorsed by the Cistercians, one of whom referred to Albi in 1189 as a 'sewer which received all the refuse and filth of the heresy'. It is certainly true that Albi was strongly anti-clerical, and with good reason, for it was an ecclesiastical fief and in 1234 its bishop, Armand Catalan, was so unpopular that he had to take refuge in the old church, having excommunicated the citizens. Nevertheless two thousand Albigeois went to help at the siege of Montségur in 1244.

Bernard de Castanet, bishop from 1276 to 1308, was the Grand Inquisitor of Languedoc and Vice-Inquisitor for the whole of France. He was particularly intransigent in his attitude to heretics, but he seems also to have paid off scores against his personal enemies of whatever religious persuasion: 'not a week went by but that some notable of Albi was seized, tortured or immured'. It was by constant extortions and the enormous revenues he received (his income from church sources was 11,000 florins a year which compares well with the 10,500 received by the Bishop of Paris) that as both spiritual and temporal overlord of the city he was able to start building the new cathedral which he dedicated to Ste Cécile. It went up by the side of the old Romanesque church, by this time in ruins, but Bernard's long-running disputes with both the municipality and the chapter led to him being fined by the King and banished by the Pope to Le Puy, where he died.

The first stone was laid on 15 August 1282 but the cathedral was not consecrated until 1480. Considering that it took two hundred years to complete, it is remarkable that the original plans were so faithfully adhered to and that the building should present so homogeneous an exterior. The crowning parapet, however, resting on arcaded corbels resembling machicolations, was added between 1849 and 1860 by César Daly who was called in to repair the roof without damaging the painted frescoes on the interior vaulting. Daly was a northerner, born in Verdun, and his work excited a good deal of protest in his own time, in much the same way as had that of Viollet-le-Duc at Carcassonne.

The huge red-brick structure, standing in a relatively uncluttered space, is one of the most imposing cathedrals in Europe. It resembles a fortress rather than a church and its terrifying austerity embodies Jehovah, for it was designed to put the fear of God into the faithful and the heretic alike. As Kipling said, 'the brick bulk of Albi cathedral seen against the moon, hits the soul like a hammer'.

The sheer walls, rising to 40 metres, are punctuated only by semicircular buttresses alternating with tall narrow windows. The belltower at the western end is a formidable keep 78 metres high with a square base and massive towers at each of the four corners. In 1485 the tower was refashioned and given three additional octagonal storeys.

The entrance to the church is by way of an impressive flight of stone steps and through, first, an ornate stone portal surmounted by an elaborately carved Gothic arch between the church and a crenellated tower. The openwork tympanum contains statues of Ste Cécile standing between Ste Marthe and Dominic of Florence, bishop in 1397–1410, who was responsible for building the portal. A further fifty steps lead up to an even larger white stone canopy of incredible exuberance covering the approach to the doorway which is surmounted by another even more flamboyant tympanum.

Although Mérimée said of the canopy that 'the imagination cannot conceive of anything more elegant or more graceful and its perfect conservation is nothing short of a miracle', he went on to complain that 'its whimsical mullions provide no shelter from the rain, the sun or the wind; it is simply there to be admired'. Whatever his strictures on this, and he continues, 'its oddness is not compensated for by its elegance', he had nothing but praise for the inside of the cathedral.

It takes an effort of imagination for us now to see it as it was originally, for at the same time as the exterior canopy was added, so too was a self-contained choir occupying and enclosing half the area. The nave has no aisles, there are no transepts and without the caesura of the choir, it must have resembled nothing so much as the whale's belly in which Jonah found himself. There was to be no avoidance of God's wrath for heretics – or for the orthodox.

It was too bleak for Louis I d'Amboise when he arrived as bishop in 1474, the year in which he installed a printing works in Albi (the third in France after those of Paris and Lyon). During his incumbency, which lasted till 1503, he set about the embellishment of the cathedral in the same humanistic spirit that had inspired his brother Cardinal Georges d'Amboise at Gaillon on the Loire. But embellishment did not mean doing away with the threat of hellfire. The whole of the western end of the church was covered with a terrifying series of paintings showing the Last Judgement, harping on the ghastly fate awaiting sinners. The seven deadly sins are graphically represented, each with an appropriate punishment: the proud are broken on the wheel, while the envious burn in a frozen river; the angry are surrounded by flames and the covetous sweat in cauldrons of molten metal; the gluttons are drowning in a sea of rotting food and fetid water, and the lustful burn in an eternal fire. The slothful, like the figure of Christ himself, were destroyed in 1693 when the wall was pierced to make a way through to a chapel on the ground floor of the tower. Paradise, where Charlemagne and St Louis amongst many others are to be found, makes a far less powerful impression, as does the

Earth. Similarities with Rogier van der Weyden's work at the Hôtel Dieu in Beaune have led to the supposition that this gigantic fresco may have been of Flemish workmanship. The choir and its screen (*jubé*), showing Burgundian or perhaps Spanish influence, was erected at roughly the same time. Augustus Hare found it magical:

A harmonious mass of labyrinthine stonework, upon which the eye can always rest without being fatigued, and can always discover something new to admire. It is said to be like lacework, but is rather like the thousand interlacing tendrils of a mossy bank, so boundless and intricate is the variety of its designs, of which each, perfect in itself, is yet subservient to the unity and harmony of the whole.[106]

There were originally over two hundred and fifty painted statues in all the niches of the screen, but only four remain, a weeping Virgin, St John, Adam and Eve. The rest of the choir however remains a riot of figures. Louis d'Amboise's nephew, another Louis d'Amboise, bishop in 1503–10, continued his uncle's work, and the ceiling of the nave was painted at his behest by two Bolognese artists from 1508 to 1514 in an altogether more gentle manner than that of the Last Judgement, with a wonderful cobalt blue background.

The Palais de la Berbie gets its name from a corruption of *bisbia* meaning bishop. It was started in 1265 under the bishopric of Bernard de Combret, though it was his successor, the villainous Bernard de Castanet who, by concentrating on enlarging and completing this dour edifice, intended similarly to cow the citizens of Albi, delayed the construction of the cathedral itself. The palace was the seat of the Inquisition, and lowered over the Albigeois until Henri IV, this time to teach the bishops a lesson, had most of its keep dismantled, leaving only the Tour Mage (or Ste Catherine) and the Tour St Michel. The palace, in pale pink brick with grey slate roofs, consists of a range of buildings giving on to sunless inner courts rather like those of the Popes' Palace at Avignon, and in one of which concerts and theatrical performances are held in summer. Its grimness is somewhat relieved by an impeccably kept garden laid out in the formal French classical style on a terrace overlooking the Tarn.

The interior was redecorated to make it less stark by later bishops in the sixteenth and again in the seventeenth century, when Louis XIV elevated the see to an archbishopric (which it remained until the Revolution, and was again from 1823 until 1905). A fine monumental staircase leads up to the galleries, for the palace is now a museum. There is an archaeological section, some good mostly seventeenth-century paintings on the first floor, and some very good early twentieth-century works on the top floors. The star attraction of the museum, though, is Toulouse-Lautrec.

Henri de Toulouse-Lautrec was born in the fine Hôtel de Bosc in the street now named for him (next door to the Musée de Cire, a sad little museum – not even real fun for children). After the death of Toulouse-Lautrec's mother, of whom so many wonderfully affectionate portraits are to be seen, Henri's great friend Maurice Joyant assembled a large collection of the artist's works. The range is impressive and instructive, from the first tentative paintings of the horses Toulouse-Lautrec so loved riding in his youth and the early portraits, to the views of the *café-concerts* and brothels of Paris in which he spent so much of his later life.

Whenever he appeared at a crowded dance hall or a smoke-filled café, he caused a sensation. Astonished, people stared at this dwarf with his two deformed legs, his over-size head, his malicious eyes peering through spectacles astride his huge nose, his bulbous lips and tousled bushy black beard.[107]

Maurice Joyant's description of his appearance is wonderfully caught in Vuillard's two remarkable portraits of him, both of which are in the museum.

The city of Albi is small and its sights well labelled, so it is easy to find one's way round. Most of the buildings, including the modern shops, are built in red brick giving it a unified aspect. Some however are in stone of which the collegiate church of St Salvy is an example. It has a fine belltower, the Tour de la Gâche, and though the church itself underwent endless rebuilding from the thirteenth to the sixteenth centuries, it retains its Flamboyant Gothic appearance. There are some splendid polychrome statues in the Burgundian style inside, and on one of the capitals in the pretty little thirteenth-century triangular cloister, there is a pope being carried away by devils, carved, one wonders, by a Cathar mason?

The Pharmacie des Pénitents, also known as the Maison Enjalbert, is a typical sixteenth-century half-timbered house, with wooden sculpted window- and door-frames, and both it and the rather grander Hôtel de Gorsse should be seen. Albi, like Toulouse, thrived on woad, and there are a number of other attractive bourgeois mansions, of which the most impressive is the Hôtel de Reynès. In brick with stone decorations, it is a refined example of Albigeois Renaissance architecture and, appropriately, now the home of the chamber of commerce.

On the north bank of the Tarn, away from the city centre in a square generously named Botany Bay, is the small museum devoted to Albi's other famous son, Jean-François de Galaup, Comte de Lapérouse. A hero of the War of American Independence, he was a sailor in the mould of Captain Cook, whom he followed to the South Seas only to be tragically shipwrecked at Vanikoro in the Solomon Islands.

Jean Jaurès found the city enchanting:

With its clear sky, the brickwork of its houses, its terraced gardens and fine bridges; with its central square open to the rays of the sun, where all the citizens foregather to enjoy its mild warmth in winter; with the imposing bulk of its cathedral set off by the delicacy of its portico at its foot; with the chalky slopes bordering it to the north, reminding one of the hills of Latium – all these would lead one to think it an Italian city, made for cultivation of the arts and of a serene philosophy. If, towards evening, you enter by way of the bridge, nothing could be fairer than these hushed quays leading up to the cathedral . . . whose rose-coloured brick combines in wondrous harmony with the yellow or purple of the setting sun.[108]

Jaurès, born in 1859 in Castres of bourgeois stock, was a brilliant scholar and taught for a time at the *lycée* in Albi and the university in Toulouse before turning to politics. He was a pacifist and on the whole a simple man whose 'trousers were less stylish than his speeches'. Jaurès became leader of the socialist party in 1905, and remained so until his assassination by Raoul Villain at the Croissant café in Paris in July 1914.

The village of Carmaux to the north of Albi is of no particular architectural interest but it played an important part in the history of the Midi. It was the centre of a modest coal-mining industry and when its miners went on strike in 1892, it attracted nation-wide attention. Jaurès, who had been elected as a republican deputy for Castres in 1885, failed to gain re-election in 1889, but his support of the miners and his conversion to socialism resulted in his being returned for Carmaux, as the first socialist deputy in the Tarn.

In 1895 the glassworkers of Carmaux, after a lockout by their employers, then also went on strike, and subsequently, with the support of both Jaurès and the Fédération Syndicale du Verre, the Verrerie Ouvrière was created. It was owned not simply by its workers but by a group of trade unions and co-operatives acting jointly. The new factory, which was actually built in Albi, was an experiment designed to symbolize the solidarity of the workers' movement and the growing power of the socialist party. Though the factory got off to a slow start, it flourished until the 1970s when it was no longer economically viable.

The railway line between Albi and Carmaux was opened in 1858 but extending it to Rodez presented engineering problems because of the depth of the River Viaur and the size of span that would be required to bridge it. A competition for its design was held in 1887 and although two plans were put forward by Gustave Eiffel, it was won by Paul Bodin. Ahead of its time both in design and technology, the Viaduc du Viaur took six years to construct and was opened in 1902. Made of steel struts which, like those of the Forth Bridge have to be repainted every twelve years or so, its single span arches 116 metres above the declivity in one graceful curve.

Close by, near Naucelles and half-way between Albi and Rodez is the château du Bosc where Toulouse-Lautrec spent much of his happy childhood. A beautiful mellow house in a rather rustic style, it has been in the hands of the same family since 1180 and was rebuilt in the late fifteenth century. While some of the rooms have been arranged as furniture displays, the château still has an undeniably lived-in atmosphere.

Toulouse-Lautrec fell when he was fifteen and broke one of his legs; a year later he fell again and broke the other and neither of his legs were to grow to full length. His parents (who were first cousins) were not themselves very tall and Henri remained of dwarf-like stature for the rest of his short life. One is particularly struck to see the marks of all the children's heights; his, at the age of eighteen, was still only 1 metre 53 centimetres. His bedroom in the château has been left as it was and there are many examples of his juvenilia as well as splendid photographs of members of his extensive family.

The road from Albi to Castres goes through the pleasant *bastide* of Réalmont, founded by Philipppe III in 1272. Its central *place* is surrounded by covered arcades and there is a good seventeenth-century church, Notre Dame du Taur, and a pretty fountain. Four kilometres to the east at St Lieux-Lafenasse, there is one of the typical farms (*métairies*) of this countryside, where the outhouses surround the main building like apses of a church.

I was told that not many visitors actually spend the night in Castres, which is a pity because it is a charming town and would be a good base for excursions, whether south across the Montagne Noire and into the Cabardès and Minervois, or east into the Sidobre and the mountains of Lacaune. (The tourist office has a good guide for walkers or cyclists called *Les Sentiers de Découverte*.) We took a risk and stayed in a hotel on the bank of the River Agout where the service was said by the Gault-Millau guide to be '*disputable*'. There was nothing at all wrong with the service and even if there had been, the view from our bedroom window would have made up for it. We faced across the river to the far bank lined with the tall narrow houses in which the weavers and dyers worked and lived. Some of them date from the fourteenth century and their façades are in neither brick nor stone but clapboard or wattle-and-daub, with open overhanging balconies. They suffered badly from a flood in the 1930s but have been restored, and some are gaily painted in white or green. Arched cellar doors in the stone foundations open straight on to the waterfront where small shrubs and wildflowers grow unheeded.

Castres was originally a Roman encampment, and St Benoît d'Aniane founded a monastery there in the ninth century. By the eleventh century the town had become the property of the viscounts of Albi, and later, though Cathar, it submitted to Simon de Montfort without a struggle. Staunchly Protestant, it was badly damaged during the Wars of Religion and became one of the fifty-one strongholds allowed after the Edict of Nantes. In the seventeenth century Castres enjoyed great prosperity from the proceeds of both the leather and the wool it processed.

Although many of the Huguenots had emigrated, and by the mid-eighteenth century religious fanaticism had somewhat abated, an incident similar to the Calas case in Toulouse (see p. 211) took place at almost the same time. Pierre-Paul Sirven's daughter, known to wish to convert to Catholicism, was found dead at the bottom of a well in 1762. Her parents, only too aware of Calas's fate, fled to Switzerland and in 1777, thanks once again to Voltaire's intervention, were found innocent.

The first mechanized wool-spinning factory was installed in 1815 and the city maintained its production of woollen cloth throughout the nineteenth century. It supplied a great deal of cloth to the army through the good offices of Nicolas Soult, one of Napoleon's marshals created Duke of Dalmatia in 1807, and whose family came from the valley of the Thoré nearby. Today Castres is still one of the most important French producers of cloth and specializes in the de-woolling of skins.

The cathedral, dedicated to St Benedict of Nursia and built

on the site of the original abbey, looks from the outside to be a typical if rather sombre Baroque church. It was started in 1678 by Guillaume Cailhau and completed in 1718 by Eustache Lagon. The interior, however, is still in meridional Gothic style. It has a huge canopy over the high altar supported on lovely red marble pillars from Caunes-Minervois, and the side chapels are filled with paintings, one attributed to Poussin and the others by local artists. Many of the furnishings come from the ruined charterhouse of Saïx nearby, and one set of pews was reserved for the municipality while another was set aside for the clothworkers (*fabriciens*).

An eleventh-century tower is all that remains of the original abbey buildings; it has two rows of lombard arcading along its two dissimilar lower storeys, to which a third was added in 1679. By its side is the entrance to the bishop's palace, which now houses the Hôtel de Ville and the museum. It was built in 1669–73 to the plans of Jules Hardouin-Mansart.

The elaborate and beautifully kept garden behind it is attributed to Le Nôtre. Certainly it displays his mathematical skills in disguising the irregularities of the terrain and his love for the formal interplay of cylinders, domes and cones. Four parterres with arabesque patterns, filled with flowers or a pale gravel, are traced out by the dark green of the meticulously clipped box and yew, and meet in the centre where a fountain plays in a circular pond.

Notre Dame de la Platé is a late Baroque church built between 1743 and 1755, with a much more elaborate façade than that of the cathedral and with a dome rising above the crossing. It too has a canopy above the high altar and a splendid organ dating from 1764.

Some dozen hôtels are to be seen scattered through the city of which the best are the Hôtel de Viviès (or de Rozel), dating from 1585, and next to it that of Jean Leroy, which is seventeenth-century. The Hôtel Poncet, of much the same date, has caryatids supporting a balustrade and an inner court-yard with a large open staircase. The Hôtel de Nayrac of 1620 is in the Toulousain style, built in brick but with stone window and door surrounds. It is well worth going into the municipal theatre, a late nineteenth-century Italianate building (in the foyer of which is the tourist office), to see the paintings of Laurens, one of which is an interpretation of Berlioz's 'Symphonie fantastique'.

The Musée Goya, which has specialized in Spanish paintings since 1946, was originally founded with the gift of three of Goya's paintings, bought in Madrid by Marcel Briguibol, whose own works include a good self-portrait. Goya's self-portrait, with spectacles perched on the end of his nose, is stunning, and the two others, *Don Francisco del Mazo*, and his largest work, *The Junta of the Philippines*, are magnificent. There is also a complete set of engravings: 'Tauromaquia', 'Los Proverbios', 'Los Disparatos', 'Los Desastros de la Guerra' and 'Los Caprichos'. Seen together they exemplify only too well Baudelaire's observation that 'the great merit of Goya consists in his ability to make horrors credible'.

Amongst the works by other atists there is an extraordinary *Flagellation* by the Catalan Luis Borassa; portraits of Philip III by Pantoja de la Cruz, a copy of the Prado Philip IV by Velazquez, and paintings by Morales, Murillo, Valdes-Leal and Zurburan.

Another museum, devoted to Jean Jaurès, is up by the old grain market built in cast iron between 1865 and 1868 and recently renovated. The open market is held in the place Jean-Jaurès and sells a good range of local produce, including *melsat*, a rather bland white sausage made from eggs and bread and unique to this region. While I am not sure that I agree with Austin de Croze that *melsat* deserves to be better known than it is, it is always good to try something new. Strangely enough it is not mentioned in Jane Grigson's *Charcuterie and French Pork Cookery*. She does however give a generic recipe for *boudin de Languedoc*, a black pudding, but it is one that few of us could attempt to make at home as the list of ingredients starts with five pints of pig's blood.

There is a big choice of *charcuterie* and hams and, in the autumn, *cèpes* and other local mushrooms. It was cheering too to find a little old man selling his own baskets made from hazel twigs, and other pretty and properly-made baskets instead of the usual inferior imported versions. What we did not find on the cheese stalls was *le chester français* which we had been told might be on sale as it is made hereabouts.

The Montagne Noire, the last outcrop of the Massif Central, presents two very different faces. Whereas that to the south, in the Aude, is arid *garrigue*, the northern face is both hillier and heavily wooded with meadowlands where sheep may safely graze.

In the thirteenth century Mazamet had a flourishing cloth trade, supplied with wool from the sheep on the Montagne Noire and dyes from the plains to the south. It continued prosperous and by the middle of the nineteenth century was importing skins to be de-woolled from the Argentine, though nowadays they come from Australia and South Africa as well. Though small, it is now a busy manufacturing centre where one can pick up bargains in the way of belts, wallets and bags, boots and jackets, especially in the emporia to the east of the town.

The small museum in the Maison Fuzier displays some basic information about the Cathars and, more interestingly, in the section called 'Mémoire de la Terre', photographs of different types of early burial and funeral rites.

Three kilometres to the south is the rather sad ruined village of Hautpoul from which the view is splendid. The drive up there is rather depressing because the road is lined with disused and decaying tanneries which, though they have not been in use for years, still have that unmistakable smell.

The road that runs west from Mazamet goes along by the River Thoré, the water of which was found to be particularly good for washing wool and tanning. The valley is edged with rather down-at-heel woollen mills and, more attractively, pine trees grown for their timber. It is worth stopping in the village of St Amans-Soult, formerly St Amans-la-Bastide, to see Maréchal Soult's mausoleum in the church. Soult, withdrawing from Wellington's army advancing up from Spain, was forced into battle at Toulouse on Easter Day, 10 April 1814, but managed to get the better part of his troops away to Carcassonne, with fewer casualties than those suffered by the Allies. Elizabeth Longford thinks that this conflict was 'the closest run thing' of the whole of the Peninsular War, and the French claim it as a victory, though Toulouse welcomed the Iron Duke with open arms. When, two days later, Wellington was told of Napoleon's abdication, he exclaimed 'You don't say so, upon my honour! Hurrah!'.[109] This sentiment was doubtless echoed by Soult who, like Wellington, went on to have a distinguished career as a politician.

The Grotte de la Devèze, some few kilometres to the east, is one of the few caves that is worth seeing if stalactites, stalagmites and other such natural concretions take your fancy.

St Pons-de-Thomières lies deep in the valley of the Jaur. It is easy to park in the square in front of the church guarded by a fine buxom oversize Marianne painted in bright green and the very antithesis of the Virgin Mary. All that remains of the abbey that was founded here in 936 is the handsome fortified church, which has undergone much rebuilding over the centuries, so that the result is an uneasy mixture of Romanesque and Baroque. The façade is Baroque but its absence of decoration gives it a rather strange appearance and it is odd to find that the interior consists only of a single wide Romanesque nave. The elaborately decorated eighteenth-century choir in splendid roseate and white marble makes up for the simplicity elsewhere; it was the work of Joseph Grimes of Caunes-Minervois (one wonders, with a name like that, where he or his family originated) and Antoine Fabre of Montpellier. There is a handsome altar table and a fine organ. The cloister was destroyed in 1785 to make way for the road which now runs past the church, but some of its capitals were saved and four are still to be seen at St Pons.

The town itself is in two parts, separated by the River Jaur.

The Ville Mage, which grew up round the abbey, still has remnants of its fortifications in two towers. The Hôtel de Ville is in the seventeenth-century former bishop's palace. The Ville Moindre, on the south bank, retains some sixteenth- and seventeenth-century houses, and has a small museum of prehistory and archaeology.

The combination of impermeable granite rock and heavy rainfall make the Monts de l'Espinousse and the Monts de Lacaune to the north an inhospitable terrain where the villages, sustained only by sheep, are few and far between. Megaliths, believed to date from about 2600 BC, abound amidst the chestnuts and beeches, some of them called menhir-statues because they have human faces carved into them.

Lacaune is the only town of any size and nowadays lives, apparently, on air. One would have thought that it would be bracing, but no, it seems to be sedative and of great comfort to people, especially children, with breathing difficulties. It is less surprising that one of its specialities is an air-dried and delicious ham. Indeed all the local *charcuterie* – salamis, sausages and the huge *boudin noir* called *calabart* – are good, if rather spicier than elsewhere.

In the past when Lacaune was a spa, it advertised the fact by erecting, in 1559, the Fontaine des Pisseurs, where four young men are immortalized in the act of demonstrating the diuretic nature of its waters.

Some fifty kilometres farther north, St Affrique lies on the edge of the Grandes Causses, as the extensive mountainous plateaux to the east are known. They are strange places and appear to be little inhabited though in fact they are dotted with hamlets and farmhouses. The Caussenards are inevitably a hardy people with a strength of will and patience inbred over long centuries of battling with the elements.

Roquefort-sur-Soulzon, on the edge of the Causse de Larzac, is the home of one of the best-known French cheeses and is certainly the only one of which Languedoc can be proud. This blue-veined cheese, made here since time immemorial, has been prized since Pliny reported it well-liked at Rome. In the Middle Ages it was actually used as a medium of exchange like gold or silver specie, and during the sixty years that the Holy See was installed at Avignon, the popes had supplies sent to them as an annual tribute.

Many later writers, including Rabelais, Brantôme and Grimod de la Reynière, have sung its praises. Casanova, entirely in character, tells of an occasion when some young woman 'nimble as doe' served him with Roquefort and a succulent glazed ham, after which he rhapsodized that 'Chambertin and Roquefort are excellent viands to revive a lover and to bring a fresh love to a prompt consummation'. Émile Zola, with his gift for acute observation and passion for hyperbolic prose, included it amongst the cheeses in his novel *Le Ventre de Paris* (centred on the former market of Les Halles in Paris). He describes Roqueforts lying 'under their crystal globes where they took on a princely aspect, a mottled and shiny complexion, streaked with blue and yellow, looking as if they had been attacked by some shameful disease of the rich who have gorged themselves on truffles'. Curnonsky was moved to a eulogy whose high-flown conclusion is a bit hard to stomach:

> it brings with it a powerful smell of the earth and an aroma of the meadow; its presence seems to open a window on distant horizons . . . it exalts and enhances our fine wines, in the way that Wagner's potent orchestration accompanies and prolongs the singer's melody, communicating to it a deeper resonance.[110]

Roquefort has been jealous of its name and reputation from 1407 when it was accorded an *appellation d'origine* by Charles VI. It won its first battle against neighbouring imitators at the *parlement* of Toulouse in 1666, and emerged victorious in a similar case in more recent times against a restaurateur in Chicago who served a cow's milk cheese labelled Roquefort. True Roquefort is made from unpasteurized ewes' milk in the caves of the mountain of Combalou. *Penicillium roquefortii* is cultivated on breadcrumbs and then injected into the raw milk, and it is its microscopic flora that produces the characteristic bluey-green veining. The cheeses are shaped and laid out on oak planks in *caves* looking much like the nave of a subterranean Gothic church. These are blessed with a constant temperature of 7–9°C and a constant humidity the whole year round. It takes three months for the cheeses to mature and then, since there are variations in the finished product, a taster is employed to decide to which country each should be allocated; the stronger ones going, for example, to Britain where the cheese is usually eaten with butter.

La Couvertoirade looks much like Carcassonne must have looked a hundred and fifty years ago, though of course on a much smaller scale. It is a fortified village where there has been little restoration to date. In 1158 the Templars built a castle, church and cemetery, (in which facsimiles of discoid stelae, two of which come from Usclas-du-Bosc, have now been placed) to succour pilgrims travelling across this Causse. The old Roman road along which they came was by then known in the *langue d'oc* as the *cami romieu*, the pilgrim, or 'romany' way.

The darkly forbidding walls of the defensive system and their square and round towers were erected between 1429 and 1455 by Déodat d'Alans for the Hospitallers who had taken over from the Templars after the latter's extinction some hundred or so years earlier, and the whole ensemble is a rare example of fifteenth-century military architecture. One of the firing apertures is in the shape of a capital 'I' and another in the shape of an exclamation mark, oddities which prompt speculation as to whether such shapes were decorative, symbolic or just technically useful.

Most of the houses are small with steps leading up to the living-quarters on the first floor. Huge dried sunflowers which open and close with changes in temperature and humidity and seem to be accurate in forecasting the weather hang on many of the shutters. There are some larger houses too, of which the Hôtel de la Grailhe with its family escutcheon is the grandest. The communal oven still exists as it does in many of the villages, and there is an elliptical stone dewpond (*lavogne*) for the summer-pastured sheep just outside the village.

From La Couvertoirade one can wriggle one's way through endlessly dramatic and savage scenery to St Jean-de-Bruel, a picturesque village with an agreeable small hotel, on to Nant along the canyon of the Dourbie and the Chaos du Montpellier-le-Vieux on the Causse Noir. Montpellier-le-Vieux is a mysterious outcrop of dolomitic rocks which look like the ruins of a petrified city and which can be explored with the help of the signposts indicating a number of circuits for walkers.

A kilometre to the south of Millau one comes upon La Graufesenque, where excavations have revealed the existence of an enormous Gallo-Roman pottery of the first century AD. There were over five hundred workshops in whose huge kilns anything up to forty thousand pots could be fired. Examples of the terracotta pots made here have been found as far afield as Scotland and Libya.

The Dourbie joins the Tarn at Millau, another leather town, ringed by wooded hills. It was for centuries renowned for its gloves and was so proud of them that its municipal officers wore them for all their ceremonies. But since they are no longer articles of common daily use, other more modish garments have taken their place. The leather is of the highest quality, soft and supple, and comes in many attractive colours.

The Musée de la Peau et du Gant, which also has a good collection of dolls, and the Musée de Millau et des Causses, with many pieces of La Graufesenque ware, are housed in a pleasant eighteenth-century building. (In passing one may note that there is a square named for the opera singer, Emma Calvé, who died here and was involved with the occultists of St Sulpice.)

From Millau the road to the north-west runs along the Tarn through a number of small villages which make good centres for walkers who enjoy a challenge. Le Rozier is one such. Many years ago we spent a night there and had an excellent meal in what was then a simple hotel. We ate spitted larks and thought nothing of it; times, and the hotel, have changed. A kilometre or so away one has the choice of driving through two equally spectacular gorges. To the east the gorges of the Jonte lead via Meyrueis directly into the heart of the Cévennes, while to the north one can drive along the Tarn, an exciting if hair-raising experience but one preferably undertaken out of season. The road twists and turns by the side of the turbulent river through the verdant rocky cliffs between the Causse de Sauveterre to the north and the Causse Méjean to the south, and with the skyline defined by a series of ever-more dramatic crenellations.

It is with some relief, if travelling in this direction, that one reaches Ste Enimie. The town, in a magnificent oasis of greenery above the river, has picturesque streets lined by stone houses whose roofs, with their round slates, glint in sun and rain alike. Ste Enimie herself, rudely referred to by the local English residents as the Holy Enema, a sobriquet the poor saint hardly deserves, was a Merovingian princess suffering from leprosy. She was miraculously cured by the waters of the Fontaine de Burle, but her recovery lasted only if she stayed by its side. The fountain is still there but there are no remains of the Benedictine priory founded in her memory in the tenth century. Her story is told in modern ceramics by Henri Constans, in one of the chapels of the fourteenth-century church, and the Vieux Logis has a room devoted to the folklore of the Gévaudan (which plays no part in this book).

At Ste Enimie we have at last reached one of the most dramatic areas of Languedoc, that region of austere beauty known as the Cévennes.

9

Camisards and Silkworms

Cévennes – Florac – Le Pont de Montvert –
Voie Regordane – Alès – Anduze – Le Mas Soubleyran –
St Jean-du-Gard – Ganges – St Hippolyte-du-Fort –
Le Vigan – Pont St Esprit – Bagnols-sur-Cèze –
Villeneuve-lès-Avignon

WHILE purists speak of the Cévenne in the singular to mean its heartland, defining the Cévennes is a bit like trying to define Languedoc itself. There are considerable differences in the geological configuration of its component parts but their remoteness and inaccessibility have given all the inhabitants a sense of common identity.

Despite accelerating depopulation, the Cévennes in general are less isolated than they were even thirty or so years ago and the remaining Cévenols a good deal less inward-looking. E. A. Martel, who systematically explored the gorges of the Tarn and the whole region in the 1880s and was one of the founders of the Club Cévenol, recorded that

> only a few years ago, the natives couldn't understand our finding it beautiful. 'It is bad country,' they would say in their rude patois, 'all rocks, no houses.' But in 1885 they were saying, 'It's true, this place is not so bad; all these posh visitors have already paid our taxes for the year'. And they were setting up shops, and building rooms to rent, and training their mules to carry the tourists.[111]

The Cévennes are indeed all rocks, but rocks of different kinds. The Causse Méjean, across which there are few roads, is a huge windswept limestone plateau with wide open views. In the past it produced some wheat and rye but was mainly dependent on sheep, and the ground floors of the isolated farmhouses served as pens for the resident flocks, for there was no transhumance here. (Transhumance is the term commonly employed for the twice-yearly migration of shepherds and their sheep from the plains up to summer pasture in the hills.) The sturdily-built houses had large roofs covered in *lauzes* (flat stones) which helped to capture the rainwater for storage.

The uplands round Mont Lozère by contrast are granitic and though there are vast grassy pastures, the poor soil, icy winds and heavy snows have made life hard for its farmers. In the summer months they welcomed the sheep from the plains, receiving in return for their grazing the droppings which helped to manure such productive land as they had. Their grey-pink houses reflect the need to shelter from this inclement environment for they are squat, with few openings, have low ceilings and were originally thatched to trap any warmth, but were given *lauze* tiles when rye was no longer grown. The best of the twentieth-century regional novelists, Jean-Pierre Chabrol commented that 'this land smells of death and broom' and

> up there when the *tramontane* begins to blow, there is a silence made by a thousand and one springs of clear water, enough water for a paradise on earth; only up there, there is not enough soil to hold it so the water runs off, spreads to the four points of the compass, melts away all over France.[112]

South of Mont Lozère, astride and across the Montagne de Bougès and down to the Corniche des Cévennes, that lovely road that winds through it and beyond it, is the true Cévenne, as Robert Louis Stevenson discovered on his travels there.

> Speaking largely, I was in the Cevennes at Monastier, and during all my journey; but there is a strict and local sense in which only this confused and shaggy country at my feet has any title to the name, and in this sense the peasantry employ the word. These are the Cevennes with an emphasis: the Cevennes of the Cevennes.[113]

Here the mountains are of schist, and space has become more restricted, with deep parallel valleys where the chestnut and mulberry grow. Narrow houses were built on the slopes of the terraced hills to catch the sun, and their top floors were often transformed into attics where silkworms could be bred. Then there is yet another area, different again, round Mont Aigoual, granitic and desolate like Mont Lozère. André Chamson described it in despair:

> Rising from a desert of lightning-struck trunks of dwarf trees, and torn-off branches covered in lichens and moss, from the bewitched landscape of a dead star, the Aigoual raises itself like the shoulder of some reclining god.[114]

Today, though still bleak, the reafforestation, mostly with pines, has somewhat softened its appearance, though Jean Carrière wrote of the harshness of life there about forty years ago in his novel, *L'Epervier de Maheux* which won the Prix Goncourt in 1972. He stressed the darker side rather than the more picturesque aspects that Chamson wrote of in many of his books, and when John Ardagh went to visit him in his chalet up near Mont Aigoual in 1988, Carrière told Ardagh that, 'the older Cévenol peasants hated me for the book but the younger ones were glad that I put my finger on the real problems and denounced a phoney folksy traditionalism.'[115]

Virtually the whole of these Cévennes are now encompassed within the Parc National des Cévennes, created in 1970 to help sustain a tolerable environment for its remaining inhabitants, to preserve local traditions and protect the wildlife. On the Causse Méjean there are wild boar, and now deer, beavers and capercaillie (*Tetrao urogallus*); and the vulture (*Gyps fulvus*) – which has become a protected species – have been reintroduced to their natural habitat.

In the wooded scrubby country of Mont Lozère and the Aigoual there are deer and moufflons (wild sheep), butterflies and wonderful dragonflies, the *Anax imperator* and the rare Alpine emerald (*Somatochlora alpestris*) amongst them; and there are known to be jenets, those shy creatures of whom it is so difficult to catch sight, in the more southerly Mediterranean parts.

One of the main information centres about the Parc is to be found at Florac, in the seventeenth-century château that was rebuilt after an earlier one had been completely destroyed in the Wars of Religion. A pleasant town, at the junction between the Causse Méjean and Mont Lozère, it is watered by the Tarn, the Tarnon and the Mimente, and fountains play in its streets. Stevenson found it 'notable besides, for its handsome women'.

His interest in the Cévennes was awakened by reading George Sand's novel *Le Marquis de Villemer* and, needing desperately to be on his own to sort out his feelings about Fanny Osbourne (whom he later married), he took himself to Le Monastier in September 1878 to begin a twelve-day walking tour. On his return he spent six months expanding his notes, adding details from topographical books and long pieces on the Camisards from the standard sources. *Travels with a Donkey in the Cevennes* was published in 1879, but without the charming little drawings (now at Yale University) that he made in his journal. In June of that year he wrote to a cousin that

it has good passages, I can say no more. A chapter called, 'The Monks', and then 'A Camp in the Dark', and a third, 'A Night in the Pines'. Each has I think some stuff in the writing . . . Whether the damned public – But that's all one. I've got 30 quid for it and it should have been 50.[116]

Stevenson set off with his recalcitrant Modestine and walked via Langogne, and across the Pic de Finiels 'which in clear weather commands a view over all Languedoc to the Mediterranean Sea. I have spoken with people who either pretended or believed that they had seen from the Pic de Finiels, white ships sailing by Montpellier and Cette'.

Although he found the stretch from Florac to Le Pont-de-

Montvert to be 'a pass like Killiecrankie; a deep turning gully in the hills, with the Tarn making a wonderful hoarse uproar far below, and craggy summits standing in the sunshine high above', at Le Pont de Montvert itself he decided that 'a subtle atmosphere distinguishes a town in England from a town in France, or even in Scotland', even though one of the first things he noticed was a Protestant temple. It is less noticeable now, but there is an ugly new building which houses the Ecomusée. The museum has sections on life in the past and what is being done to preserve it, for example by the restoration of buildings like the belltowers known as *clochers de tourmente*. These are to be found around Mont Lozère, a predominantly Catholic area where the bells called the faithful to Mass or simply marked the hours for the workers in the fields. It is also said that in times of storm the bell was rung continuously by day and by night to help travellers find their way. One of the favourite stories told round the fireside at the evening gatherings or *veillées*, was of the *curé* who rang his bell for three days and three nights by threading the bellcord through his bedroom window and attaching it to his foot. Examples of *clochers de tourmente* are to be seen at Serviès, Ouitet, Les Sagnes, Auriac and La Fage; it takes about four or five hours to drive round and see them all.

At Vialas, some few kilometres to the east of Le Pont-de-Montvert, the most attractive building is the Protestant temple. It is low-lying, with sloping *lauze*-tiled roofs, and were it not for its bell, one would take it for a smart set of cottages. There is a rather grand hotel there which makes a good base from which to explore the Voie Regordane, an ancient road which runs through nearby Génolhac.

The main route from Nîmes and Montpellier to Paris went through Alès to Le Puy-en-Velay, and this Cévenol stretch has been known from time immemorial as the Voie Regordane. No one is quite sure where its name came from and recent scholarship suggests that although the Romans may well have used the road, it long pre-dates them. It is thought to have originated as a *draille* – an unmade path on uncultivable land used by man and beast during the transhumance.

The earliest references are to a 'chemin de Saint-Gilles' and it is mentioned in an epic poem of the end of the twelfth century when Guillaume d'Orange (whom we met at St Guilhem-le-Désert) travelled along it on his way to recapture Nîmes from the Saracens. His knights (being good classical scholars) succeeded in their mission by hiding in barrels and thereby entering the city undetected.

When Languedoc became part of France at the end of the thirteenth century, the Rhône became and remained for centuries the main artery of transport and the Voie Regordane lost much of its importance. Most of it was cobbled rather than paved to avoid huge ruts being made by the cartwheels, but even so it must have made for a bumpy ride. By 1668 when Monsieur de Froidour was sent to inspect it and report on its condition, he found it had fallen into a sorry state. Now the D906 goes along odd stretches of it, and many of the Grandes Randonnées, the walkers' paths, follow its tracks, so ramblers can combine enjoyment of the natural beauties of the scenery with an element of exploration.

Génolhac is a typical 'village-rue', where the houses, in granite, run either side of a long main street. It has kept some vestiges of its distant past as an important stopping-place on the Voie Regordane, and it is worth looking for the characteristic façades that indicate which of the buildings served as warehouses. They commonly had two high-arched openings through which the carts could enter to unload their goods, and by their side a rectangular door which gave on to the staircase leading to the dwelling-rooms above. Génolhac was also a nail-making town, though it has nothing to show for that. A square tower remains of the twelfth-century château and there are vestiges of a fine Romanesque house by the side of the contemporaneous church of St Pierre, which has undergone many alterations, not least in 1885 when the chevet was replaced. Only the façade and its doorway is original; the gabled *clocher-peigne*, with its four arcades, is sixteenth-century.

Clochers-peignes are narrow, flat belfries with openings in which the bells are suspended, and are typical of the Cévenol

Romanesque style. There are dozens of them around, but like the châteaux hereabouts, are mostly in dire need of repair.

An excursion to the north of Génolhac takes one to Concoules, where there was a priory belonging to the abbey of Chaise Dieu. It was originally built to provide lodging and subsistence for the abbey's servants sent south into Languedoc to buy wine, oil, herbs and onions there. The early twelfth-century church of St Etienne has a fine *clocher-peigne* above a low gable and a seventeenth-century tribune in the interior.

Beyond Villefort, La Garde-Guérin remains a picturesque village with its paved streets and simple houses. It was founded by the bishops of Mende, who in the tenth century installed a community of nobles called *pariers* to escort travellers (for a fee) along these robber-infested roads. There were twenty-seven *pariers*, each of whom had a fortified house. Only a handful of the houses are left, and there are only a few remains of both the ramparts and the keep of the fortified castle. The Romanesque church of St Michel has a good barrel-vaulted ceiling.

The road back from La Garde-Guérin through Villefort and to the east of the D906 gives one an opportunity to see a number of spectacular châteaux and more charming small churches. The château of Brésis is in ruins; only the apse and parts of the walls of Notre Dame de Bonnevaux are still standing; and at Aujac both the church of St Martin and the château are in the last stages of dilapidation. The church at Sénéchas has however recently been restored and, though it is not always open, it is worth going to see it for the exterior alone, and for the lovely granite houses in the vicinity. Two particularly interesting Grandes Randonées start here.

Bessèges is altogether larger, and another 'village-rue', long and strung out. It was a prosperous coal-mining town but in 1861 a disastrous flood at Lalle killed 105 miners. There is an unusually good bookshop in the main street. Jean-Pierre Chabrol comes from nearby Chamborigaud, where there is a lovely single-span fifteenth-century bridge, the Pont de Rastel, with a spinning mill by its side.

Portes is to be found a little further south, an important stopping-place as it was at the junction of the *draille* leading from Provence up to Mont Lozère. It has a magnificent château, also in ruins, but ruins caused as much by man as by time. Excessive and thoughtless mining, especially after the First World War, has resulted in subsidence, and indeed the village itself, which clustered round its feet, had to be rebuilt some distance away. The early part of the château is fifteenth-century, with splendid machicolations and a small round watch tower, like a ship's prow, built precipitously out over a spur; additions were made some two hundred or so years later.

Although the countryside in the Cévennes is so beautiful that it might not matter much if one never saw a building at all, it is depressing that so many of them are in such a ruinous state. Albeit belatedly, efforts are being made to save some of them, just as they are to record living memories before they too are lost. Two-thirds of the indigenous population has gone and only a few summer residents have taken their place. Life has changed so radically in these villages that it is good to find people like Monique Manifacier, the schoolmistress at Mallenches (so small a hamlet that it does not figure on the maps), interviewing and publishing the recollections of some of the older inhabitants. The 84-year-old Xavier Mouline told her about his childhood:

Our village was not a wealthy one. The principal crop was chestnuts, the basic food of both man and beast. And even on them we economized . . . After that came rye and a little wheat . . . add to that potatoes, and garden produce from what has now become one huge bramble patch.

Every house had some silkworms though not in large quantities for lack of leaves to feed them. So we went to spend the summer months elsewhere. Hiring fairs were at Vans or St Ambroix in April and we would return home for the summer tasks of haymaking and harvest until June. After that we able-bodied men would go in a team to Mont Lozère or La Margeride; we would be reaping all day long. Then we would leave for the wine harvest in the south.[117]

Alès, known as one of the gateways to the Cévennes, is in some senses a frontier town as it lies on the edge of the mountain and the plain, in a loop of one of the many Gardons (the Gardon d'Alès). Here chestnut trees, so characteristic of the uplands, and olive trees, the very epitome of the Mediterranean, grow together.

Like much but not all of the Cévennes, Alès was profoundly Protestant, and although the Edict of Nantes had ostensibly ended the civil wars, after Henri IV's death there was to be recrudescence of religious revolt. Henri, Duc de Rohan, son-in-law to the great Sully, led the Protestants in Languedoc, but by now they were on the defensive. The General Synod of the Reformed Churches of France met in Alès in 1620 and two years later Louis XIII appeared in person at the head of the royal troops and defeated Rohan. Nothing loth, Rohan tried again, but after being beaten by Condé in 1629, submitted and accepted the *Grâce* of Alais (as Alès was spelled until 1926). This Act stripped the Protestants of their strongholds and political privileges, but they were allowed to continue to worship in their own way and in their own temples. In 1694, some nine years after the Revocation of the Edict of Nantes, Louis XIV, intent on rehabilitating Catholicism, made Alès into a bishopric.

The cathedral of St Jean is sadly undistinguished. It is a clumsy mixture of styles, with a Romanesque façade, a Gothic belltower and neo-Classical walls, with a neo-Gothic meridional interior. The bishop's palace, built between 1724 and 1741 by Rollin, is a good deal more attractive, and is now occupied by the Caisse d'Epargne.

Vauban was instructed to erect a royal fort on the site of the old château which, in 1789, was turned into a prison. As it still serves the same function one can only catch a glimpse of it set back behind the Jardins du Bosquet where there is a rather indifferent statue to Louis Pasteur. This was put up to commemorate Pasteur's years working there in 1865–9 trying to find an antidote to the parasite that in 1855 had attacked the silkworm. He did, but not in time to save the catastrophic decline of the industry which impoverished so many of the peasant producers.

In the nineteenth century, Alès enjoyed a new lease of life, though to see the city today one would not have thought that it had been a thriving coal-mining centre. André Chamson's family settled there at the time that it was a town

> newly caught-up in the fever of business, a town of commerce and industry, where the chances of growing rich did not seem too remote. For long years before that, the old city, curved like a wing in the bend of the Gardon river, had nestled undisturbed behind its fortifications, not far from Anduze, a town of potters and small craftsmen. Coal and iron had transformed Alès into an industrial centre. Within a few years, it was surrounded by new suburbs, and a population of more than thirty thousand had grown up round the mines with their huge pithead wheels, round the black wilderness of slag-heaps where grass no longer grew, and the workshops spitting brilliant sprays of sparks. It drew into itself all the wealth of the region. With its collieries and foundries, its iron and steel works, its warehouse and storage depots, it was rather like one of the mushroom cities of the New World, a sort of Chicago raised upon old-world foundations.
> But it was a Chicago without a future . . .[118]

Chamson was writing in 1957 and his pessimism was justified; since then all the mines but one have been closed. A fascinating underground museum, the Mine-Témoin, has recently been opened in one of the old mine-shafts and covers all aspects of mining. The largest collection of mineralogical specimens in France is to be seen in the Ecole de Mines, founded in 1843.

Alès also boasts an archaeological and fine arts museum, the Musée municipal du Colombier and the Musée-Bibliothèque Pierre-André Benoit (PAB). The last is housed in the château de Rochebelle, refashioned at the end of the eighteenth century in neo-Classical style by François Pierre de Tubeuf, a mine-owner. Pierre-André Benoit, sculptor, poet and printer of limited-edition books, has given the city both his collection of paintings by artists such as Picasso, Braque, Picabia and Miró, and his extensive library, which includes examples of the books he has printed. The only remaining piano factory in France is also to be found at Alès and concerts are held in the old glassworks, the Verrerie de Rochebelle, a fine example of restored industrial architecture.

The château de Rousson, just off the road going north to St Ambroix, is worth a short visit. It is an early seventeenth-century square building with four towers at each corner and is, unusually, full of good period furniture.

Anduze is sometimes called the 'Geneva of the Cévennes', for it was a powerful Protestant stronghold; indeed all its fortifications were destroyed in 1629 and only the Tour de l'Horloge of 1320 is still standing. It is now a rather cosy small town which has made much of its living from glazed ceramic pots; they were supplied to the Orangerie at Versailles in the eighteenth century and are still being produced. The only drawback is that the larger ones, lovely for the garden, are rather bulky to transport. There is an odd little fountain of 1648 capped with polychrome tiles in the Burgundian manner; one of the largest Protestant temples in France, rebuilt in 1823; and in the Parc des Cordeliers, a statue of the *trobairitz* Clara d'Anduze.

A little steam train, not yellow this time, puffs and toots in and out of the tunnels and round the hills from Anduze to St Jean-du-Gard. On the way it stops at the Bambouseraie de Prafrance, an enormous botanical garden started by Eugène Mazel (whose date of birth seems unknown and who 'disappeared' in 1882) who went to China and Japan to study mulberry trees. Today the garden is almost entirely devoted to bamboo of which there are more than a hundred varieties growing there. One walks through great forests of over-arching plants, through water gardens filled with lotus and water-lilies, nursery gardens and greenhouses. All kinds of artefacts – from plant-holders to furniture – made from this versatile plant are on sale. If the Bambouseraie seems foreign to these parts, the same cannot be said about the museum devoted to the history of Protestantism at Mialet.

Just as the west of Languedoc is branded with the memory of the Albigensian Crusade and the disappearance of the Cathars, so the Cévennes are marked by a more recent episode in the history of religious intolerance. Gide remembered his grandfather talking of the 'persecutions that had dealt so unsparingly with their ancestors, or at least a certain tradition of resistance'. Once again it was a king of France who set about eradicating non-conformity by the sword, and while the Huguenots had nothing in common with the Cathars, they were to suffer in similar ways.

In the early sixteenth century the Reform movement spread from Geneva, brought across the Rhône and up the two Gardon rivers by itinerant pedlars, Bibles in hand. It took hold rapidly in the Cévennes where puritanism and asceticism accorded well with the spirit of Cévenol independence, and the new ideas met with fervent approval from the wool-carders, silk merchants and cobblers. By 1600 there were virtually no Catholic Masses being held in the Cévennes.

Although with the Edict of Nantes of 1598 the Protestants had been granted freedom of worship and certain political privileges, the Peace (or *Grâce*) of Alais, only some thirty years later, was the first step in renewed royal and episcopal hostility to members of what was sneeringly called the 'Religion Prétendue Réformée'. By 1669 the Huguenots (as the Protestants were less prejudiciously and more commonly called) were no longer allowed to hold office. Even though they were responsible for much of France's economic vitality, in 1683 Louis XIV authorized the *dragonnades*. In these, troops were employed to enforce conversions to Catholicism, since preachers even as persuasive as Fénelon had, like St Bernard of Clairvaux before him, failed to achieve them by more rational means. Two years later all Huguenot services were made illegal, their pastors exiled and their temples demolished.

Despite wholesale emigration (and many of the silk-workers came to England and settled in Spitalfields) and mass apostasy, a hard core of Huguenots remained in the Cévennes. They continued to hold prayer meetings and Bible readings behind closed doors or in deserted places, even though they well knew that if they were discovered the pastors would be executed, the men sent to the galleys and the women imprisoned for life. From 1685 onwards, with the arrival of Nicolas de Lamoignon Basville as Intendant, forced conversions became ever more numerous as the methods employed became ever more draconian. Villages were razed, their inhabitants deported and children removed from their families. A hideous atmosphere of repression prevailed, but Protestantism did not die; it simply went underground. The fire of prophetism smouldered beneath the embers of the *dragonnades*, and the faith was to be fanned back into life by a number of artisans, peasants and shepherds, illiterate save for their knowledge of the Bible, but possessed by religious frenzy.

The event, however, that sparked off the uprising of 1702 in the Cévennes was, once again, a murder. On 24 July 1702, at Le Pont de Montvert, Abraham Mazel and 'Esprit' (Pierre) Séguier, two of the apocalyptic visionaries, and some fifty enraged Cévenols killed the Abbé François du Chayla (or Chaila), Inspector of Missions for the Cévennes. Chayla was, says Stevenson in one of my most treasured quotations, 'a conscientious person, who seems to have been intended by nature for a pirate, and now fifty-five, an age by which a man has learned all the moderation of which he is capable'.

Moderation was certainly not to be much in evidence on either side during the ensuing war. Some fifteen hundred Camisards, as they came to be called because they sacked a shirt (*chemise/camisa*) factory and dressed themselves in the clothes they found there, held twenty-five thousand royal troops at bay for the better part of two years. Although they were not well co-ordinated and operated only in small groups, their knowledge of the terrain ensured that their guerrilla tactics were effective even against such experienced soldiers as the Maréchals de Broglie, Montrevel and Villars.

The King's forces were under the overall command of Basville whom we have encountered before. Stendhal, who saw Basville's portrait in Montpellier (it is now in the Musée Fabre), thought he looked 'aristocratic, dull and stately', but Saint-Simon was his usual waspish self:

> For very many years Languedoc had been suffering under the tyranny of Bâville . . . a shrewd and intelligent man, well-informed, energetic, industrious, but sly, utterly ruthless . . . Above all, he had a lust for power, crushing all opposition, ready to stick at nothing in order to gain his ends . . .[119]

It was no simple matter for Basville to suppress the revolt, for according to Voltaire

> a large portion of the country secretly befriended [the Camisards.] Their war-cry was: *No taxes and liberty of conscience*; and it won over the populace on every hand . . . The reverses sustained by the king's arms at that time gave encouragement to the fanatics of Languedoc who, looking to Heaven for help, received assistance from the Allies.[120]

The Camisard leaders, like the Camisards themselves, were artisans or peasants. They were Abraham Mazel, born in St Jean-du-Gard; Roland (whose real name was Pierre Laporte) who combined wool-carding with gelding pigs; and Jean Cavalier, a shepherd and baker's apprentice, the only one with any real organizational ability.

Every kind of atrocity took place during the two years that the war lasted until Maréchal de Villars, by now the military commander, persuaded Cavalier, who has been described as a 'Cromwell *manqué*, and with the same vanity', to negotiate. Villars offered to make Cavalier a colonel and let him raise a regiment of Camisards to go and fight in Spain with whom France was then at war. Cavalier accepted but his fellows thought they had been betrayed and he had to flee in the summer of 1704. He did indeed later command a regiment in Spain, but against the French. In 1738 he became lieutenant-governor of Jersey and, a year later, a major-general in the British army. One at least of the Allies got their money's worth. (In 1707 a coffee-house called The Camisards opened in St Martin's Lane, London.)

Roland was captured a month after Cavalier's defection and the fighting came to an end, though the Cévennes were left depopulated and impoverished for years. The persecution of the Protestants continued intermittently, as witness the Calas and Sirven cases, but the Camisard rebellion was the last religious and the last peasant war in France.

The history of this appalling episode is told in the Musée du Désert with a wealth of detail and documentation. The museum, tucked away at Mialet in a peaceful green enclave, is in the Mas Soubeyran, the seventeenth-century house where Roland was born. Here the term 'désert', taken from the Old Testament – 'And thou shalt remember all the way [sic] which the Lord thy God led thee these forty years in the wilderness' (as the St James Version translates it) – denotes both a period, from the Revocation of the Edict of Nantes in 1685 to the Edict of Tolerance in 1787, and a place, a cave or just a remote spot in the countryside where the faithful could risk meeting.

The museum is in two parts. In the Mas itself the rooms have been furnished to give a vivid impression of a typical Cévenol household. There is a fine collection of Bibles, Communion plate and *méreaux*, the tiny lead tokens issued to members of each church to avoid infiltration by government spies. There is also an ingenious pulpit made as part of a grain tub and into which it could be folded at the first cry of alarm. The second part of the museum is in a rather unattractive modern building called the 'Mémorial' in which there is a reconstruction of Marie Durand's cell in the Tour de Constance at Aigues-Mortes, and some fascinating exhibits, not the least of which are a collection of Huguenot jewellery and a galley-oar, 12 metres long and weighing 130 kilograms. Five men would have been chained to oars such as this and it brings vividly home what risks the Huguenots were prepared to take for their faith.

Thousands of Protestants gather early in September each year from all over France for prayer meetings at the Mas Soubeyran to honour their ancestors and reaffirm their own beliefs.

*

St Jean-du-Gard, where Stevenson sold his donkey Modestine, is another pleasant small town with some attractive houses and a *filature* (spinning-mill) built in 1838. Known as the Maison Rouge, it is now occupied by a furniture factory and is the only one out of twenty in the town not to have been demolished. The Musée des Vallées Cévenoles is in a rambling seventeenth-century staging inn and imparts a good deal of information despite its slightly chaotic layout. It has domestic and agricultural tools, including several *bâts*, the packsaddles in which virtually everything was transported. Many were hinged at the extremities to make unloading easier and in the centre so that they could be laid flat to make beds for the muleteers. *Bâtard* as the word for a child born out of wedlock has been traced to the randy habits of the muleteers on these *bâts*.

The room devoted to silkworms is of the greatest interest. Silk weaving was firmly entrenched in Lyon by 1550 but the silk thread had to be imported and was expensive. Henri IV thought that encouraging sericulture in France would be one way of re-establishing economic prosperity after the havoc caused by the Wars of Religion. In 1603 he had 60,000 young mulberry trees imported from Italy and to set the example planted 20,000 of them in the Tuileries Gardens in Paris. He also erected a model *magnanerie* (a silkworm-rearing shed) there. Over the next five years some four million *Morus alba*, the white-fruited mulberry tree, were raised by the professional nurserymen of Tours and Nîmes (including our old friend Traucat), and hundreds of thousands of silkworm eggs were distributed with them.

It was not until a century later, when the exceptionally cold winter of 1709 killed enormous numbers of the chestnut trees on which the Cévenols had so largely depended, that sericulture became the prime, rather than a secondary, occupation in the area. It was so successful that the mulberry tree was soon dubbed the *arbre à or*, whereas the chestnut had been the *arbre à pain*. Raising silkworms and spinning silk were both perfect employments for a cottage industry.

The female of the *bombyx mori* moth lays three to four

hundred eggs which have to be stored at a low temperature until they are ready to hatch into grubs, caterpillars or worms. This stage must coincide with the appearance of the first mulberry leaves. Locke tells of one common method used by his landlady to ensure that this happened.

> This day Mme Fisket's silk worms began some of them to work. She took eggs and wrapped them up in a linen cloth on Good Friday and so wore them in some warm place about her night and day till the Monday following they were hatched. They usually put the eggs hatching in Holy Week, but that which best governs the time is the budding of the mulberry trees, that the worms, when hatched, may have food.[121]

In the museum there are examples of these linen bags, which the women wore between their breasts, though Locke is too fastidious to say so.

Once the eggs are hatched the grubs have to be fed five or six times during the day and twice or three times more at night with an enormous quantity of chopped-up leaves. The grubs increase their weight by 10,000 times between birth and maturity. During the course of a month they shed their skins four times and measure about five centimetres. At this point the worms stop feeding, attach themselves to a twig (or these days plastic contraptions called *hérissons*, because they look like hedgehogs) and start to spin a cocoon of silk thread around themselves. In three days of ceaseless spinning, the thread, in one continuous length of about 1,500 metres, is ejected in short loops in a figure-of-eight pattern which involves the creature in 300,000 movements of its head. The worm is now a tiny shrunken insect wrapped inside the cocoon and, temporarily worn out, goes to sleep. Two days later it moults yet again, and develops a hard skin. Ten to twelve days later still the chrysalis, as it has now become, swells and emerges from the cocoon in what the Chinese described as 'the great awakening', the Greeks the 'psyche' and the sericulturalists the 'imago' or perfect silk moth. The moths mate immediately, and the female lays eggs twice within two to three days, and then dies, a victim to its *raison d'être*.

While the best cocoons are allowed to hatch into moths for breeding purposes, if the silk is to be harvested, the chrysalis must be killed before the moth emerges or else the thread will be spoiled. The cocoons are therefore put into boiling water, which not only kills the chrysalis but makes it easier to find the starting-point of the thread for reeling.

Both rearing the silkworms and spinning the silk could be done in the farmhouses without too much special equipment. The eggs were distributed by brokers who also collected and marketed the thread, enriching themselves as well as the peasants, whose only income it now became. Each *magnanier* reared an average of 200 kilograms of cocoons which produced about 60 kilograms of raw silk. *Magnaneries* were added as upper storeys to the houses and many examples of this characteristic domestic architecture can still be seen.

By the end of the eighteenth century, with the coming of industrialization and machinery, spinning mills were erected, usually on the outskirts of the towns or villages where there was plenty of light, for it was delicate work, and almost always undertaken by women. Alas, not a single one remains in its original state, but a number of them are being brought back into use. An organization called Le Chemin de la Soie is busy restoring some, which can be visited, or turning them into museums. They are to be found at Molezon (Magnanerie de La Roque); St Nazaire-des-Gardies (Domaine Séricole de Puechlong); Monoblet (Filature de Gréfeuilhe); Molières-Cavaillac (La Maison des Magnans); and Valleraugue (Filature Le Mazel). A derelict *filature* by the crossroads at the Lassalle turning on the road between St Jean-du-Gard and Anduze at the Pont de Salindres still has its fine double staircase reserved for the women workers and there is a handsome ruin of another huge one by the side of the Hérault at Laroque, just south of Ganges.

It is a beautiful drive from St Jean-du-Gard through Lassalle to St Hippolyte-du-Fort, in the charmingly named Cigaloise, which has a museum entirely devoted to silk in an old barracks complex. Here the Musée de la Soie concentrates on the processes involved after the silkworm has done its work, and one is shown how the cocoons were heated, and the silk reeled and spun. The boutique there sells silk underwear, beautiful but expensive shirts, and lengths of material.

Ganges is another, rather more bustling silk town, famed for the stockings it supplied to Louis XIV and thereafter to the rich until cheap nylons brought demand for them to an end. It also became notorious for a macabre saga that took place there in the middle of the seventeenth century.

Diane de Joannis Roussant married as her second husband the Marquis de Ganges in 1658. (His brother, the Comte de Ganges was married to Jeanne de Gévaudan, with whom both Basville and Bonzi were in love, and for whom the latter built the Hôtel de Ganges in Montpellier.) Some years later the Marquis and his two other brothers, the Abbé de Ganges and the Chevalier de Ganges, started behaving in what can only be called a Grand Guignol manner. The Marquise, a considerable heiress, by now realizing that she had been married only for her money, made a will in her mother's favour and registered it at Aix-en-Provence. When her husband discovered this he was so angry he asked the Abbé to avenge him and smartly took himself off while his brother did so.

The Abbé started by poisoning Diane's food but to no effect and then persuaded her, with greater success, to get her to make a new will in favour of her husband. Although she did so, Diane did not revoke the earlier one. Notwithstanding, on 17 May 1667 the Abbé laced her purgative with poison and when this failed to work, he stood over her with more poison in one hand, a pistol in the other and the Chevalier, his sword at the ready, by his side. 'Madame', said the Abbé, 'it is time to die: here are iron, fire and poison. Choose.'[122]

The poor woman drank the poison and while the two villains went to fetch the family chaplain to give her the last sacraments, she tied her sheets together, let herself out of the window and fled to a neighbouring house. The Abbé and the Chevalier tracked her down and the Chevalier struck her twice with his sword while the Abbé took a pot shot at her, and missed. Both men by now sure, in spite of their incredible bungling, that the Marquise was dead or at least dying, then took to their heels. In fact neither of Diane's wounds was fatal but she died of poisoning on 5 June.

The Abbé and the Chevalier had left the country but the Marquis was arrested and tried by the *parlement* of Toulouse. His property was confiscated, his patent of nobility abolished and he was exiled for life. The Abbé eventually went to Holland where, under a false name, he found work as a tutor to a young nobleman. He fell in love with one of the girls of the family and proposed to her but as he had not revealed his aristocratic origins the union was thought unseemly. Love overcame fear about his past misdeeds and when he revealed who he was, he was dismissed. But his inamorata followed him to Amsterdam where he made a great show of remorse, and ended his days as a Protestant.

It was a tale that kept the court gossips and letter-writers busy for years and inspired the Marquis de Sade to write *La Marquise de Ganges*, a book which ran to five hundred pages.

If the behaviour of the aristocracy sometimes left much to be desired, that of the peasants some hundred years later evoked nothing but admiration from Arthur Young:

> Every man has an olive, a mulberry, an almond, or a peach-tree, and vines scattered among them; so that the whole ground is covered with the oddest mixture of these plants, and bulging rocks that can be conceived. The inhabitants of this village [Sauve, to the east of St Hippolyte-du-Fort] deserve encouragement for their industry; and if I was a French minister, they should have it. They would soon turn all the deserts around them into gardens. Such a knot of active husbandmen, who turn their rocks into scenes of

fertility, because I suppose THEIR OWN, would do the same by the wastes, if animated by the same omnipotent principle.[123]

When Adrienne Durand-Tullou went from Nîmes in 1937 to be village schoolmistress at Rogues just south of Le Vigan, she was struck rather by 'a feeling of having left a welcoming and easy-going world and entered another, enigmatic and severe'. However, she came to love this countryside and its people; she married a local peasant (her word), and has since become a great authority on local anthropology. In 1965 she fulfilled one of her ambitions by going with the shepherds up to the summer pasture lands along the drovers' paths (*faire la draille*). They set off on 9 June.

At the first glimmer of dawn, the doors were flung open wide in front of the straining mass, in prey to the mysterious call of the heights. No force could have held them in the sheepfold. The beasts knew that the moment had come to depart; driven by instinct, they rushed forth headlong. A winding river of fleeces flowed out from the yard with a fantastic chorus of bleating, a veritable hymn to the new, nature and open spaces. With the bleats there mingled peremptory barking, hoarse shouts and more tuneful cries. So began the concert of the sheep-bells. The *dralhaus* (the big bells for the transmigration); the *clapas* and the *clapetas* (the small bells worn by young sheep): *montem, montem* (up we go) proclaimed the first; *devalem, devalem* (we go down) declared the second; *benlèu, benlèu* timidly ventured the last.[124]

I met a farmer in St Jean-du-Gard who told me that thirty years ago he and his father and their dogs took two flocks each of about two hundred sheep up to pasture with three shepherds in front, three behind and one on each side. The sheep with their brandmarks and coloured pompons made a jolly sight as they travelled along the *drailles* and through villages where everyone turned out to watch the procession and the shepherds had their work cut out, he said, in trying to prevent a nifty thief from nabbing a fat ewe for his wife's pot.

The journey of 120–150 kilometres took a week and they all

returned in the middle or at the end of September. Nowadays most of the sheep are transported by lorry but one flock of about 2,000 head still goes up via St Jean-du-Gard early each summer. My friend said he only partially regretted the passing of the *drailles*, because his nostalgia was tempered by memories of the discomforts, and the loneliness. One gets some idea of the discomfort and the danger from seeing, in the museum at Le Vigan, one of the shepherds' portable cabins and a dog-collar spiked to keep the wolves at bay.

Le Vigan is a cool, sympathetic town proud of its two native heroes to whom statues have been erected. The Chevalier d'Assas, whose courage Voltaire so admired, was caught by the enemy while reconnoitering on his own in a wood during the battle of Klostercamp in 1760. Ordered at bayonet-point to keep silent, he alerted his regiment by calling out 'A moi, Auvergne, the enemy is here', and was promptly killed. Sergeant Triaire was also a redoubtable soldier, who served in Bonaparte's army and distinguished himself at the battle of Castiglione. During the Egyptian campaign he blew up the magazine, and himself, to prevent Turkish troops from taking the fort of El Arich.

But the special attraction of Le Vigan is the Musée Cévenol in a building that has successively been a tannery, a silk-spinnery and a glove factory and is on the banks of the River Arre by the side of a Romanesque bridge, where there was once a Benedictine abbey. The different areas of the Cévennes are explained with acceptable didacticism and two rooms are devoted to the crafts of the past; basket-work, glass-blowing, tinning, woodwork and pottery. Furniture and some beautiful silk clothes are also displayed, and one is shown how wool and silk were treated. There is much about local food and wine too; the vine and chestnuts, (*chataignes* are wild chestnuts and *marrons* cultivated and grafted on to chestnut root-stocks); pigs and home-made *charcuterie*; sheep and goats, and *pélardons*, the cheeses made from their milk.

M. Betham-Edwards, who edited the centennial edition of Arthur Young's *Travels in France* and thought it fitting to follow in the Suffolk squire's footsteps to see the countryside for herself, had comments as perceptive as his to make. 'The Gard,' she said

> is by no means one of the most favoured departments. The phylloxera and the silkworm pest have greatly affected the prosperity of both town and country, yet the stranger halting at Le Vigan . . . finds himself amid a condition of things usually regarded as Utopian – a cheerful, well-dressed, self-supporting population, vagrancy unknown, and a distribution of well-being perhaps without a parallel in any part of Europe. Again and again will occur to his mind the famous passage with which Virgil concluded his second Georgic, that beautiful picture of pastoral happiness, which if imaginary in old Roman days, is so often realized in the rural France of our own.[125]

A. S. Byatt, who has a house just outside Le Vigan, paints a similar picture, if not of pastoral happiness, of a food-shopper's heaven:

> Every Saturday everyone goes to market, to bring or to buy, cheeses, sheep, goat, cow, freshly dripping and damp, or drily wrinkled like old wax seals, tubs of curds, heaps of fresh mussels and oysters, a *camionette* with a tank of weaving river-trout, heaps of vegetables, all uneven and gleaming and locally grown, melons and redcurrants, honey from high pastures, quails and ducks, alive in coops or neatly dissected on stalls.[126]

However Virgilian the countryside and whatever the choice of foods available in the market at Le Vigan, it is salutary if depressing to find a recipe for *aigo boulido* (boiled water) in a slim booklet called *La Cuisine Cévenole*. It was admittedly only consumed for breakfast and was not considered a main dish, which was just as well, since it consisted only of water, garlic, salt, olive oil, nutmeg and bread. Not everything was so sparse, though for centuries the staple food came from chestnuts

which, as the same little cookery book explains, 'have a high
calorific value and in terms of nutrition some similarities with
wheat; they are recommended for people suffering physical and
mental debility, convalescents and those prone to varicose veins
and piles'.

Apart from game and freshwater fish, the most substantial
food comes of course from the sheep; both mutton and lamb are
served in any number of different ways, and one of the local
specialities is tripe. The Cévenols are occasionally referred to
derogatively as *manje-tripes* and a bullfight in Alès in May 1990
was advertised as the 'Feria des Mangetripes'. I have to confess
that I rather share Henry James's views about tripe since an
incident some thirty years ago when we found ourselves without
plans for the night and just stopped in a village hoping for the
best. It was hot and we were tired, and anyhow there was no
choice, so we sat ourselves down in the hotel restaurant. As
there was no menu we looked forward to taking pot luck. The
pièce de résistance turned out to be a dish of hard little bits of
gristle swimming about in fat. One mouthful and I was a
member of the resistance, but alas, by this time the village
worthies had heard us talking English and the mayor came over
to introduce himself and shake our hands. He told us that we
had arrived at the centre of the world as he sat himself down
beside us, intent on a lengthy conversation. 'Eat up', he said,
'eat up'. We somehow felt that the honour of Great Britain was
at stake, and did so. One consolation was the wine with which
we washed down each greasy gobbet; there was plenty of Côtes
du Rhône from the nearby vineyards of Tavel, so loved by
Philippe IV, and Lirac, so much appreciated by the popes at
Avignon.

Pont St Esprit was originally called St Saturnin-du-Port and
grew up round a Cluniac foundation in the tenth century. Its
strategic position led to its rapid expansion and made a bridge
across the Rhône a commercial necessity (the Romans had built
none between Vienne and Arles).

The bridge was put up between 1265 and 1309 by the Confrérie of the Frères Pontifes, an association of clerical and lay volunteers, who raised the money for it by subscription. It is said that twelve men worked on it, with the help of a mysterious thirteenth – the Holy Ghost. It has been considerably extended since then and is now nearly a kilometre long; nineteen of its twenty-five arches are the medieval ones. Shipping found it difficult to manoeuvre under the bridge and there were so many disasters that Stendhal recommended the removal of one of its piers. 'So notorious was its reputation', he was told, 'that when fear gives them the courage to brave the stares and quips of all the passers-by, the timorous, both women and men, are put ashore upstream of the bridge, to be picked up again a hundred paces below it'.

At the western extremity of the bridge vestiges of the early fourteenth-century Hospice du St Esprit and the ruins of a somewhat later collegiate church, with a Flamboyant Gothic portal (1475–7), still stand within the rather gloomy remains of the demolished citadel. The latter was built by Maréchal Ornano in 1585 and later enlarged by Vauban.

A handsome monumental double staircase erected on the quai de Luynes in the nineteenth century leads to the large *place* above, from which there is a magnificent view across the river. The *place* was formerly a cemetery and was surrounded by sanctuaries. There remain the churches of St Pierre, rebuilt by Franque between 1779 and 1784, but now deconsecrated and closed; St Saturnin, the parish church, started in 1340 and only completed some hundred and fifty years later; and the chapelle des Pénitents, with an attractive Baroque façade of 1656 and a bizarre little nineteenth-century arch perched on the roof above the entrance.

There are some seventeenth-century hôtels in the main part of the town and the Musée Paul Raymond in the former Hôtel de Ville has an important collection of apothecaries' jars from the pharmacy of the Hospice du St Esprit, including some lovely Montpellier ware.

*

Bagnols-sur-Cèze, originally a spa, was a flourishing silk town from the seventeenth century onwards and has since become the centre for Côtes du Rhône wines, which have been transported for centuries in barrels simply labelled 'CDR'. The centre of the town is the arcaded place Mallet where the market was held, but it is now disfigured by doing duty as a car park. It is dominated by the Tour de l'Horloge, erected in the fourteenth century by Philippe IV and surrounded by mostly seventeenth-century golden limestone houses, amongst them the Hôtel Mallet (the municipal library), the Hôtel de Marmier, and next to it the Hôtel Madier in which the Hôtel de Ville and the museum of fine art are to to found. Bagnols was one of first towns to have a municipal museum. It was started in 1859 by Léon Alègre in one room into which he crammed everything regardless, from fossils to steam engines. After his death it was run by his daughter but in 1917 the painter Albert André was pressed to become curator

> by a strong-minded citizen who was at one and the same time acting magistrate, municipal councillor and a pork butcher. My friend was a pork butcher in name only for, in keeping with the traditions of the south, he left the labours and the cares of his business to his wife so as to give all his attention to politics, literature and art. He had attached me to his pretty town by ties of sausages and tripe sausages (*andouillettes*) which his wife prepared to perfection.[127]

André feared the quality of the *andouillettes* might deteriorate if he refused the offer, but he found the butcher's conclusion irresistible: '"it's a foot in the stirrup; today Bagnols, tomorrow the Louvre." That clinched it.' André recounted this to Renoir, who often stayed with him at his family home nearby. 'My friend,' Renoir said,

> all my life I've dreamed of such good fortune. Accept! Just because once in my life I refused the charge of the museum which Gambetta offered me, in one of those moments of despondency when I had thoughts of giving up painting for good – there's no reason why you should follow my example. Accept: stuff painting.[128]

André took the job, and made the museum famous. In the winter of 1923/4 the local firemen, holding their annual celebrations in the same building, set fire to it and a large number of paintings and objects were destroyed. André told his Parisian friends of the disaster and many of them, including Monet, Marquet, Signac, Bonnard, Vollard, Clemenceau and Durand-Ruel gave him replacements for the paintings that were lost.

The most remarkable piece of sculpture is a bronze made in about 1903 by Camille Claudel. *L'Imploration* expresses only too eloquently her desperation at the ending of her liaison with Rodin. The gift in 1971 by George Bresson and his wife Adèle, of whom there is a fine portrait (1908) by Kees van Dongen, of paintings by Marquet, Bonnard and Matisse and others has added immeasurably to the collection. There are also works by nineteenth-century Lyonnais painters such as Louis Carrand, François-Auguste Ravier and François Vernay.

The town also boasts a museum devoted to archaeology and it is intriguing that it has an obscure connection with the Jacobites. In 1700 the Comte de Lussan's daughter married the Duke of Albemarle, one of James II's bastards. After his death, much to her mother's snobbish disgust, she married Lord Forth, whose uncle, the Earl of Perth and father, the Earl of Melfort had both followed James II into exile in France. Lord Forth took part, as a major-general, in the 1715 Jacobite uprising by the side of the Old Pretender, and two of his sons were with Charles Edward (who, it will be remembered, was married to Louise de Stolberg) at Culloden. The family house, the Hôtel Melfort, is still to be seen at 15 rue Crémieux and there was a promenade at Bagnols still called 'la Milorde' until the early years of this century.

Le Puy Andaon was a prehistoric site where, in the tenth century, the important Benedictine abbey of St André was built to serve travellers on one of the major pilgrim routes. During the thirteenth century, when Languedoc became part of France, the kings protected the abbey and a new town –

Villeneuve-lès-Avignon – was built. Of the keep erected by Philippe IV in 1293–1307 to protect his bank where the Pont St Bénézet debouched, only the tower remains; it was given a new storey, added in 1360, and the little watch-tower dates from the fifteenth century.

In 1307, to escape from the feuding amongst the aristocratic families in Rome, the papacy removed itself to Avignon encouraged by Philippe IV, who thought he could more easily control the popes if he had them nearer at hand. Clement V, a Frenchman, moved into the bishop's palace and it was his successor, Clement VI, who started the new Palais des Papes in 1334. Although the papacy moved back to Rome in 1377, by which time there had been seven Frenchmen on the seat of St Peter, many of the cardinals remained in Avignon during the Great Schism with an anti-pope at their head.

Since Avignon was too small to accommodate all the cardinals they installed themselves in Villeneuve-lès-Avignon. They built fifteen or so sumptuous hôtels, known here as *livrées*, and the town is often referred to as a *ville cardinalice*.

Jean II built the Fort St André on a high grassy mound by the abbey between 1362 and 1369 so that he could keep an eye on the popes across the Rhône. It has immense encircling walls which are pierced only by one great gateway flanked by massive twin towers. Apart from the little twelfth-century chapel of Notre Dame de Belvezet, there are few remains of the abbey though there is a large terrace and a magnificent Italian-style garden from which one gets a splendid view across the river.

In 1352 the conclave at Avignon elected as pope Jean Birelle, the General of the Carthusians (an order founded in 1084 by St Bruno). He declined to serve because he thought he was not worthy of such high office. Cardinal Etienne Aubert was then chosen in his place and took the name of Innocent VI. Innocent decided to transform his *livrée* in the Val de Bénédiction into a monastery to honour Birelle, and gave the land to the Carthusians. Work on the Chartreuse started in 1356 and was continued after Innocent's death by his nephew. The whole ensemble covers a huge area, which is all the more astonishing as in the early days of the Chartreuse there were only twelve Fathers, though their number was doubled later.

The entrance to the cloister is through a monumental gateway added in 1644. The buildings which one visits consist of the mid-fourteenth century small cloister, the chapter house, the sacristans' courtyard with a well and a fine staircase, the church, the refectory and the offices, all of which were used by the whole community. The Fathers lived in their own tiny two-roomed cells, which had a small courtyard with a latchet giving on to the large cloister.

Innocent VI, at his own request, was buried in the chapelle de la Trinité in the church, where the wall frescoes are attributed to Matteo Giovanetti, who also worked at the Palais Neuf at Avignon in about 1354–5. Innocent's white marble tomb is magnificent; his effigy, by Barthélemy Cavalier, lies on an arcaded dais beneath an elaborate canopy sculpted with figures and Gothic pinnacles. In 1835 when Mérimée saw it, it was in use as a rabbit hutch, but it was obviously in better condition when Locke was there: 'In their chappell Pope Innocent the 6th lies interd; he died 1362, & in a litle chappel in their convent stands a plain, old chair where he was infallible. I sat too little a while in it to get that priviledg.'[129]

Virtually none of the *livrées* themselves remain but the hôtel of Pierre de Luxembourg, a young cardinal who died there in 1385, still stands, albeit refashioned in the seventeenth century when it was given a new façade and a monumental staircase. Cinq-Mars' friend De Thou was held prisoner here in August 1642, before they were both taken upstream by the dying Richelieu to be executed in Lyon. Alfred de Vigny, in his novel *Cinq-Mars, ou une conjuration sous Louis XIII*, imagines Richelieu trailing them behind him as,

flaunting to all eyes on both banks the indulgence of his hatred, he slowly mounted the river on barges with gilded oars, bedecked with his own colours and coat-of-arms, himself reclining in the first, and towing his two victims in the second at the end of a long chain . . . Often, of an evening . . . the two young prisoners could be seen standing, each supporting the other, and watching with unclouded brow the river waters glide swiftly by.[130]

The Hôtel de Pierre de Luxembourg underwent many vicissitudes, and in 1876 two Lyonnais silk-workers installed their looms in it. It was subsequently used as a chemist's shop and a chair factory but now it is a museum. Among the many treasures are a very beautiful seated ivory Virgin and Child where the figures gracefully follow the curve of the elephant tusk. It dates from 1320–30 and in style is typical of contemporary Parisian ivorywork. There is also a second Virgin and Child in alabaster from the east of France or the Rhineland. It is double, with both Virgin and Child depicted on each face, and was perhaps intended to be seen from either side of a choir screen.

The great masterpiece, however, is *Le Couronnement de la Vierge*. It was so to speak 'discovered' by Mérimée in 1835 when he saw it hanging in the bedroom of the Superior of the Hospice. Attributed variously to Giotto, Dürer, Jan van Eyck and Fouquet, it was not until 1938 that Charles Sterling conclusively proved it to be by Enguerrand Quarton. Quarton was born in Picardy and worked in Avignon from 1447 to 1466.

The painting, dateable to 1453–4, is a powerful and elaborate composition. The Virgin is shown in the centre with two virtually identical figures of God on each side of her, holding above her head a crown surmounted by the Holy Ghost shown as a dove. Red seraphim stand in serried ranks and little blue ones peep their heads through the clouds on either side of this dominating central group with the Virgin's dark blue robe swirling below. To one side are groups of patriarchs, prophets, apostles and founders of religious orders, and on the other, nobles, bourgeois and the common people, many of them clearly portraits of contemporaries. Below are imaginary and imaginative small townscapes of Rome and Jerusalem, and below them again, Purgatory and Hell.

The contract (*prix-fait*) for the work exists and goes into great detail about the commissioning of the picture. It not only specified the price and delivery date, but laid down the exact iconography and colours to be used. Although Quarton did not follow his instructions to the letter, he produced a truly magnificent painting in which he combined the skills of a miniaturist with the broad sweep of a master.

There are many good paintings in the museum, by Philippe de Champaigne and Nicolas Mignard (who worked in Avignon from 1636 to 1660) in particular, and a rather odd one called *The Martyrdom of the Carthusians in England* by an anonymous hand, which records an occasion sometime between 1535 and 1540 when Henry VIII had eighteen of the Fathers put to death. Sadly, Villeneuve's other great painting, the *Pietà*, also by an unknown artist, was sold in 1905 to the Louvre, but a copy of it now hangs in one of the chapels of the fourteenth-century collegiate church of Notre Dame, founded by Cardinal Arnaud de Via, and where there is a particularly impressive marble altar under which lies the figure of Christ by Antoine Duparc (1745). The cloister was built in the garden of the cardinal's *livrée*.

Once the Great Schism was over and the papacy firmly ensconced in Rome again, Villeneuve-lès-Avignon reverted to being just another small town. Since 1954, however, it has had a new lease of life for it has become home to the workers in the atomic plant at nearby Marcoule.

Here on the banks of the mighty Rhône, which for centuries drew a line between Languedoc and Provence, we have come full circle, for we are barely thirty kilometres from Beaucaire. Nuclear fission is indeed a far cry from the gentle love of Aucassin and Nicolette; we have I hope come a long way from the attitude prevalent in the past, exemplified by Stendhal in *Le Rouge et Le Noir*, when Julien Sorel tells M. de la Mole that he is leaving, only to be asked 'where for?':

'For Languedoc.'
'Oh no, please don't, you are destined for higher things; if you must go, it should be for the North.'

If all I have achieved in writing this book is to prove Stendhal wrong in this one respect, I shall be content.

Appendix 1

Chronology

Only the accession dates for the more important kings and counts are given here; for other details, see the Index.

Middle Pleistocene	Early form of man found at Caune de l'Arago, Tautavel
Late Palaeolithic	Cave paintings at Niaux; traces of early man at Le Mas d'Azil
BC 600	Agde founded by the Phoceans as a trading post
BC 3rd century	Arrival of Volcae Tectosages and Volcae Arecomici
BC 218	Hannibal crosses Languedoc
BC 118	Narbo Martius (Narbonne) founded by Romans; Via Domitia started
27 AD	Provincia Narbonensis created by Romans
c.250	Martyrdom of St Sernin at Toulouse and St Paul Serge at Narbonne
413	Arrival of Visigoths from Eastern Europe
507	Battle of Vouillé; Franks under Clovis defeat Visigoths
6th century	Visigoths found Kingdom of Septimania (or Gothia)
719	Saracen raids start
732	Battle of Poitiers; Charles Martel defeats Saracens
789	Guillaume d'Orange (St Guilhem) awarded County of Toulouse
865	Creation of Catalan March (Roussillon)
1027	Synod of Toulouges proclaims Truce of God
1071	Guillaume IX, Duke of Aquitaine
1093	Raymond IV, Count of St Gilles/Toulouse

1096	Urban II preaching First Crusade
1105	Bertrand, Count of Toulouse
1112	Alphonse Jourdain, Count of Toulouse
1137	Louis VII, King of France
1148	Raymond V, Count of Toulouse
1152	Eleanor of Aquitaine marries Henry Plantagenet
1154	Henry Plantagenet succeeds to throne of England
1172	County of Roussillon left to counts of Barcelona and Aragon
1177	County of Cerdagne left to counts of Barcelona and Aragon
1180	Philippe II (Auguste), King of France
1194	Raymond VI, Count of Toulouse
1198	Innocent III, Pope
1204	Pedro of Aragon marries Marie of Montpellier
1202–4	Fourth Crusade
1208	15 January; murder of Pierre de Castelnau at St Gilles
1209	22 July; sack of Béziers
1213	Battle of Muret; Pedro II of Aragon killed
1218	Death of Simon de Montfort at third siege of Toulouse
1222	Raymond VII, Count of Toulouse
1223	Louis VIII, King of France
1226	Louis IX (St Louis), King of France
1229	Treaty of Paris (or Meaux): Languedoc made into two *sénéchaussées*: Beaucaire and Carcassonne; Toulouse university founded
1233	Inquisition founded by Pope Gregory IX
1244	Fall of château of Montségur
1249–71	Jeanne de Toulouse and Alphonse de Poitiers rule Languedoc
1251	Seventh Crusade
1255	Fall of château of Quéribus
1258	Treaty of Corbeil confirms Roussillon and Cerdagne to Aragon
1270	Eighth Crusade
1271	Languedoc accrues to French crown on death of Alphonse de Poitiers and Jeanne de Toulouse
1276	Kingdom of Majorca founded

1285	Philippe IV (le Bel), King of France
1290	Counts of Foix inherit Béarn
1311	Death of Jaime I (II) of Majorca
1317	Creation of archbishopric of Toulouse and new bishoprics
1337	Creation of governorship of Languedoc
1344	End of the Kingdom of Majorca
1349	Montpellier sold to French crown
1355	Black Prince's *chevauchée*
1360	Languedoc made into three *sénéchaussées*: Toulouse, Carcassonne and Beaucaire
1360–1450	Famine kills one-third of population
1418	Estates of Languedoc authorized to meet at will
1443	*Parlement* re-established at Toulouse
1461	Louis XI, King of France
1462	Catalan revolt; Roussillon and Cerdagne occupied by the French
1464	Fair of Beaucaire gets new commercial privileges
1478	Cour des Aides established in Montpellier
1493	Treaty of Barcelona: Roussillon and Cerdagne returned to Spain
1523	Chambre des Comptes established in Montpellier
1539	Edict of Villers-Cotterets imposes French as official language on the whole country
1560–98	Wars of Religion
1563	Henri I de Montmorency, Governor of Languedoc
1589	Henri IV, King of France
1598	Edict of Nantes proclaims freedom of worship for Protestants
1610	Louis XIII, King of France
1619–29	Duc de Rohan's revolts
1629	Peace of Alais (Alès) removes Protestants' political privileges
1632	Henri II de Montmorency executed
1643	Louis XIV, King of France
1659	Treaty of the Pyrenees: Roussillon and Cerdagne ceded to France
1666–81	Building of the Canal du Midi
1685	Revocation of the Edict of Nantes
1702	24 July; Abbé du Chayla murdered

1702–4	Camisard war in Cévennes
1709	Bitter winter destroys many chestnut trees
1715	Louis XV, King of France
1761–2	Calas affair (Toulouse); Sirven affair (Castres)
1787	Edict of Tolerance
1791	Creation of *départements*
1793	Federalist movement
1814	Battle of Toulouse; Wellington defeats Soult
1839	Railway opened from Montpellier to Sète
1863	Phylloxera louse attacks vines
1892	Coal-miners strike at Carmaux
1896	Workers' co-operative Verrerie Ouvrière opens at Albi
1907	Demonstrations by *vignerons*
1955	Creation of Regions of Languedoc-Roussillon and Midi-Pyrénées
1963	Coastal resorts started

Appendix 2

Main Museums

Days and times of opening have not been given because they are liable to change, especially with the season. The majority of museums are open most days during July and August; some are opened for groups only, by arrangement, in the winter months. The current *Guide Michelin* will have the most up-to-date telephone numbers for the Syndicats d'Initiative or Tourist Information Offices which, even if closed, may give recorded information about local sights.

If you are planning a holiday which includes seeing a specific museum, it is as well to check first to avoid being disappointed.

Agde
  Musée Agathois 'Escolo dau Sarret', rue de la Fraternité,
  tel. 67 94 82 51
Albi
  Musée Toulouse-Lautrec, Palais de la Berbie, tel. 63 54 14 09
  Hotel du Bosc, rue Toulouse-Lautrec, tel. 63 46 01 87
  Musée Lapérouse, square Botany Bay, tel. 63 46 01 87
Alès
  Mine-Témoin, Chemin Cité Ste Marie, tel. 66 30 45 15
  Musée municipal du Colombier, Château du Colombier,
  tel. 66 86 30 40
  Musée-Bibliothèque Pierre-André Benoit, 52 Montée des Lauriers,
  Rochebelle, tel. 66 86 98 69
Avignonet-Lauragais
  Centre Pierre-Paul Riquet, Port Lauragais, tel. 61 27 14 63
Bagnols-sur-Cèze
  Musée Léon Alègre, Hôtel de Ville, tel. 66 89 60 02
  Musée d'Archéologie rhodanien, Maison Jourdan, 24 avenue Paul
  Langevin, tel. 66 89 74 00

Beaucaire
Musée municipal de la Vignasse, Château, tel. 66 59 47 61
Béziers
Musée des Beaux-Arts, Hôtel Fabregat, place de la Révolution,
tel. 67 28 38 78
Musée des Beaux-Arts, Hôtel Fayet, 9 rue de Capus,
tel. 67 49 04 66
Musée St Jacques, Caserne St Jacques, tel. 67 49 34 00
L'Espace Paul-Riquet, 7 rue Massol, tel. 67 28 44 18
Bosc, Naucelles
Château du Bosc, tel. 65 69 20 83
Bouzigues
Musée de la Conchyculture, 4 rue Saint Nicolas, tel. 67 78 33 57
Cap d'Agde
Musée d'Archéologie Sous-Marin et Subaquatique, Mas de La
Clape – Cap d'Agde, tel. 67 26 81 00
Carcassonne
Musée du Château Comtal, Château Comtal, La Cité,
tel. 68 25 01 66
Musée des Beaux-Arts, 1 rue de Verdun, tel. 68 47 80 90
Castres
Musée Goya, Hôtel de Ville, tel. 63 59 62 63
Musée Jean Jaurès, place Pélisson, tel. 63 72 01 01
Céret
Musée d'Art Moderne, rue Jean Parayre, tel. 68 87 27 76
Casa Catalane de la Culture, place Picasso, tel. 68 87 00 36
Cordes
Musée Charles Portal, tel. 63 56 00 40 (Mairie)
Musée de l'Art du Sucre, place de la Bride, tel. 63 56 02 40
Elne
Cloître d'Elne, Cathédrale, tel. 68 22 05 38
Ensérune, Nissan-lès-
Musée National d'Ensérune, tel. 67 37 01 23
Foix
Musée de l'Ariège, Château, tel. 61 65 56 05

Frontignan
Musée de Frontignan, 3 bis rue Lucien Salette, tel. 67 48 25 25
Gaillac
Musée Philadelphe-Thomas, rue Philadelphe-Thomas,
tel. 63 57 36 31
Musée, Château du Parc, tel. 63 57 18 25
Ille-sur-Têt
Exposition permanente, Hospice d'Ille, tel. 68 84 83 96
Lavelanet
Musée du Textile et du Peigne à corne, 65 rue Jean Jaurès,
tel. 61 01 22 20
Le Pont-de-Montvert
Écomusée du Mont-Lozère, tel. 66 45 80 73
Le Vigan
Musée Cévenol, 1 rue Calquière, tel. 67 81 06 86
Lézignan-Corbières
Musée de la Vigne et du Vin, 1 rue Necker, tel. 68 27 37 02
Limoux
Musée Petiet, Promenade du Tivoli, tel. 68 31 11 82
Lodève
Musée Fleury, Hôtel du Cardinal de Fleury, tel. 67 44 08 63
Mas d'Azil, Le
Musée de la Préhistoire, tel. 61 69 97 22
Maureillas-las-Illas
Musée du Liège, tel. 68 83 30 19
Mazamet
Maison Fuzier, rue des Casernes, tel. 63 61 43 43
Mialet
Musée du Désert, Le Mas Soubeyran, tel. 66 85 02 72
Millau
Musée de Millau et des Causses, Hôtel Pegayrolles, place Foch,
tel. 65 59 01 08
Musée de la Peau et du Gant, Hôtel Pegayrolles, place Foch,
tel. 65 59 01 08
Site archéologique de la Graufesenque, Route de Millau,
tel. 65 60 11 37

Montauban
  Musée Ingres, Hôtel de Ville, tel. 63 63 18 04
  Musée du Terroir, place Antoine Bourdelle, tel. 63 66 46 34
  Musée d'Histoire Naturelle, place Antoine Bourdelle,
  tel. 63 63 10 45
Montpellier
  Musée Fabre, 13 rue de Montpelliéret, tel. 67 66 06 34
  Musée Sabatier-d'Espeyran-Cabrières (c/o Musée Fabre)
  Musée de la Société Archéologique, 5 rue des Trésoriers de
  France, tel. 67 52 93 03
  Musée du Vieux-Montpellier, Hôtel de Varennes, 2 place
  Pétrarque (no telephone)
  Musée Fougau, Hôtel de Varennes, 2 place Pétrarque (no
  telephone)
  Musée Atger, rue École de Médecine, tel. 67 66 27 77
  Musée de la Pharmacie, Faculté de la Pharmacie, avenue Charles-
  Flahaut, tel. 67 63 20 47
  Musée de l'Anatomie, rue Ecole de Médecine, tel. 67 60 73 71
Montségur
  Musée de Montségur, Mairie, tel. 61 01 10 27 (c/o)
Narbonne
  Musée d'Art et d'Histoire, Palais des Archevêques,
  tel. 68 32 31 60
  Musée Archéologique, Palais des Archevêques, tel. 68 32 31 60
  Musée de l'Horreum, rue Rouget de l'Isle, tel. 68 32 31 60
  Musée Lapidaire, Église Notre Dame de Lamourguier,
  tel. 68 32 31 60
  Crypte archéologique de St Paul Serge, place Dupleix,
  tel. 68 32 31 60
Niaux
  Grotte, tel. 61 05 88 37
  Musée de Niaux, Arts et Traditions populaires de l'Ariège,
  tel. 61 05 88 36
Nîmes
  Musée des Beaux-Arts, rue Cité-Foulc, tel. 66 76 70 76
  Musée du Vieux-Nîmes, place aux Herbes, tel. 66 36 00 64

Musée Archéologique, 13 bis boulevard de l'Amiral-Courbet, tel. 66 67 25 57

Perpignan

Musée Hyacinthe Rigaud, 16 rue de l'Ange, tel. 68 35 43 40

Musée Catalan des Arts et Traditions Populaires, place de Verdun, tel. 68 35 66 30

Pézenas

Musée de Vuillod-St-Germain, 3 rue Albert-Paul Alliès, tel. 67 98 14 15

Pont St Esprit

Musée Paul Raymond, place de l'Ancienne Mairie, tel. 66 39 09 98

Port Lauragais *see* Avignonet-Lauragais

Prades

Musée Pablo Casals, rue Victor Hugo, tel. 68 96 27 58

Rivesaltes

Musée Joffre, 1 rue Maréchal Joffre, tel. 68 64 24 98

Sète

Musée Paul Valéry, rue François Desnoyer, tel. 67 46 20 98

St Antonin-Noble-Val

Musée du Vieux Saint-Antonin, place de l'Hôtel de Ville, tel. 63 30 63 47 (Office de Tourisme)

St Gilles-du-Gard

Musée de la Maison Romane, place de la Maison Romane, tel. 66 87 40 42

St Hippolyte-du-Fort

Musée de la Soie, place du 8 Mai, tel. 66 77 66 47

St Jean-du-Gard

Musée des Vallées Cévenoles, 95 Grand'Rue, tel. 66 85 10 48

St Laurent-de-Cerdans

Musée de l'Espadrille, rue Joseph Nivet, tel. 68 39 50 06

St Pons-de-Thomières

Musée de Préhistoire, rue du Barry, tel. 67 97 22 61

Ste Enimie

Arts et Traditions populaires, Le Vieux Logis, tel. 66 48 53 44

Stes Maries de la Mer, Les

Musée Baroncelli, rue Victor Hugo (no telephone)

Tautavel
Musée de la Préhistoire, La-Tour-de-France, tel. 68 29 07 76
Toulouse
Musée des Augustins, 21 rue de Metz, tel. 61 23 85 07
Musée St Raymond, place St Sernin, tel. 61 22 21 85
Musée Paul Dupuy, 13 rue de la Pleau, tel. 61 22 21 83
Musée Georges Labit, 45 rue des Martyrs de la Libération, tel. 61 22 21 84
Salles historiques, Capitole, place du Capitole, tel. 61 22 29 22 ext 3412
Musée du Vieux-Toulouse, 7 rue de May (no telephone)
Musée d'Histoire Naturelle, 35 Allées Jules-Guesde, tel. 61 52 00 14
Galerie municipale du Château d'Eau, 17 place Laganne, tel. 61 42 61 72
Villeneuve-lès-Avignon
Musée Hôtel Pierre de Luxembourg, rue de la République, tel. 90 25 45 03

Appendix 3

Local Dishes

A short list of the local dishes which you might be lucky enough to be offered, and with which you might be unfamiliar.

aigo bullido/aigo bouïdo: bread and garlic soup

aïoli/aillade: mayonnaise with garlic and sometimes walnuts

alicuit/alicot/aligot/alycuit: poultry stew, mostly giblets

amenlous/amellonades: almond pastries

anchoiade: anchovy spread

beurre de Montpellier or *de Languedoc:* butter made with herbs, anchovies, garlic, etc.

bistorto/coucou/coco: brioche

bougnette: large sausage or – in the Cévennes – a pancake

bouillinade: thick fish stew

bourride: fish stew

brandade de morue: an emulsion of salt cod, olive oil and garlic

cabassol: tripe, head or feet of sheep

calabart/galabart: very large black pudding

cabecou: fresh goat cheese

caladons: small dry cakes

cargolade: snail stew

cassoulet: rich bean stew. See pages 191–2

causalade: omelette with peppers, wild asparagus or hop shoots (*jets d'houblon*), pinenuts and garlic

cognes: see *gâteaux de poivre* below

confit d'oei or *de canard:* preserved goose or duck

criadillas: bull's testicles – politely referred to as *rognons blancs* (white kidneys)

escargots: snails

escuedella de nadal: stuffed turkey

flaunes/flauzonnes/flônes: cheese cake made from ewe's milk

fouace: brioche with angelica

fougassettes: small cake-like biscuits

gâteaux de poivre: biscuits rolled in pepper

gimblette: fruit paste

gras-double: tripe

manouls: stuffed veal tripe

melsat: a white sausage. See
    page 238
Mirepoix: a basic sauce made
    from diced onions, carrots and
    celery to which ham is
    sometimes added
omelette languedocienne: see
    causalade above
oreillettes: sweet batter cakes.
    See page 49
pan bagna/pa y all: baked sticks
    of bread coated with oil and
    garlic
pannequets: pancakes
    sometimes filled with
    Roquefort
pélardon/péral/péraldou: ewe's
    or goat's milk cheese
petits pâtés de Pézenas and *de
    Béziers:* small mincemeat

pastries. See page 70
pissaladière: an onion tart
    decorated with olives and
    anchovies
ragoût languedocien: stew of
    chicken giblets
rhubarbe: scrapings of blue
    cheese (Roquefort) potted
    with *eau-de-vie* and covered
    in pepper
rouille: mayonnaise with garlic,
    cayenne pepper, tomatoes,
    and sometimes bread-
    crumbs
tielle: pasty with tomatoes and
    squid or calamares
touron: soft nougat
trénels: tripe with ham, garlic
    and eggs
tripoux: tripe

Sources

Unless credited otherwise the translations are by Roger Toulmin.

1 Sulpicius Severus, *Dialogues*, and Gregory of Tours, *Historiae* quoted by Edward James in *The Origins of France From Clovis to the Capetians, 500–1000* (Macmillan, 1982)

2 Quoted by Fernand Braudel in *The Identity of France*, vol. 1, translated by Sian Reynolds (Collins, 1988)

3 Henry James, *A Little Tour in France* (Heinemann, 1922)

4 Jethro Tull, *The New Horse-houghing Husbandry: or, an Essay on the Principles of Tillage and Vegetation* (London, 1712) quoted by John Lough in *France Observed in the Seventeenth Century* (Oriel Press, 1984)

5 Ellis Veryard, *An Account of Diverse Choice Remarks . . . Taken in a Journey through the Low Countries, France, Italy and parts of Spain . . .* (London, 1701) quoted by J. Lough, *op.cit.*

6 Geoffroi de Vigeois, *Monumenta Germaniae Historia*, ed. G. H. Pertz (Hanover) quoted and translated in Richard Barber, *The Knight and Chivalry* (Longman, 1970)

7 Thomas Platter, *Journal of a Younger Brother; The Life of Thomas Platter as a medical student in Montpellier at the close of the Sixteenth Century*, translated and introduced by Seán Jennett (Frederick Muller, 1963)

8 Stendhal (Marie Henri Beyle), *Mémoires d'un Touriste*, vol. 1 (Michel Levy Frères, 1874)

9 Stendhal, *op.cit.*

10 Felix Platter, *Beloved Son Felix; The Journal of Felix Platter as a medical student in Montpellier in the Sixteenth Century*, translated and introduced by Seán Jennett (Frederick Muller, 1961)

11 Jean-Jacques Rousseau, *Les Confessions* (Éditions Jules Tallendier, 1927)
12 Henry James, *op.cit.*
13 Rousseau, *op.cit.*
14 Arthur Young, *Travels in France during the years 1787, 1788, 1789*, edited by M. Betham-Edwards (George Bell and Sons, 1889)
15 Tobias Smollett, *Travels through France and Italy*, edited by Frank Felsenstein (Clarendon Press, 1979)
16 André Gide, *Si le grain ne meurt* (Gallimard, 1920)
17 Thomas Platter, *op.cit.*
18 Jean Racine, *Oeuvres*, vol. 6 (Hachette, 1865)
19 Laurence Sterne, *Letters*, edited by Lewis Perry Curtis (Clarendon Press, 1935)
20 Elizabeth David, Postscript to 'Confort anglais, French fare', *An Omelette and a Glass of Wine* (Jill Norman Books, Robert Hale, 1984)
21 Prosper Mérimée, *Lettres de Prosper Mérimée à Ludovic Vitet* (Plon, 1934)
22 Vincent van Gogh, *Further Letters of Van Gogh to his brother, 1886–89* (Constable, 1929)
23 L. Figuier, *Le Gardien de la Camargue* (Hachette, 1862)
24 John Locke, *Travels in France, 1675–1679, as related in his Journals, Correspondence and other papers,* edited by John Lough (Cambridge University Press, 1953) quoted in J. Lough, *op.cit.*
25 Locke, *op.cit.*
26 Stendhal, *Mémoires d'un Touriste*, vol. 3, *Voyage dans le Midi* (Librairie Ancienne Honoré Champion, 1932)
27 Elizabeth David, 'The Markets of France' (first published in *Vogue*, March 1960; quoted in *An Omelette and a Glass of Wine*)
28 Henry James, *op.cit.*
29 François Rabelais, *Oeuvres Complètes* (Pléiade edition, Gallimard, 1941)
30 Thomas Wentworth, *Diary*, (Wentworth Woodhouse Papers, Sheffield Central Library, Str. P. 30) quoted by J. Lough, *op.cit.*
31 Sterne, *op.cit.*
32 Stendhal, *op.cit.*, vol. 3

33 Quoted by Bernard Sournia in 'La place Louis-le-Grand', in *Monuments Historiques*, No. 120, March–April 1982 (CMNHS)

34 Ranulph Glaber, quoted by Jean Hubert in *Larousse Encyclopedia of Byzantine and Medieval Art*, edited by René Huyghe (Paul Hamlyn, 1963)

35 Edward James, *The Origins of France*, *op.cit.*

36 Smaragdus, quoted in *Languedoc roman*; *le Languedoc méditerranéen*, 2nd edition (Zodiaque, 1985)

37 Léon Daudet, *Devant la douleur* (Nouvelle Librairie Nationale, 1915)

38 Hippolyte Taine, *Journeys through France, being Impressions of the Provinces* (T. Fisher Unwin, 1897)

39 Paul Valéry in a letter to the mayor of Sète, December 1925

40 Paul Valéry, 'Le Cimetière Marin', Gallimard; translated by C. Day Lewis in *Collected Poems 1954*, Jonathan Cape and The Hogarth Press, 1954

41 Thomas Platter, *op.cit.*

42 Steven Runciman, *The Medieval Manichee; A Study of the Christian Dualist Heresy* (Cambridge University Press, 1960)

43 Pierre Belperron, *La Croisade contre les Albigeois, et l'union de Languedoc à la France, 1202–49* (Plon, 1944)

44 Guillaume of Tudela, *La Chanson de la Croisade contre les Albigeois* (Renouard, 1879)

45 Caesar of Heisterbach, *Dialogus miraculorum*, dist. 5, cap 21, quoted in Elie Griffe, *Le Languedoc cathare de 1190 à 1210* (Letouzy et Ané, 1971)

46 Grimod de la Reynière, letter to Restif de la Bretonne, quoted in Henri Gault and Christian Millau, *Guide Gourmande de la France* (Hachette, 1970)

47 Alexandre Dumas, *Le Grand Dictionnaire de Cuisine*, Cercle du Livre Précieux (Tchou, 1985)

48 Young, *op.cit.*

49 Locke, *op.cit.*

50 Ausonius quoted in Henri-Paul Eydoux, *Les Grandes Heures du Languedoc* (Librairie Académique Perrin, 1973)

51 Prosper Mérimée, *Notes d'un Voyage dans le Midi de la France* (Librairie de Fournier, 1835)

52 Stendhal, *op.cit.*, vol. 3

53 Stendhal, *ibid.*

54 Louis XIII, from Goulas, *Mémoires de Louis XIII* vol. 1, quoted and translated in A. Lloyd Moote, *Louis the Just* (University of California Press, Berkeley, 1989)

55 Victor Hugo, *L'Homme qui rit* , Librairie Internationale, 1969

56 Henry James, *op.cit.*

57 D. D. R. Owen, review in *Times Literary Supplement* 5 January 1990 of *The Voice of the Trobairitz; Perspectives on the Women Troubadours*, edited by William D. Paden (University of Pennsylvania Press, 1989)

58 Marina Warner, *Alone of All Her Sex, The Myth and the Cult of the Virgin Mary* (Weidenfeld and Nicolson, 1976)

59 Runciman, *op.cit.*

60 Eydoux, *op.cit.*

61 Pierre des Vaux-de-Cernay, quoted by H.-P. Eydoux, *op.cit.*

62 Richard Ford, *Gatherings from Spain* (1846) quoted by Peter Sahlins in *Boundaries: The Making of France and Spain in the Pyrenees* (University of California Press, Berkeley, 1989)

63 S. Baring-Gould, *The Book of the Pyrenees* (Methuen, 1907)

64 Thomas Platter, *op.cit.*

65 Baring-Gould, *op.cit.*

66 Jean Leymarie, *Fauvism*, translated by James Emmons (Skira, 1959)

67 André Derain, *Correspondence, Lettres à Vlaminck* (Flammarion, 1955)

68 Leymarie, *op.cit.*

69 A. S. Byatt, in *The Independent Magazine*, 3 March 1990

70 Augustus Hare, *South-Western France* (George Allen, 1890)

71 Baring-Gould, *op.cit.*

72 Thomas Merton, *The Seven-Storey Mountain* (Sheldon Press, 1975)

73 Rudyard Kipling, *Souvenirs of France* (Macmillan, 1933)

74 Nancy Mitford, *The Sun King* (Hamish Hamilton, 1960)

75 Eugen Weber, *France, Fin de Siècle* (Harvard University Press, 1986) and quoting from Henry Beraldi, *Cent Ans aux Pyrénées*, 1900

76 A. Leroi-Gourdan, *Préhistoire d'Art occidental*, quoted by Jean Clottes in 'La Grotte de Niaux', in *Monuments Historiques*, no. 118, Nov.–Dec. 1981 (Caisse Nationale des Monuments Historiques et des Sites (CMNHS))

77 Young, *op.cit.*

78 Lévis-Mirepoix, Duc de, *Montségur* (Michel, 1972)
79 Runciman, *op.cit.*
80 Stendhal, *op.cit.*, vol. 3
81 May McKisack, *The Fourteenth Century 1307–99* (Clarendon Press, 1959)
82 Stendhal, *op.cit.*, vol. 3
83 Mérimée, *Lettres, op.cit.*
84 Eugène Viollet-le-Duc, letter to his wife and father, quoted by Pierre-Marie Auzas in *Eugène Viollet-le-Duc, 1814–1879* (CMNHS, 1979)
85 A. W. Raitt, *Prosper Mérimée* (Eyre and Spottiswoode, 1970)
86 Taine, *op.cit.*
87 Yvan Christ, 'Chronique du règne de Mérimée' in 'La Table Ronde', March 1962, quoted by Raitt, *op.cit.*
88 Henry James, *op.cit.*
89 Young, *op.cit.*
90 Hans Christian Andersen, *The Story of My Life* (Sampson Low, Son, and Marston, 1871)
91 H. C. Clos-Jouve, quoted in Gault and Millau, *op.cit.*
92 Locke, *op.cit.*
93 Mérimée, *Lettres, op.cit.*
94 Taine, *op.cit.*
95 Charles Bertie, *Diary of a Journey in France 1660–1662* (Historical Manuscripts Commission, 1942) quoted by J. Lough, *op.cit.*
96 Young, *op.cit.*
97 Ford Madox Ford, 'Dinner with Trout' (first published in *Vogue*, New York; reprinted in *The Compleat Imbiber*, no. 14, edited by Cyril Ray, 1989)
98 Anthony Blunt, *Art and Architecture in France, 1500–1700* (Penguin, 1973)
99 Henry James, *op.cit.*
100 Rabelais, *op.cit.*
101 Antoine Bourdelle quoted by Ionel Jianou and Michel Dufet in *Bourdelle* (Arted, Editions d'Art, 1970)
102 Wentworth, *op.cit.*
103 Merton, *op.cit.*
104 Merton, *op.cit.*
105 Albert Camus, in preface to *Cordes en Albigeois*, Claire Targuebayre (Privat, 1954)

106 Hare, *op.cit.*

107 Maurice Joyant, quoted by Pierre de Gorsse in *Albi/Cordes* (Alpina, 1963)

108 Jean Jaurès quoted in *Histoire d'Albi*, edited by Jean-Louis Biget (Privat, 1983)

109 Broughton (Hobhouse) I, 290, quoted by Elizabeth Longford in *Wellington: The Years of the Sword* (Weidenfeld and Nicolson, 1969)

110 Curnonsky quoted in Gault and Millau, *op.cit.*

111 E. A. Martel, *Les Cévennes et la Région des Causses* (1890) quoted by Eugen Weber, *op.cit.*

112 Jean-Pierre Chabrol, *Les Rebelles* (Plon, 1965)

113 Robert Louis Stevenson, *Travels with a Donkey in the Cevennes* (Kegan Paul and Co., 1879)

114 André Chamson, *L'Aigoual* (Espace Sud, 1986)

115 John Ardagh *Writer's France* (Hamish Hamilton, 1989)

116 Stevenson to his cousin Bob, quoted by Richard Holmes, *Footsteps* (Hodder and Stoughton, 1985)

117 Xavier Mouline in an interview with Monique Monifacier, 'Lou Rebieure' (*Le Revoir*), no. 17, 1990

118 André Chamson, *A Time to Keep*, translated by Erik de Mauny (Faber and Faber, 1957)

119 Saint-Simon, Duc de, *Historical Memoirs*, edited and translated by Lucy Norton (Hamish Hamilton, 1967)

120 Voltaire, *The Age of Louis XIV*, translated by Martyn P. Pollack (Dent, 1926)

121 Locke, *op.cit.*

122 *Dictionnaire des Femmes Célebres*, 1830

123 Young, *op.cit.*

124 Adrienne Durand-Tullou, *Le pays des asphodels*, (Editions Payot, 1989)

125 Miss Betham-Edwards' introduction to Arthur Young, *op.cit.*

126 Byatt, *op.cit.*

127 Albert André, quoted by Alain Girard, *Le Musée de Bagnols-sur-Cèze*, from Marius Mermillion, *Cahiers d'aujourd'hui*, Paris, 1927

128 Renoir, quoted in Alain Girard, *op.cit.*

129 Locke, *op.cit.*

130 Alfred de Vigny, *Cinq-Mars, ou une conjuration sous Louis XIII* (Quantin, 1889)

Further Reading

Nearly all the books listed in the Source notes have good material on Languedoc and Roussillon. Unfortunately there is relatively little on the area in English, but the most recent general works are: James Bentley, *Languedoc* (George Philip, 1987); Andrew Sanger, *Languedoc and Roussillon* (Christopher Helm, 1989); Rex Grizzell, *Auvergne and the Massif Central* (Christopher Helm, 1989); Andrew Sanger, *South-West France*; *Aquitaine, Gascony, the Pyrenees* (Christopher Helm, 1990); John Sturrock, *The French Pyrenees* (Faber, 1988).

Whether or not one can read French, the absolutely essential guidebooks are *Languedoc-Roussillon* and *Toulouse-Midi-Pyrénées* in the Hachette *Guides Bleues* series; and good but much shorter, *Gorges du Tarn–Cévennes–Bas Languedoc* and *Pyrénées Roussillon –Albigeois* in the Michelin Green Guide series.

The two volumes in the Larousse series *La France et ses Trésors* – Aude Grouard de Tocqueville, *Languedoc-Roussillon* (1989) and Françoise Legrand, *Midi-Pyrénées* (1989) – have wonderful colour illustrations and brief but helpful texts. Jacques Durand, *Le Languedoc des Cévennes à la Mer* (Rivages, 1983) has rather moodier photographs and a poetic text.

Selection from Stendhal's travel notes has been published in an English translation (not used here) by Elisabeth Abbott in *Travels in the South of France* (Calder and Boyars, 1971) and André Gide's *Si le grain ne meurt* has been translated into English as *If It Die . . .* , by Dorothy Bussy (Penguin Books, 1977). (This translation not used here.) Emmanuel Le Roy Ladurie has written three relevant books, all of which are interesting: *Montaillou, Cathars and Catholics in a French Village 1294–1324*, translated by Barbara Bray (Scolar Press, 1978); *Love, Death and Money in the Pays d'Oc*, translated by Alan Sheridan (Scolar/Penguin, 1982/1984); and a short work in French, *Histoire de Languedoc* (Presses Universitaires, 1974).

Henri-Paul Eydoux, *Monuments méconnus: Languedoc and Rous-*

sillon (Librairie Académique Perrin, 1979) is full of good things, as is Marcel Girault, *Le Chemin de Regordane* (Lacour/Colporteur, 1988) which suggests walks along the Voie Regordane. For greater detail, the volumes published by Editions Privat in Toulouse are invaluable. Of these, the *Histoire du Languedoc*, edited by Philippe Wolff is the most general, and there are single volumes on the cities of Albi, Béziers, Carcassonne, Montauban, Montpellier, Narbonne, Perpignan and Toulouse.

Romanesque churches are covered by *Languedoc roman: le Languedoc méditerranéen* (2nd edition, 1985); *Haut-Languedoc roman* (1978); and *Roussillon roman*. *Itinéraires romans en Roussillon* (1977) proposes a number of circuits; all are published by Zodiaque and are beautifully illustrated. For additional detail, especially on ruined and out-of-the-way churches, see *Eglises romanes oubliées du Bas Languedoc*, Pierre A. Clément (Presses du Languedoc, Max Chaleil, éditeur, 1989).

The *Canal du Midi*, Odile de Roquette-Buisson (Thames and Hudson, 1983) is both informative and attractive.

The cookery books are all, alas, in French save for Elizabeth David, *French Provincial Cookery* (Michael Joseph, 1950; Penguin Books, 1970). Curnonsky and Austin de Croze, *Les Trésors Gastronomiques de la France* (Librairie Delagrave, 1933) is very basic and Alain Degond, Joseph Caracci, Francis Carcel, Marcel Dutot, *Les Recettes de la Table occitan – Midi-Pyrénées* (Librairie Istra, 1977) rather chattier. Albin Marty, *Fourmiguetto, Souvenirs et Recettes de Languedoc* (Editions Creer, Nonette, 1978) has, as its title implies, more than just recipes. François Beaulieu, *Les meilleurs recettes du Languedoc-Roussillon* (Ouest France, 1984) and *La Cuisine Cévenole* (Revue mensuelle de l'Association 'Terre Cévenole', 1988) are both useful but slight.

Index

Page numbers in *italic* refer to quotations